# Feeding Frenzy

# Feeding Frenzy

WILLIAM STERNBERG
and
MATTHEW C. HARRISON, JR.

*A Donald Hutter Book*

HENRY HOLT and COMPANY

NEW YORK

*For Ellen and Scott*
*W. S.*

*For Judy, Cecily, and Page*
*M. C. H.*

Copyright © 1989 by William Sternberg and Matthew C. Harrison, Jr.

Published by Henry Holt and Company, Inc.,
115 West 18th Street, New York, New York 10011.

Published in Canada by Fitzhenry & Whiteside Limited,
195 Allstate Parkway, Markham, Ontario L3R 4T8.

Library of Congress Cataloging-in-Publication Data
    Sternberg, William.
        Feeding frenzy / William Sternberg and Matthew C. Harrison, Jr. —
    1st ed.
            p.   cm.
        "A Donald Hutter book."
        Includes index.
        ISBN 0-8050-1063-7
        1. Wedtech (Firm) 2. Defense contracts—Corrupt practices—United
    States.   I. Harrison, Matthew C.   II. Title.
    HD9743.U8W437   1989
    363.1'323—dc20                                                    89-15262
                                                                         CIP

Henry Holt books are available at special discounts
for bulk purchases for sales promotions, premiums,
fund-raising, or educational use. Special editions
or book excerpts can also be created to specification.

    For details contact:

    Special Sales Director
    Henry Holt and Company, Inc.
    115 West 18th Street
    New York, New York 10011

First Edition

Designed by A. Christopher Simon
Printed in the United States of America
10 9 8 7 6 5 4 3 2 1

# Contents

v

# Contents

# Preface

WILLIAM STERNBERG

Many Americans remember January 28, 1986, as the day the space shuttle *Challenger* exploded. I remember it as the day the *Challenger* exploded while I was at Wedtech.

I was then a Washington-based business journalist working on a feature story about a fast-growing defense contractor in the Bronx. The morning of the twenty-eighth, I flew to New York City to interview Wedtech's vice-chairman, Fred Neuberger, at the company's pontoon production plant on 149th Street.

I had first heard of Wedtech in 1984, when I was the Washington correspondent for some small papers in Michigan. Wedtech had used Washington connections to acquire a bankrupt shipyard in the Upper Peninsula. More than a year later, my interest was further piqued when I saw Securities and Exchange Commission filings showing that the company's annual sales had risen from $10 million to $100 million in just a few years.

About a month before the *Challenger* disaster, I had gone to the Bronx to tour Wedtech's facilities and interview Neuberger. (Wedtech's chairman, John Mariotta, was said to be in Puerto Rico and unavailable for comment.) When it came time for the interview, however, Neuberger informed me that Wedtech was in the registration period for a stock offering and the lawyers had told him he shouldn't talk about the company.

I grumbled something about wishing Neuberger had told me this before I left Washington. He apologetically offered to pay for my return visit. Regarding the offer as innocent but mindful of accepting anything of value from those I was writing about, I declined. The interview was rescheduled for January 28, five days after the stock sale.

The *Challenger* disaster occurred at 11:39 A.M., while I was waiting for Neuberger in the reception area. It was the first thing he mentioned when he ushered me into his office. I was shaken; Neuberger seemed surprised but otherwise showed little reaction.

At the rear of Neuberger's spartan office was a window overlooking the production floor. On the wall was a humanitarian award he had received from a medical school. Neuberger was a shirt-sleeve executive—open collar, no tie, a cigarette in his hand. A smooth talker with a twinkle in his eye, he deftly fielded a number of questions about the business and its future.

Wedtech, he said, was looking forward to graduating from the program that set aside government contracts for minority companies. He praised local politicians who'd gone to bat for the company. Despite disagreements with his longtime partner Mariotta, their relationship was "always good." He said he'd like to see Wedtech reach $500 million in sales within two years.

He went on to expound on his business philosophy—"I always believe in overpaying my management. If you overpay, you get." Asked if the company's rapid growth made him nervous, he replied, "Nothing makes me nervous. Being poor makes me nervous." The impression he left was that of a bright wheeler-dealer, hardly a shady character.

In connection with my research at that time, I also interviewed a Washington consultant named Richard Ramirez who had helped Wedtech acquire the shipyard in Michigan. Ramirez compared the chaotic, ethnically diverse atmosphere at Wedtech headquarters to the popular television series, "Hill Street Blues." I liked the analogy and used it in my article.

By early 1987, however, it had become apparent that the executives at Wedtech and their cronies—including Neuberger and Ramirez—were the robbers, not the cops. I became fascinated with how the "shining star" of the government's minority business program was really a Potemkin Village. For the next eighteen months, I covered the unfolding scandal for *Crain's New York Business*, during which time I met Matt Harrison.

## MATTHEW C. HARRISON, JR.

In the late winter of 1986, I was preparing to leave the army after twenty years as an infantry, intelligence, and electronic warfare officer. I asked Bob Cresci, a close friend who was working in the financial community in New York City, for suggestions about companies to contact. Cresci knew a management consultant who had done some work for Wedtech; she had told him that the company, a rapidly growing defense contractor, badly needed competent managers. Cresci suggested to me that I get in touch with Wedtech.

In March I looked up Wedtech in the Standard & Poor's reference and wrote a blind letter to Anthony Guariglia, who was listed as the president; I enclosed a copy of my resumé and asked for an interview. A few weeks later, I received a call from Margie Colon, Guariglia's secretary, scheduling an interview in New York.

At that first interview, I met with Guariglia, Fred Neuberger, and Larry Shorten, a vice-president, in Guariglia's office. Guariglia started the interview by telling me that the senior executives of Wedtech were entrepreneurs with a lot of street smarts but that the company had grown to the point where it could no longer be managed "off the back of an envelope." It needed, he said, some people who were familiar with administering and managing large organizations, people who could establish and execute management systems.

Guariglia told me that they were interested in hiring a vice-president of administration and asked if I was interested. I said I was. At that point, Neuberger took his cigar out of his mouth and growled, "How much you want?" Fresh from reading numerous books on job-hunting and interviewing, all of which advised to avoid the compensation question until the second or third interview, I tried to duck Neuberger's query. "Aw, bullshit," Neuberger said, "you got some idea how much you want, we got some idea how much we're willing to pay. Give me a ball-park number." Seeing no room to maneuver, I named a figure. "Fine," Neuberger said, and left the room.

Several weeks later I had a second interview, this time talking with Mario Moreno, Wedtech's executive vice-president. After some further negotiations over salary, Guariglia offered me the job. I was delighted. It wasn't so much that the salary was higher than that offered by other companies (it was, but considering the cost of living in the New York area, not significantly so); my excitement stemmed from the fact that the opportunity looked so perfect. It appeared as though I were being offered the chance to join a young company and be part of its growth. I saw the opportunity to get more responsibility and make more of an impact than would be possible in a larger, more established firm. I accepted the offer.

I started working full time in the Bronx in July 1986 but only began to suspect that I had not made a wise career decision when the press reports of Wedtech corruption began to appear in the fall. After Wedtech filed for bankruptcy, I was selected to continue with the company, working with the creditors to liquidate Wedtech, providing assistance to federal and local prosecutors, and supporting the litigation that arose in the wake of the scandal.

# 1

# A Hero for the Eighties

**O**n March 6, 1984, the presidential campaign was at the top of the news.

The Democrats were engaged in their quadrennial bloodletting. Sen. Gary Hart had become the surprise front-runner in the contest for his party's nomination, upsetting Walter Mondale in the New Hampshire primary and Maine caucuses. This Tuesday evening, Hart would make it three wins in a row, overwhelming the former vice-president in Vermont. Meanwhile, Sen. John Glenn and the Reverend Jesse Jackson were hoping to score well in the "Super Tuesday" primaries one week later. All in all, the race for the Democratic nomination gave every indication of being bitter and prolonged.

The Republicans had no such problem. They knew who their candidate was going to be—Ronald Reagan, the incumbent president and one of the most popular politicians in American history. Despite their strong advantages, the Republicans were taking nothing for granted. They wanted to do more than just return Reagan to the White House. They wanted him re-elected by a margin that would renew his mandate of four years earlier. They wanted his coattails to be long enough to increase G.O.P. strength in Congress.

Accomplishing these goals would require money, lots of money,

1

and here the Republicans looked to New York City, the mother lode of campaign cash. What power is to Washington, money is to New York. The posh Waldorf-Astoria Hotel, at Park Avenue and Fiftieth Street in midtown Manhattan, was a natural site for tonight's $1,000-a-plate dinner to benefit the Reagan re-election campaign.

It was a dreary day in New York—overcast, with drizzle and temperatures around forty degrees. The city's once-proud basketball and hockey franchises, the Knicks and the Rangers, were both mired in third place. Reports from spring training in Florida—where the Mets had a rookie pitcher named Dwight Gooden and the Yankees were converting ace left-hander Dave Righetti to a reliever—did little to relieve the late-winter blahs.

Inside the Waldorf, however, the mood was anything but blah. One of the contenders for the title of Grand Hotel of New York City, the Waldorf had welcomed many distinguished visitors in its time. Although the staff liked to pretend a presidential visit was nothing out of the ordinary, it was difficult to maintain an air of imperturbability with Secret Service agents swarming about the premises. The presidential advance team had already been on site and underfoot for a week; a White House cook was in the hotel's kitchen to prepare the president's meal. An edgy expectancy was in the air.

Five miles to the north, across the Harlem River in a less favored part of the city, anticipation over Reagan's visit was also building. Executives of the Wedtech Corporation, a small defense contractor in the South Bronx, would be attending the dinner at the Waldorf. John Mariotta, the chairman and chief executive officer, and Mario Moreno, the executive vice-president, had each purchased a table of ten tickets for $10,000.

It was a lot of money, but they could afford it. Mariotta in particular was flush. As a result of a public offering of Wedtech's stock the previous summer, the semiliterate machinist had become an overnight millionaire. On this particular day, Wedtech's common stock had closed at a bid price of $21 a share in over-the-counter trading. That made Mariotta's holdings worth, on paper, more than $32 million.

Wedtech's nouveau riche executives were excited, and more than a little awed, to be moving into such unfamiliar circles of money, power, and connections. For Mariotta, a high school dropout from Spanish Harlem, and Moreno, a South American immigrant, it was heady stuff to be listed as leading contributors to the fundraising event, along with David Rockefeller, Brooke Astor, Estée Lauder. But unknown to Mariotta, the evening held in store for him a moment that he wouldn't have even dared to dream about when he began his adventures in the business world.

The president had begun the day with a speech to the National Association of Evangelicals in Columbus, Ohio. Preaching to the converted, Reagan declared that under his administration Americans were regaining their moral bearings and "turning back to God."

From Columbus, Reagan flew to New York to attend the dinner at the Waldorf, officially billed as "Salute to Victory II." Demonstrators against the president's policies in Central America gathered outside the hotel, but the police kept them a good block away.

While Reagan mingled with state Republican leaders at a private reception in the hotel, the dinner guests filed into the ballroom through the mirror-lined Silver Hallway. Like the rest of the Waldorf, the Grand Ballroom was beginning to show its age. The third-floor room was getting a little shabby at the edges, the paint a little dull in bright light.

But tonight the lights were subdued, and the room—the only four-story ballroom in the world—looked resplendent with its deep blue carpet and peacock blue paneled walls. An enormous crystal chandelier hung high over two tiers of boxes, which in turn overlooked the expansive dining area. The seventeen boxes were festooned with red, white, and blue bunting and American seals. A large foamboard sign spelling out "Salute to Victory" on a blue backdrop was mounted on the stage.

Around seven P.M., the president entered the ballroom to enthusiastic applause and took a seat at the dais between Charles A. Gargano, who was running Reagan's re-election campaign in New York, and George L. Clark Jr., the New York State Republican chairman. Nancy Reagan sat on the other side of Clark. Among the others at the head table were Sen. Alfonse D'Amato, the first-term Republican from New York; Samuel Pierce, the secretary of Housing and Urban Development; John Shad, chairman of the Securities and Exchange Commission; Frank J. Fahrenkopf, chairman of the Republican National Committee; and Jonathan Bush, brother

3

of the vice-president. Reagan, D'Amato, and Pierce flashed the "V" for victory sign to the gaggle of news photographers.

Gargano, a former building contractor who had served as a mass transit administrator in the Reagan administration, welcomed the crowd. He recounted how nervous he had been about making sure the event went off without a hitch. The tension had eased, he said, when a friend told him: "Look, Chucky baby, what's there to be worried about?"

After a dinner of pasta, salad, and veal, Gargano introduced Clark, the state G.O.P. chairman. Clark, in turn, introduced Reagan. At 8:38 P.M., the president rose to speak.

Reagan acknowledged Gargano and others at the head table, then launched into a partisan campaign speech covering the accomplishments of his administration. He previewed the themes the Republicans would hammer home throughout this election year.

"Does anyone want to go back to that double-digit inflation of four years ago?" the president asked.

"No!" the audience hollered.

Still using Jimmy Carter as a whipping boy, the president drew the biggest laugh of the evening when he compared his Democratic predecessors to Donald Duck's nephews. During the Carter administration, Reagan said, the country was being led by people "with good intentions and bad ideas—people with all the common sense of Huey, Dewey, and Louie."

He praised Senator D'Amato and the Republicans in New York's congressional delegation, especially Rep. Barber Conable, who was retiring. Then, as the speech drew to a close, Reagan departed from the standard campaign rhetoric. The president, with his actor's sense of timing, typically ended his speeches with uplifting anecdotes. Tonight would be no exception. He proceeded to heap extraordinary praise on a businessman in the audience, a man who had never held public office and who was known to only a handful of those at the dinner:

> Real progress in this country can be traced to the work of conscientious and hardworking individuals . . . One such person is John Mariotta, who's providing jobs and training for the hardcore unemployed of the South Bronx.
>
> Born of Puerto Rican immigrants and having served in the United States Army, Mr. Mariotta has had all the ups

and downs associated with entrepreneurship. And today, through Wedtech, he not only has built a successful corporation, he's helping hundreds of people who would otherwise be condemned to menial jobs or a life on the dole.

And what gave Mr. Mariotta the courage to keep going when others quit? He tells us it was his faith in God. Now, his faith has moved mountains, helping hundreds of people who'd almost given up hope.

People like John Mariotta are heroes for the eighties.

After a few closing remarks, the president headed back to Washington, where his nominee for attorney general, Edwin Meese III, was in the midst of a tough confirmation hearing before the Senate Judiciary Committee. The fundraiser had been a huge success, netting $550,000 for Republican campaign coffers.

John Mariotta, meanwhile, was flabbergasted. The short, stocky executive hadn't known this was coming. As the dinner ended and reporters crowded around, thrusting microphones at Mariotta's long face, he looked more than a little scared.

Mariotta's responses to reporters' questions were rambling and disjointed. The fifty-four-year-old Hispanic businessman with the unfashionably long sideburns talked about Wedtech as the solution to urban problems. He tried to say that Wedtech was the "penicillin" that would cure the diseases of the inner cities, but he stumbled badly on the word. He went on to praise the president for his inspirational leadership.

That night, millions of television viewers tuning in to the late-night newscasts saw clips of the president's speech and then the interview with Mariotta in his tuxedo and frilled shirt. It was more than a good story; it was good theater.

What the president and the press, and the people watching television, and the people in the ballroom didn't know was that the whole inspirational story was a fraud. Wedtech, Mariotta's success, was built on lies and theft and bribery.

Just short of five years later, on a cold January morning, John Mariotta, the hero for the eighties, would walk through the gates of the Allenwood Federal Prison Camp in Montgomery, Pennsylvania, to begin serving an eight-year sentence. By then, Wedtech would be in bankruptcy, and the jobs the president had mentioned with such pride would be gone. All that remained would be a scandal stretching from the South Bronx to the White House, one that would ruin political careers and sully some of the nation's most prestigious financial institutions.

But, on this day, John Mariotta was a celebrity.

Given what was to follow, it was perhaps only appropriate that this hero for the eighties and his crony, Mario Moreno, had stolen the $20,000 used to pay for their two tables at the gala "Salute to Victory" dinner.

# 2

# The Wasteland

**B**y the time the company that was to become Wedtech was founded in 1965, the South Bronx was well on its way to becoming a national symbol of urban blight. An exodus of businesses and middle-class residents, accompanied by waves of arson and looting, had left vast stretches of the borough looking like a war zone. Pervasive poverty, rampant crime, drugs, a lack of skilled labor—all cast heavy clouds over the "business climate" of the South Bronx.

Amid the rubble, it seemed hard to imagine that the Bronx had once been a bucolic region of farms and country homes. The borough was named after Jonas Bronck, a Swede who'd begun farming the rolling wilderness during the 1600s. In the early nineteenth century, the area was settled by Irish immigrants who'd worked on the railroads and Germans fleeing political persecution. They were soon joined by wealthy New Yorkers coming north to build country homes.

When New York City annexed the Bronx from Westchester County and extended the Third Avenue elevated train northward, a wave of Jewish and Italian immigrants, fleeing the tenements of Manhattan's Lower East Side, soon followed. In the early 1900s, the Grand Concourse was built to connect Manhattan with the parks of the Bronx. The Concourse was to be the Park Avenue of the Bronx, only wider and more lushly landscaped.

By the 1920s, the borough was a bastion of the burghers. The streets were lined with prosperous-looking townhouses. Yankee Stadium opened in 1923, and many of the ballplayers lived at the plush Concourse Plaza Hotel during the season. More than thirty classic Art Deco buildings were built along the Concourse during the 1930s and 1940s. The term South Bronx itself was unknown. People referred to the individual neighborhoods—Mott Haven, Port Morris, Tremont, Highbridge, Melrose, North New York and Morrisania. After World War II, a new wave of immigrants changed the character of those neighborhoods. By the late 1940s, the South Bronx—as social workers began to call it—was beginning decades of economic decline. Puerto Ricans became the dominant ethnic group, bringing with them the crime and poverty that often accompany the newly arrived and relatively powerless. Despair flourished and buildings burned. New highways sliced through the old neighborhoods, and middle class residents fled to the suburbs or the massive Co-op City development.

By the time the decline bottomed out, the Bronx had lost hundreds of companies, tens of thousands of jobs, and more than 100,000 residents, or some 14 percent of its population. It was as if a city the size of Albany, New York, had been abandoned. The term South Bronx acquired such a stigma that businessmen who remained began an effort to change the name. One real estate broker urged that "South Bronx" be banished from business usage because it "connotes only decay, deprivation, and decadence in the eyes and minds of most Americans." Proposed new names included "Lower Bronx," "Downtown Bronx," "New Bronx," or, in the trendy suggestion of Mayor Edward Koch, "SoBro."

It was amid this atmosphere of decay, deprivation, and decadence that John Mariotta attempted to build a business. Starting a business anywhere is difficult; doing so in the burned-out, boarded-up South Bronx was unusually so. Only a native of the area might have been brave—or rash—enough to try.

The machine shop that would become Wedtech was founded in late 1965 by Mariotta and Irving Lonstein. The two scraped up approximately $3,000 for their start-up capital. Lonstein, a fatherly businessman who had been impressed with Mariotta's determination and mechanical skills, would take care of the paper-work and bring in contracts. Mariotta's job was to run the shop.

The new company on 148th Street, a couple of blocks east of the Grand Concourse, was a modest enterprise, occupying about two thousand square feet of space and employing just three workers. It was dubbed the Welbilt Electronic Die Corp. and was to special-ize in making dies—the patterns or templates used in manufactur-ing. Lonstein considered the name "Welbilt" lucky because he had repaired Welbilt batteries during World War II. Dies for manufac-turing electronic equipment needed to be particularly precise, so a company name suggesting the capability to produce such dies created a good impression.

The week before Welbilt was incorporated, Mariotta married Jennie Caballero, whom he had met three years earlier at a social club dance. Both were thirty-six at the time of the wedding; it was the second marriage for both.

With a new wife to support, Mariotta threw himself into his work. He ordered raw materials, laid out die work, set up ma-chines, and trained new workers. At the end of a seven-day work week, he generally took home a salary of $150.

Despite Mariotta's long hours, Welbilt did not prosper. The com-pany hobbled along with small government contracts and occa-sional commercial jobs. Lonstein was hardly around. Living in Florida in semiretirement, he would come up during the week to do the books, and virtually nothing in the way of marketing.

When a major customer ran into financial problems and wouldn't pay Welbilt for work it had done on a large contract, Lonstein, whose wife was suffering from cancer, decided he didn't need the headache of Welbilt. He told Mariotta to go find himself a new partner.

John Mariotta couldn't afford to be choosy. In June 1970, people weren't exactly lining up to invest in a struggling machine shop in the heart of the South Bronx, run by a loud, quick-tempered, semiliterate high school dropout with a history of business failures.

In fact, the only potential partner the desperate Mariotta could find was Fred Neuberger, himself a tapped-out co-owner—of Fleet-wood Metal Products, a sheet metal concern on Whittier Street in the Bronx.

Welbilt had obtained some subcontract work from Fleetwood and had helped bail Fleetwood out of one particularly difficult job. Now Mariotta approached Neuberger and tried to convince him to come in as a partner. Mariotta was nothing if not persistent. After three days of badgering, Neuberger agreed. But he didn't want to carry Lonstein. So Mariotta and Neuberger bought out Lonstein for $2,400–$1,200 apiece. Neuberger had to borrow the money, using his old Buick as collateral.

Perhaps only in the roiling ethnic melting pot of the Bronx could two men with such varying backgrounds and talents wind up as business partners.

John Mariotta was the elder of two boys born to John and Germina Mariotta. His father was a talented but alcoholic tool- and die-maker, his mother a devout "Holy Roller" Baptist. His grandfather had come to Puerto Rico from Sicily, which accounted for the Italian surname.

Young John grew up in the slums of Spanish Harlem and the Bronx. He made only fitful progress through the New York City public school system, largely because of his poor speech—teachers said he had "marbles in his mouth"—and a chaotic home life. The boy particularly dreaded Fridays, when his father would get paid and come home in a drunken rage. John, his mother, and his younger brother, Mario, would take refuge in the New York City subways—a relatively safe haven in those days.

Despite lofty ambitions and a fascination with chemistry, John failed to get into the prestigious Bronx High School of Science. In one of the many contradictions that mark this complex man, Mariotta bemoaned this rejection for years afterward, even while asserting that he was unable to write and barely able to read. He settled for the Bronx Vocational High School, where he learned his father's trade.

Leaving Bronx Vocational after a year, young Mariotta worked in a series of machine shops and soon became convinced he'd rather be his own boss. After a stint in the army during the Korean War, he returned to a small storefront shop he had established with his father and brother in 1949. The shop made machines to cover jewelry boxes with cloth. Hardly in a growth industry, the business collapsed in 1957, when Mariotta's father died at age fifty-seven of Asiatic flu and his brother died of pneumonia eight months later. At first the despondent Mariotta worked in a couple of other machine shops, but then, still infected by the entrepreneurial bug, he attempted to establish a business on Long Island. The attempt failed, and he turned to Lonstein to start up Welbilt.

Neubergers' background was more exotic. Born in Romania at the dawn of the Nazi era, Neuberger spent his early childhood hiding in cellars as Jews around him were taken away to extermination camps. He later recalled one occasion when he was rounded up in a street raid and taken to a commercial railroad yard. Neuberger, a small boy whose growth had been stunted by illness, managed to escape through some slats and make his way home.

As the Romanian fascists, the Iron Guard, grew increasingly vicious, Neuberger's parents arranged for their son to join a group of young people leaving for Palestine. When the train taking the group broke down, the youths made the rest of the journey on foot. The trek took four weeks during which they subsisted largely on raw potatoes from the fields. Neuberger's immediate family survived the Holocaust, but virtually all his other relatives perished.

In Palestine, the short, scrappy teenager watched the British turn away thousands of Jewish refugees. Enraged, he joined the underground movement. Neuberger would later tell associates that he had worked in the underground with the notorious Stern Gang during Israel's War of Independence. He would regale Mariotta with stories about shooting people in the war and delivering "care packages"—bombs—to the British. How much of this was fact and how much Neuberger's habitual, tough guy braggadocio is hard to determine. A leading Israeli historian of the liberation movement has said that he never heard of Neuberger.

In any event, the Holocaust clearly left Neuberger with a thinly disguised contempt for the norms of civilized society. Getting him to wear a tie was a major ordeal. He once testified in federal court with a toothpick dangling from the side of his mouth.

"Society," he would tell Mariotta, spitting on the floor, "it's a farce. They kill six million of my people. And you call this society? Hah!"

Over the years of their partnership, Neuberger and Mariotta would fight frequently—usually at the top of their lungs, sometimes physically. Mariotta developed a psychological explanation for his constant warfare with Neuberger. It came from one of several rabbis with whom Mariotta was friendly.

"John," Mariotta quoted the rabbi as telling him. "You are putting a conscience on him. And he does not want a conscience, John.

11

He's aggravated because he saw six million with a conscience and . . . they went to the slaughter like lambs. And he does not want a conscience."

After emigrating to the United States in 1947, Neuberger went to school while working as a blacksmith, machinist, and fixture builder. After receiving a bachelor's degree in mechanical engineering from New York University in 1954, he co-founded Fleetwood Metal in the Hunts Point section of the Bronx. The business supported Neuberger and his partner, Murray Brown, for several years but fell on hard times in the late 1960s. When he grudgingly agreed to Mariotta's entreaties to join Welbilt, Neuberger could hardly have imagined that the decision would bring him fortune and a certain measure of fame.

Mariotta and Neuberger were indeed an odd couple. Mariotta spoke an idiosyncratic blend of English sprinkled with Spanish and Yiddish; Neuberger was a member of the Mensa society of geniuses and was fluent in as many as eight languages. Mariotta was a devout Christian and devoted husband, Neuberger a less-than-devout Jew and shameless womanizer. Mariotta was exceedingly generous; Neuberger gave to charity grudgingly.

Still, each brought certain talents to the table. Mariotta had the street smarts, the mechanical ability, and the rapport with the workers on the shop floor. Neuberger had the intellect, the engineering background, and the marketing know-how. They shared an overriding interest in making money. Together, they were an engaging duo—Mariotta the inarticulate entrepreneur reaching for a piece of the American dream, Neuberger the smooth-talking brains behind the operation.

Shortly after they became partners, Mariotta and Neuberger faced a pressing problem. Of all the sites available in the South Bronx, the city of New York had chosen Welbilt's block to be part of the new Lincoln Medical Center complex. The company would have to move. This wasn't such a tragedy: a gang called the Young Lords had been terrorizing businesses in the 148th Street corridor. The problem was that even though the city was willing to reimburse moving costs, Welbilt didn't have enough cash to pay a rigger to move the machinery.

Mariotta and Neuberger managed to locate 3,000 square feet of space in a windowless, one-story building at 1049 Washington Avenue in the blighted Melrose section of the Bronx. The L-shaped brick-and-cinder-block building was "between a dope pusher and a car thief," Mariotta would say later. Legend has it that Mariotta financed the move by investing in a six-pack of beer. The beer lured a group of derelicts who helped lug the tools and equipment to the new site.

Neuberger hustled a few commercial contracts, but Welbilt was always on the brink of collapse. Its sales for all of 1973 were only about $200,000. Neither Mariotta nor Neuberger knew much about accounting systems, and bookkeeping remained a constant problem.

At one point, Neuberger brought his wife, Helen, in to help with the books. Helen was Fred Neuberger's second wife. His first marriage, to a social worker, had ended in divorce. Acquaintances recall the first marriage as a mismatch, mainly because Fred Neuberger's compassion for the downtrodden, his first wife's professional concern, was minimal at best. Although unpolished and crude, Neuberger had little tolerance for those he considered to be his intellectual inferiors, even though he could exude charm whenever it came to picking up women or making a deal.

Helen Manlow Neuberger, his second wife, was a beautiful, pale, glassy-eyed former model with a history of mental illness and drug abuse. In 1972, Fred and Helen Neuberger moved from Palmer Avenue in New Rochelle to a house on West Walnut Street in the city of Long Beach, Long Island. According to Mariotta, the Neubergers were a "wild" pair who thought it amusing to get into a movie, or out of a restaurant, without paying. When they fought, which was frequently, they would slam car doors violently, and Mariotta was enlisted to do repair work. Helen Neuberger was not well suited to working in the bookkeeping department of a struggling machine shop in the South Bronx.

"She was wigged out of her mind," Mariotta recalled. "Why does a person drink four bottles of extra-strength cold medicine?

"She hires an individual that tells me he called up for a gypsy cab and he got the wrong number. And she put him into the books. He doesn't know nothing about books!'

"I told Fred, 'Hey, Freddie, you take that woman out of my place. Freddie, I'm no headshrinker. She's not normal . . . Either you take her out or you will lose face if I take her out. If you need her salary, stay with her salary, but please, for the well-being of the business, for the well-being of my mind, take her out.'"

The bookkeeping crisis was finally resolved in 1973 when Welbilt hired Ceil Lewis, who had answered an ad in the *New York Post*. Because of the company's financial straits, the new $175-a-week clerk was pressed into some unorthodox duties. During one cash crunch, Lewis reportedly got $2,000 off a loan shark in the men's room of a plant in Hunts Point, a particularly tough area of the Bronx. Given Welbilt's chronically precarious situation, she became adept at fending off creditors. Checks were mailed unsigned, or to the wrong company. "John and Freddie are in the hospital," callers were told.

The year after Lewis joined the company, tragedy struck. On September 9, 1974, Helen Neuberger was found dead in the bathroom of the Long Beach house. She was thirty-six.

Fred Neuberger told police Helen had shot herself with the automatic 9mm pistol he kept in the house. Jennie Mariotta's brother-in-law, who was staying in the house with Fred Neuberger at the time, corroborated the story. Although suspicions arose later, the authorities ruled the death a suicide.

Following Helen's death, Neuberger began devoting more time and energy to Welbilt. With the company's finances remaining troubled, Neuberger went down to the bid room at the federal Defense Contract Administration Service on Hudson Street in Manhattan. He combed through all the open contracts. Finally he came across one to manufacture filters for Bell helicopters. The bid documents were virtually illegible.

"We bid on it," he told Mariotta.

"You're crazy," Mariotta shot back.

"*You're* not crazy?" said Neuberger.

"Freddie, I can't read these films."

"If you cannot read these films nobody else can read these films, and we are going to get the job."

In bidding on—and getting—the job, Neuberger and Mariotta paid little heed to whether they could actually make a profit on it. What mattered was getting cash into the company's coffers—fast. It was an attitude that would become a credo.

Neuberger also began to focus on ways the company could turn its ghetto address and Mariotta's Puerto Rican heritage to its advantage. The answer was a program of the federal government called Section 8(a).

The 8(a) program was one of the Johnson administration's responses to the urban riots of the late 1960s. It involved earmarking government contracts to be awarded noncompetitively to minority

14

businesses. In theory, this program would help revitalize the urban ghettos by providing upward mobility and jobs. In reality, it was a recipe for scandal. Determination of which contracts were set aside, and which contractors they were set aside for, was based on political and racial considerations, not economic ones. Nevertheless, the program had bipartisan backing: it appealed to Democrats' traditional concern for the welfare of minority groups and to Republican belief in bootstrap self-help.

The minority business program also appealed to shrewd wheeler-dealers and self-promoters like John Mariotta and Fred Neuberger. Neuberger looked into the program requirements.

"Do you mind being a minority?" he asked Mariotta.

"What do you mean, minority?" Mariotta responded.

"Puerto Rican."

"I *am* Puerto Rican."

With that, the pair decided to apply for acceptance into the set-aside program. There was just one hitch: under the federal regulations, the company had to be at least 51 percent owned by a qualified minority, and Mariotta and Neuberger had a 50–50 split.

To qualify legally, all they needed to do was transfer another 1 percent to Mariotta. But they were concerned that a 51–49 percent split might lead the government to think Mariotta was simply a front for a nonminority owner. So Neuberger transferred enough stock to Mariotta to make it appear that Mariotta owned two-thirds and Neuberger one-third. And just so there should be no question of convenience of timing, they backdated the transfer three years to 1972. Of course, the two-thirds, one-third setup was purely for public consumption. Mariotta and Neuberger made a handshake agreement to keep a 50–50 split.

On September 25, 1975, based on the false application, the U.S. Small Business Administration accepted Welbilt into the set-aside program.

As part of the filing with the SBA, Fred Neuberger signed a statement promising that he would "conduct my business affairs in an ethical manner." It was a pledge he hardly gave thought to when, that same year, he set up a secret checking account at the Bronx branch of Banco Popular de Puerto Rico in the name of F.H.J. Associates. The initials stood for Fred, Helen, and John. (Mariotta would later claim, implausibly, that the letters really stood for Fred & Helen Jewelry, because Neuberger had relatives in the diamond business.)

The F.H.J. account was initially created to handle what Neu-

15

berger called "brokerage"—taking orders for machined parts at a certain price, finding another company to produce them for less, and pocketing the difference as profit. For a small businessman to set up a vehicle to hide a little money from the Internal Revenue Service was not unusual. The F.H.J. account, however, would in time swell into a huge corporate slush fund through which millions of dollars would flow. Ceil Lewis's duties expanded to include bookkeeping for the new account.

Once in the 8(a) program, Welbilt's prospects began to brighten. Mariotta had managed to put together a capable little jobbing shop. The first 8(a) contract, in September 1976, was for $809,656, or more than double the company's sales the previous year. Next came a $2.5 million contract to make a component, called a bell crank, of the General Electric engines that propel the F–104 Phantom jet. Hardly satisfied, Welbilt set its sights on a $10 million contract for kits to overhaul the cooling system on an armored personnel carrier, a tanklike vehicle designated the M–113.

After years of struggle in an urban wasteland, John Mariotta's grandiose dreams were beginning to seem less fanciful. He began to talk of building a General Motors in the Bronx.

Fred Neuberger just laughed. "Are you smoking the happy weed," he asked, "or are you mainlining?"

# 3

## Two Marios and a Miracle

**I**n October 1977, President Jimmy Carter paid a dramatic visit to the South Bronx, a visit that brought home to the nation stark images of urban decay. Standing amid the rubble on Charlotte Street a few blocks from the Welbilt plant, Carter pledged to help revitalize the area. He appointed one of his White House aides, Jack Watson, to coordinate plans for federal assistance. Hugh Carey, the governor of New York, urged Watson to direct some defense contracts to the South Bronx.

All this high-level government concern for the Bronx piqued the interest of Mariotta and Neuberger, who could recognize a marketing opportunity as well as anyone. Quickly they honed a pitch presenting Welbilt as a "redevelopment role model" for the area, and for entrée into the Carter White House they turned to a law firm— Fried, Frank, Harris, Shriver & Kampelman—they had retained a few months earlier to handle their government contracts work. A partner at the firm's Washington office, Kenneth S. Kramer, wrote to Watson on Wedtech's behalf. A few days later Watson responded with a handwritten note saying he had asked his staff to review the materials Kramer had sent. Mariotta also signed off on letters to Carter and Watson, mentioning the company's rapid growth and search for a larger plant. But if Mariotta and Neuberger expected the Carter White House to find and finance a new facility

17

for them, they were sorely disappointed. Watson replied that he had referred Mariotta's letter to bureaucrats at the SBA and the New York City Office of Economic Development. Mariotta's letter to Carter was answered by a functionary in the Department of Housing and Urban Development.

While the company made little headway with the Carter administration, its pitch did attract the attention of the press. Things in the South Bronx had been so bad for so long that any glimmer of success qualified as news.

One of the first stories about Welbilt appeared in the old *New York Tribune*. Written by Mort Young, the January 13, 1978 article first described the surrounding neighborhood: "It seems that no coin phones, no mailboxes, stand on [the] streets. To mail a letter, or to receive one, you drive to the Post Office. There are no police visible . . . Cars go through red lights and park anywhere. There is no law, only huge watchdogs loping down back alleys."

Young went on to quote Mariotta as calling Welbilt the "ray of hope" that Carter missed.

Carter may have missed Welbilt, but the *Trib* story whetted the appetite of at least one local politician. Soon after the article appeared, U.S. Rep. Mario Biaggi, the veteran Democrat whose congressional district included part of the Bronx, paid a courtesy call. Biaggi's interest was a little surprising because Welbilt had no facilities in his district. Nonetheless, Mariotta and Neuberger gave their very important visitor the grand tour.

Biaggi was a big man in the Bronx, beloved by his constituents. With his husky build, dark suits, and curly gray hair, he exuded power. Before turning to politics, Biaggi had been a highly decorated member of the New York City Police Department. A limp—the result of a thirty-year-old leg injury suffered when he subdued a runaway horse—underscored his "hero cop" image.

Like Mariotta, Biaggi had started life humbly in upper Manhattan. Born in 1917 to Italian immigrants living in a tenement on East 106th Street, he grew up during the worst years of the Great Depression. His mother, Mary, was a charwoman; his father, Salvatore, a marble cutter. After high school, Biaggi worked in a braid factory, then in a post office, before winning admission to the police department in 1942.

Less than eighteen months after joining the force, he shot and killed a suspect who tried to stab him with an icepick. That earned him the first of twenty-one citations he would receive in his career.

18

As early as the mid–1950s, however, rumors began to circulate that Biaggi was "mobbed up"—that is, had ties to organized crime. (A Welbilt executive would eventually recall a visit to Biaggi's congressional office in the Bronx. Several black limousines were parked in front and some men were inside talking in what the executive believed to be Sicilian. When the executive asked who the men were, Biaggi's law partner put a finger to his temple, pointed like a gun, and said, "That's why nobody messes with the congressman.") In 1955, Biaggi was reassigned after a surprise inspection found him absent from his Queens detective command. Other questions lingered after a 1959 incident in which Biaggi, off-duty and in civilian clothes, shot and killed a man. Biaggi said the armed man had forced his way into the back seat of a car Biaggi was driving and ordered him to a remote spot. There, Biaggi maintained, he managed to draw his revolver and fire. A police investigation cleared Biaggi of any wrongdoing; he was, in fact, decorated for heroism. But Mario Merola, the Bronx district attorney who later reinvestigated the incident, came to suspect that Biaggi may have gotten away with murder.

A major reason for Biaggi's visit to Welbilt was to drum up some business for the law practice he shared with Bernard G. Ehrlich. Biaggi had interrupted his police career in 1960 and enrolled at New York Law School at the urging of the school's dean, who had heard the policeman speak. Because he had not gone to college, Biaggi needed, and obtained, special permission to pursue a law degree. He graduated in 1963, then retired from the police department in 1965 without returning to duty. Because of the leg injury, he received a 75 percent disability pension of $10,000 a year.

Biaggi's legal career started slowly. He failed the New York bar examination twice before passing in 1966. But he made the right political contacts and ran for Congress in 1968, winning easily as a Democrat with Conservative Party endorsement. His campaign slogan was, "I'm for you. It's that simple." Once in office, he endeared himself to voters by attending personally to requests as mundane as Social Security checks and passports. He tried to mediate the conflict in Northern Ireland and spoke passionately on behalf of Soviet Jews, the elderly, and victims of child abuse.

Biaggi's "law and order" background made him a leading candidate for mayor of New York City in 1973—until it was reported that he had invoked the Fifth Amendment during a federal investigation of private immigration bills. At first Biaggi denied the report, but after it was confirmed that he had refused to answer about thirty questions related to his personal finances, his candidacy died. The following year, the congressman was named in a paternity suit brought by a former campaign worker; the suit was resolved in Biaggi's favor. By the time Biaggi came to Welbilt, while it seemed clear he could be a congressman as long as he wanted, his aspirations for higher office had been dashed.

The tour went well enough. Biaggi said he was pleased to see a business growing in the Bronx, that Mariotta and Neuberger were doing a good job, and that they should feel free to call on his law firm if they needed any help. Mariotta and Neuberger didn't agree on much, but they concurred that it would help to have such a powerful friend. The following year, they engaged the services of Biaggi & Ehrlich for an initial retainer of $20,000 for two years. It was clear to Mariotta and Neuberger that they were paying not so much for legal expertise as for political clout.

At about the same time, another Mario began performing important functions for Wedtech. Mario Moreno, a native of Colombia with a master's degree in business administration from New York University, appeared to be the "numbers man" Mariotta and Neuberger had needed so long and now so desperately if they were to deal successfully with bankers and government agencies.

Moreno had met Mariotta through the Urban Business Assistance Corporation, an affiliate of the NYU business school that provided free assistance to minority businesses. As a volunteer at UBAC, Moreno spent five months helping Welbilt prepare the paperwork for a $250,000 bank loan. At Moreno's urging, Mariotta began attending the night classes Moreno was conducting on business management. Mariotta was an eager if not particularly brilliant student. After about a year and a half, he decided it was easier to hire an expert than become one. Over drinks at the top of the World Trade Center, Mariotta asked Moreno to come to work for Welbilt, telling him, "There are too many MBAs on Wall Street and not enough in the South Bronx."

Moreno had worked as a financial analyst for several shipping and freight companies but had not been a resounding success in the business world, never making much more than $30,000 a year. Welbilt was not even close to being a big-league company. At Welbilt, Moreno's superficial knowledge of financial analysis seemed profound and his formal speech and thick Spanish accent (he called the boss "Joan Mah-ree-OH-tah") suggested old-world charm and polish.

Moreno's new professional opportunity meshed nicely with his personal plans. While looking to leave his troubleshooting job at a shipping company, he had also been looking to leave Luz, his wife of seventeen years. He seized the moment, going into the catering business with his new "companion," Caridad Vazquez, and becoming a three-day-a-week consultant to Welbilt at $150-a-day.

About a year later, Moreno learned through a conversation with Neuberger that the two-thirds, one-third ownership agreement was a sham, and that Neuberger and Mariotta had the handshake agreement to split everything 50–50. Although Moreno had been taught about business ethics, this revelation of a fraud against the government apparently did nothing to dampen his association with the company.

Learning the ropes of the 8(a) set-aside program, Welbilt was starting to get a steady stream of small defense contracts. In the late 1970s its sales were running about $1.5 million a year. Unfortunately, cost controls were virtually nonexistent, and by early 1980 the company was again on the verge of bankruptcy. The two Marios helped save the day.

Moreno met Biaggi at the congressman's office on Pelham Parkway. The only way to prevent the company's demise, the consultant explained, was to expedite a direct loan and a loan guarantee from the U.S. Economic Development Administration. Biaggi directed an aide to contact the EDA loan officer in Philadelphia. The aide did, and by the end of February Welbilt had a direct loan for $2 million and a $2.2 million loan from Citibank that was 90 percent guaranteed by the federal government.

Welbilt had outgrown its plant on Washington Avenue, and it used $1.1 million of the Citibank money to acquire a three-story, red brick building at 595 Gerard Avenue, near Yankee Stadium. Compared to the desolate Washington Avenue site, Gerard Avenue was a veritable hotbed of economic activity. Across the street were maintenance facilities for the U.S. Postal Service and the New York City Department of Sanitation. At break time and lunch time, mobile canteens would park outside the Welbilt entrances, selling rice and beans. Workers could walk a couple of blocks to the check-cashing establishment on 149th Street, or to Glacken's Bar for the regular—a three-ounce shot of rum mixed with Coke. Hookers gathered at 150th Street and River Avenue to offer their services.

To the north of the newly acquired building were Yankee Stadium and the Bronx House of Detention. A steady stream of blue-and-orange Corrections Department buses, with steel mesh on the windows, ferried prisoners to and from court appearances. Just southwest of the plant was the gritty, bustling Bronx Terminal Market, where loads of fresh produce were broken down and sold to the city's retailers. The market offered good buys on fruits and vegetables but also attracted rats to the neighborhood. Unsold fruit was often dumped into the streets to rot, giving the area a particularly pungent aroma during the summer.

The streets surrounding the new plant were lined with abandoned or stolen cars in various states of decomposition. Under the Major Deegan Expressway, an al fresco auto "chop shop" seemed to operate twenty-four hours a day, seven days a week, illuminated and heated by fires in fifty-five-gallon drums. Piles of discarded tires nearly obscured the Department of Sanitation's "NO DUMP-ING—MAX. FINE $1,500" sign.

The headquarters building itself was nothing fancy. The 110,000-square-foot structure was almost thirty years old. Formerly occupied by National Shoe Company, it covered about an acre. The parking lot took up another acre. To get from floor to floor, you took a "Bronx elevator"—a flight of stairs. The top floor housed the administrative offices. Viewed from above, this floor resembled a hollow square enclosing a gravel-covered courtyard, littered with discarded signs and lumber. The offices ran along the outside of the square off both sides of a corridor. For a time, when break-ins by neighborhood junkies were particularly frequent, German shepherds were turned loose in the courtyard at night. The bottom two floors, large but low-ceilinged, were devoted to manufacturing.

After installing $1.7 million worth of machinery, Welbilt held an opening ceremony on June 12, 1980. Mariotta invited a priest, a rabbi, and a minister to the event. He explained this ecumenical approach by saying, "I am not going to take any chances."

Also on hand for the festivities were Biaggi and the Bronx congressman who represented the district in which Welbilt was located, Robert Garcia. Mariotta thanked them for leading him through "the federal maze." He also singled out for praise José Aceves of the Latin American Manufacturers Association in Washington and Ivan Irizarry of the New York regional office of the Small Business Administration.

"Without them, this miracle wouldn't have happened," Mariotta declared buoyantly in his high-pitched, squeaky voice.

Not one to be left out, Neuberger, with a keen eye for symbolism, told the *New York Daily News* that the company had saved an apple tree in the new parking lot.

"Sparing that tree cost us four parking spaces and a couple of hundred dollars additional on the paving contract, but we think it's worth it," he said.

With the company ensconced in its new home, a sense of excitement about Welbilt began to grow. The work force swelled to a seventy-person mix of Puerto Ricans, blacks, Indians from India, Soviet Jews, and a couple of token American whites. Mariotta's infectious enthusiasm spread to the office staff and the factory floor. Welbilt was shipping high-quality products, though not necessarily on time or on budget.

"Things were happening. The sky was the limit. Everyone was on a high," recalled Edward D. McCarthy, who was hired in 1979 fresh out of law school to handle contract administration.

It didn't take McCarthy long to realize that life at Welbilt would be somewhat different from life at, say, Grumman or General Dynamics. One day the young lawyer saw the principals of the company engaged in a heated dispute. Mariotta put Neuberger in a headlock and screamed into one of his ears. After the tirade ended, Neuberger turned his head, gestured to his other ear, and told Mariotta, "Now do *this* one!"

After a while, McCarthy and other workers just shrugged off such incidents. No one at Welbilt had ever worked for a Fortune 500 company, so they had no means of comparison. They became immune to the daily insanity. To them, it was the norm.

Not long after Wedtech moved into its new home, presidential candidate Ronald Reagan emulated Jimmy Carter and visited the South Bronx. Standing amid the rubble and the burnt-out shells of abandoned buildings, Reagan declared Carter's efforts to have been a failure.

"I've got a record as governor of California in which we didn't try to do things by the government route," the Republican candidate said. "We used the people and we got jobs for the people in the private sector, the kind of jobs that have got a future."

Reagan went on to pledge that, if elected, his administration would provide incentives for private companies in places like the South Bronx, creating employment and hope for ghetto dwellers.

Welbilt's executives listened attentively—even Fred Neuberger, who had given $1,000 to the Committee for the Re-Election of Jimmy Carter.

# 4

## The Small-Engine Contract

**E**ven before Ronald Reagan toured the South Bronx, Welbilt had been eyeing what would be the most ambitious undertaking in its brief history—a contract to build small engines for the U.S. Army.

The army was in the market for six-horsepower engines similar to, but larger than, those that power an ordinary lawnmower. While the typical lawnmower engine can be produced for less than $200, the army spends more than $1,000 for each of its engines.

Military engines cost more because they have to be made more rugged and reliable than their civilian counterparts, an expensive process known as "gold plating." The engines in question were designed primarily for such functions as powering the portable generators that provide electricity for much of the army's tactical communications equipment. By the late 1970s, the army needed to buy replacements for many of the 120,000 such engines in the hands of the troops.

Through José Aceves, the forceful, mustachioed chairman of the Washington-based Latin American Manufacturers Association, Mariotta and Neuberger learned in 1979 that the engine contract might be set aside for a minority company.

The purchase was to be made under a Carter administration pilot program. The government contracts that had been typically

25

awarded under the Section 8(a) law to minority firms were for services or construction. The pilot program was intended to broaden Section 8(a) opportunities by directing some fairly large contracts to disadvantaged businesses. In theory, the bigger contracts would help the minority firms grow faster and become more sophisticated.

For the small-engine contract, the army planned to team an inexperienced minority firm with an established engine manufacturer. After several major companies rejected the army's proposal, the Avco Corporation finally agreed to act as a sponsor.

Initially Aceves had hoped to get the army engine contract for his own company, Hartec Enterprises Inc., but a survey by the army's Troop Support and Readiness Command (TSARCOM, the army organization responsible for providing engines to troops in the field) revealed a few problems—namely, that Hartec had no facilities, no personnel, and no production plan. So Aceves brought the contract to Welbilt's attention, hoping that Hartec could at least get subcontracts for some of the components.

To Mariotta the news was exciting. Such a contract would put Welbilt a lot closer to the big league. It would give the company a chance to make an entire product, not just pieces of someone else's product. If Welbilt was to become another General Motors, building engines would be the natural first step.

Neuberger, however, was cool to the idea. He pointed out, not unreasonably, that Welbilt had never built any kind of engines before, much less ones that met the military's stringent quality standards.

This difference of opinion was aired in the usual fashion one Saturday morning during a meeting of senior management—Mariotta, Neuberger, and Moreno—in the conference room at 1049 Washington Avenue. Mariotta became enraged when he learned that Neuberger had not returned one of Aceves's phone calls. To Mariotta, Aceves was important and had to be treated with respect and courtesy. Mariotta was a strong supporter of LAMA and had helped bail the association out of financial trouble in 1977. The Mexican-born Aceves, meanwhile, was an ardent advocate for Hispanic businesses, particularly the three or four like Welbilt that were augmenting his salary with monthly retainers on the side. At high volume, Mariotta told Neuberger that he considered it an intolerable affront not to have returned a call from Aceves. Neuberger, never one to back away from a good fight, screamed back.

For the inarticulate Mariotta and the combative Neuberger, words hardly sufficed. Before long, the two began ripping pictures off the walls and throwing them at each other. Soon they were hurling the metal chairs stationed around the table.

By the time Moreno was able to establish a cease-fire, the two executives were bleeding from cuts on their arms, and the conference room was a shambles. After a brief cooling-off period, however, the partners left the meeting laughing together, the decision having been made to pursue the engine contract. Questions about how to build the engines could wait until later.

When the Small Business Administration formally withdrew Aceves's company as its candidate for the contract and substituted Welbilt, Mariotta and Neuberger had gotten over the first hurdle. The next was the army itself.

The official responsible for the acquisition of new engines was Thomas J. Keenan, TSARCOM's director of procurement in St. Louis. Faced with growing complaints from the field about an engine shortage, Keenan was anxious to start production of replacement engines and frustrated by the SBA's problems finding a qualified minority contractor. Although the army had agreed initially to have the contract set aside, Keenan was becoming convinced that the contract should be removed from the 8(a) program and be awarded in the regular manner—through competitive bidding to a mainstream manufacturer.

But Welbilt's appetite for the big time had been whetted, and company officials were not about to watch passively while such a plum of a contract was snatched away. When it came to winning, John Mariotta sounded like Vince Lombardi. "When I was in the service, they never taught me how to surrender," he would say. "You have to keep on and on and on and on. You never say die."

Under pressure from both LAMA and the SBA, Keenan agreed to give one last shot to a minority contractor. He sent two of his industrial specialists to the Bronx to review Welbilt's capabilities. What they found was a largely empty building—Welbilt's new headquarters at 595 Gerard—containing a couple of sophisticated metal-cutting machines. With this Welbilt was claiming it could build the high-quality engines the army needed! The specialists reported back to Keenan that Welbilt was doing good work "at the level they were doing it," but the company didn't seem capable of producing military-standard engines.

27

Still, the army was required under the pilot program to notify the SBA that it was soliciting bids for 13,100 six-horsepower engines. TSARCOM calculated that the fair-market price (the cost of production plus a reasonable profit) for the contract was $19 million, or $1,485 per engine. The estimate was based on the previous purchase of engines from Chrysler Corporation, adjusted for inflation.

On February 27, 1981, Welbilt submitted a proposal, prepared by Avco, to build the engines for $99.9 million, or about $7,600 apiece. The Welbilt-Avco bid was 500 percent above what the army considered fair. Not surprisingly, it provoked hysterical laughter at TSARCOM headquarters, which promptly asked the secretary of the army to withdraw the engine purchase from the 8(a) pilot program.

Welbilt professed outrage. The $99.9 million proposal, Mariotta and Moreno contended, was entirely Avco's work. Welbilt hadn't even received it from Avco, they said, until the day before it was due at TSARCOM. Avco may have factored in the enormous costs of starting an engine production line from scratch with an inexperienced work force, but the view from the Bronx (totally unsubstantiated) was that Avco and Keenan were conspiring to eliminate Welbilt from the picture. Accordingly, Welbilt broke with Avco and began submitting its own proposals to the army. Welbilt dropped the price first to $45 million and then to just under $39 million. Welbilt executives explained that awarding their company a single contract to build all the engines, rather than a series of contracts, would produce economies of scale.

Mariotta also trotted out some rather dubious calculations designed to make Welbilt's proposal look like the best bargain since the Dutch bought Manhattan. If Welbilt got the contract, he asserted, 300 new jobs would be created, 80 percent of which would go to welfare recipients. Taking 240 people off the welfare rolls would save the government $20,000 per year, per recipient, resulting in a "special added discount to the taxpayer" of $24 million over the five-year life of the contract!

Keenan wasn't impressed with Mariotta's New Math. He estimated Welbilt's costs could be as high as $57 million. Welbilt's new proposals had come in with virtually nothing in the way of supporting documentation. On April 13, 1981, TSARCOM formally rejected the company's $39 million proposal.

With that, Keenan jumped to the top of Welbilt's enemies list, a list that would become populated over the years by bureaucrats trying to follow the rules and protect taxpayers' money despite intense pressure from the company's political patrons.

Welbilt's executives tended to personalize every dispute. Thus, they regarded TSARCOM's reluctance to entrust an important contract to an unproven manufacturer as a case of an individual, Keenan, thwarting a fledgling minority enterprise through an arbitrary and unreasonable exercise of power.

Keenan was a formidable adversary. He had joined TSARCOM in 1973 as deputy procurement director; six years earlier, he had received a law degree from Catholic University in Washington, D.C. (The Welbilt crowd, having been told that Keenan had received the standard Juris Doctor degree, took to calling him "Dr. Keenan.") By 1977, Keenan had been promoted to procurement director. Evidently he was good at what he did: in 1980, he received a Presidential Meritorious Service Award.

Mariotta, Neuberger, and Moreno began to focus on ways to outmaneuver their nemesis. Joining them in the battle was David S. Epstein, a Bronx-born, Harvard-educated writer and urban affairs specialist. Epstein, who had been introduced to Welbilt in 1979, preached what Mariotta and Neuberger seemed to be practicing—employing the unemployable, utilizing the useless. He signed on as a public relations consultant.

"It's a very good thing you are doing," Epstein told Mariotta and Neuberger. "I can make you famous."

Convinced that Keenan was their problem, Welbilt's management team hit on the idea of hiring a private detective to investigate Keenan's personal life. With any luck, the detective would dig up some dirt that could be used to blackmail their nemesis, or at least to destroy his credibility. Convinced they were facing institutional discrimination, the Welbilt officers also wanted an investigation of John O. Marsh, Jr., the secretary of the army.

Epstein called an acquaintance named Harold Lipset, a San Francisco private eye who specialized in electronic surveillance and industrial espionage. Lipset advised that costly spying on a mid-level bureaucrat and the secretary of the army was not likely to solve the company's problems. What Welbilt needed was a friend in high places.

Lipset suggested that Welbilt get in touch with E. Robert Wallach, a successful San Francisco personal injury lawyer with whom he had worked. Wallach was a close friend of Edwin Meese

III. Meese, then counselor to Ronald Reagan, was being referred to in the media as the "deputy president." Now *that* was clout.

A meeting was quickly arranged, and Wallach flew to New York. Mariotta, Neuberger, and Moreno decided the famous lawyer from the West Coast deserved V.I.P. treatment, so they picked him up at his Manhattan hotel and drove him to the Bronx.

Trim, tanned, and balding, Wallach was about average height, but he seemed shorter because he generally kept his head slightly bowed. He had an earnest demeanor and bushy eyebrows that overhung spaniel-like brown eyes. Born in the Bronx in 1934 to a Jewish family of modest means, Wallach had moved with his mother to the West Coast after his parents' divorce.

Wallach had met Meese in 1957 at the Boalt Hall School of Law on the University of California, Berkeley, campus. Working together on the moot court team, they became fast friends. After law school, Meese went into public service, first with the Alameda County district attorney's office and later on the staff of Gov. Ronald Reagan. Wallach, meanwhile, developed a highly lucrative private practice representing the victims of auto accidents, airplane crashes, and medical malpractice.

Meese and Wallach tended to opposite ends of the political spectrum. While Meese made his reputation as a hard-line conservative, Wallach was fond of telling people that his socialist grandfather had been active in the Workmen's Circle and had instilled in him the traditional liberal ideals. He was elected president of the Bar Association of San Francisco in 1975 on a platform of advancing the interests of women and minorities and improving legal aid for indigents; he also did a great deal of pro bono work. He was so ostentatious about his do-gooderism, however, that some colleagues found the man obnoxious. Egocentric to an extreme, Wallach mounted a quixotic bid for the U.S. Senate in 1976, promising to decriminalize the possession of marijuana and strive for nuclear disarmament. He lost, receiving only 2.2 percent of the vote in the Democratic primary.

Even by California standards, Wallach was something of an odd duck, a man who seemed to cultivate eccentricities. Like the poet e.e. cummings, he spelled his name entirely in lower-case letters, a practice that began when a high school teacher encouraged Wallach to assert his individuality. West Coast associates called him "small case bob." He was a health fanatic, a vegetarian, and an avid jogger. After the break-up of his marriage in the mid–1970s, he reportedly became a modish dresser, wore a fresh yellow rose in his lapel each day, had hair transplants, tooled about town in a vintage Jaguar, and was trailed seemingly everywhere by a golden-haired dog, a Saluki named Sally.

On this April day in 1981, the Welbilt executives were less concerned about their visitor's idiosyncrasies than with making a good impression. As they pulled up to the plant, the sentimental Wallach was immediately struck by the realization that the building was four blocks from the Grand Concourse, where he had spent the first years of his life.

Mariotta, Neuberger, and Moreno guided Wallach through the run-down offices on the top floor of the building at 595 Gerard, then downstairs to the shop floor. Wallach was amazed. Here in the South Bronx was an immaculate industrial operation with a full Saturday shift of minority workers operating sophisticated, computerized equipment. Mariotta exuded charm and sincerity. He knew all the employees by their first names. The pictures on the walls were of their families, or of Christ. No pinups. No porno.

There was more. Upstairs, Wallach was shown the room set aside for chapel worship, something he had seen only on military bases. He was taken to the research and development section, populated by the Soviet Jews whom Mariotta called his brain trust. The group went to lunch at a restaurant in Spanish Harlem, El Deportiva, and schmoozed about their lives and backgrounds.

By the end of the lunch, the officers had pushed all the right buttons. "They told me their life stories in three hours," Wallach would recall, "and I loved them. I loved them. I thought they were terrific. By the end of the day, I was sold. I was very impressed."

Wallach imagined that not only he but also his friend Ed Meese, the counselor to the president of the United States, would be excited to hear this story of a minority-owned company blossoming amid the urban wasteland—proof of the administration's belief in the powers of free enterprise.

Wallach was an inveterate memo writer. Within a few days of his trip to the Bronx, he dashed off a missive to Mariotta—the first of more than 250 he would send company executives on subjects ranging from procurement strategy to proper dietary habits. The memo urged Mariotta to prepare a promotional brochure for "the right person"—Meese, presumably—containing background on the company and photos of happy workers. Wallach particularly wanted a picture of the employee who kept "a picture of Christ on his workstand."

With Wallach on board, Welbilt had an important new ally in the war against Keenan. Mario Moreno promptly informed Welbilt's contracts lawyer in Washington, Timothy Sullivan, that the company had retained "the finest trial lawyer in the United States." Hmmm, that's interesting, thought Sullivan, who had never heard of Bob Wallach.

It didn't take long for Wallach to call Sullivan to say that he was going to be overseeing Welbilt's legal strategies from that point forward, and that Sullivan's role would most likely be reduced. The two arranged to meet at the Army and Navy Club. After a memorable display of name-dropping, Wallach told Sullivan he didn't think the thirty-three-year-old Detroit native was powerful enough to represent Welbilt in Washington. He even asked Sullivan to recommend firms with more horsepower and prestige.

Understandably, Sullivan was taken aback. He had been working with Welbilt for five years, had even ventured a number of times to the South Bronx. The blond, green-eyed attorney had spent his career learning the intricacies of government contract law. Suddenly this California trial lawyer was going to come in and show the boys in D.C. how things were done?

When it came to consultants, the attitude among Welbilt management seemed to be the more, the merrier. If having one entrée into the White House was good, two would be twice as good.

With this philosophy in mind, Epstein called an old Harvard classmate, Charles Dickey Dyer III, who was related by marriage to Vice-President George Bush. It was a tenuous connection—Dyer's younger sister was married to Barbara Bush's older brother—but even tenuous connections had to be pursued in the battle against Keenan. Dyer, a Princeton, New Jersey, management consultant, was active in Republican politics and had connections with certain G.O.P. congressmen.

Dyer was briefed on the Welbilt story and said he would to try to help the company win the engine contract. His standard fee was $120 per hour, but he agreed to defer payment of one-third on the understanding that if Welbilt received the engine contract, he would get twice the deferred amount.

Like Wallach, Dyer went to work quickly, dashing off memos to two G.O.P. congressmen from New Jersey and a note to Bush telling the vice-president that Welbilt was "a good company." A separate Dyer letter to Secretary of the Army Marsh was long on giddy boosterism and short on facts:

> The Reagan/Bush Administration has committed itself to try to reduce waste, abuse, fraud and deceit in government operation and procurement . . .
>
> Based on the voluminous record I've been asked to examine regarding the [engine contract], it looks like your bureaucracy is misbehaving. This time, or course, won't be the first time.
>
> This time, however, if you can make them behave, it will rebound spectacularly to the credit of the Reagan/Bush Administration, since all of you who are part of it can allege truthfully that you've invented the double whammy for the 80s: lower cost military hardware which eradicates welfare.
>
> Visual [sic] the scene, Mr. Secretary! Mr. Reagan stands in the exact same spot in the South Bronx rubble where Mr. Carter made his failed promise. He announces the Republican solution to reduced military hardware costs: engaging the private sector to convert welfare payments into factory payrolls producing top quality military hardware. Thanks to SBA, you have found Welbilt Electronic Die Corp., the fellows who know how to perform this minor miracle.
>
> That's good for the Republican Party; that's good for the people of the South Bronx; that's good for the American people!

Unfortunately for Mariotta and his cohorts, the approximately $15,000 they ended up paying Dickey Dyer to churn out such prose doesn't appear to have affected the outcome of the engine contract decision. Nor is there any evidence that Bush himself intervened. Still, Dyer's letter spelled out clearly the political considerations at play in the Welbilt case.

Showing a keen understanding of the separation of powers, the Welbilt officials didn't neglect the legislative branch in their quest for the engine contract.

Representative Biaggi, whose law firm was receiving ever larger retainers from Welbilt, enlisted the help of Rep. Joseph P. Addabbo, a Democrat from Queens who held influential posts with both the House Small Business Committee and the Defense Appropriations Subcommittee.

Biaggi also turned to New York's freshman Republican senator, Alfonse M. D'Amato. During the 1980 election, Biaggi had thrown his weight behind an organization called Democrats for D'Amato that helped the little-known Long Island politician win the Senate seat in a close three-way race. Now it was time for Biaggi to call in the favor.

Biaggi's law partner, Bernie Ehrlich, prided himself on being a well-informed insider, so he took great pleasure in announcing to the Welbilt executives that he was going to be named as an unpaid military adviser to D'Amato. His daughter, Robin, would later go to work on D'Amato's staff in Washington. D'Amato had run on a platform of doing more for New York interests. As a newly elected conservative Republican with a newly elected conservative Republican in the White House, D'Amato impressed Welbilt officials as a potentially valuable ally.

In fact, D'Amato delivered almost immediately. Trooping into Biaggi's office one day, Mariotta, Moreno, and Ehrlich mentioned they could use the senator's help with the army contract. Biaggi picked up the phone.

"Al, I have the people from Welbilt here and they would like to ... have a talk with you on this problem that they have," Biaggi said.

With that, the threesome took off for the other side of Capitol Hill; there they were soon meeting with the senator and one of his aides. The wiry, hard-charging D'Amato, a self-styled "Mr. Fixit" for New York interests, told the aide to develop an information paper on what could be done to help Welbilt. The senator also signed off on a note to Marsh, calling on the army secretary to allow "a competent, growing firm like Welbilt a fair opportunity to meet the army's needs."

Rounding out Welbilt's expanding arsenal of supporters were Phillip V. Sanchez and Stephen Denlinger.

Sanchez, the former U.S. ambassador to Honduras and Colombia during the Nixon and Ford administrations, had been a leading Hispanic supporter of Reagan and was being considered for a job with the new administration. Mariotta had met him at Hispanic political and business meetings. When Welbilt retained him at $1,000 per month to provide advice and exert pressure, Sanchez promptly wrote to Lyn Nofziger, then head of the White House Office of Political Affairs, urging that Mariotta be photographed with President Reagan. Such a presidential photo session would "yield significant political pluses for our administration," Sanchez asserted.

Denlinger, meanwhile, had taken over as head of the Latin American Manufacturers Association after a bitter fight with Aceves. Like Aceves, he quickly realized that lobbying for Welbilt would be a nice way to supplement his income. Denlinger urged Hispanic members of Congress to side with Welbilt in the struggle with the army; he also extolled the company's virtues in letters to such top White House aides as Meese, Nofziger, Elizabeth Dole, Michael Deaver, and James Baker.

Under normal circumstances, Keenan's rejection of Welbilt's $39 million proposal would have been the end of the matter. But Welbilt didn't operate under normal rules.

Fortunately for Welbilt, the Small Business Administration was in its corner, and SBA officials refused to accede to the army's desire to withdraw the engine contract from the set-aside program. As a result, the company found itself in the enviable position of having one agency of the government arguing with another on its behalf.

While the bureaucrats wrangled on, Welbilt decided that its immediate objective should be to force the army to conduct an "audit" and a related "technical review." Not only would this give Welbilt a chance to sell its cost calculations, it would also delay the army's final decision (although Keenan, understandably, thought he had made that in April).

Wallach quickly grasped the significance of the audit. Since the initial lunch with the Welbilt officials, he had been getting regular reports on the status of Welbilt's efforts to obtain the engine contract, which in turn he had passed on to his friend, Ed Meese, in memos and phone calls. Frequently, Wallach would send the memos to Meese's home in McLean, Virginia, so Meese would be more likely to read them. It is also likely that Wallach personally provided Meese with information about Welbilt during a spring weekend drive to West Point, where Meese's son, Michael, was a cadet.

35

In a May 11 letter to Meese, Wallach suggested that Welbilt's request for an audit might be "too conservative" an approach. Direct intervention by Defense Secretary Caspar Weinberger or Army Secretary Marsh might be all that was needed "to accomplish the task," Wallach wrote.

Meese, a bluff and genial sort, seemed oblivious to the possibility that his friends might have ulterior motives for doing him a favor or asking him to do one for them. The presidential counselor apparently saw nothing wrong in Wallach's using his special access to promote a private interest's efforts to influence an army procurement decision. In fact, he agreed that it might be possible to arrange a meeting between Welbilt's principals and either Marsh or Weinberger. He also asked his staff to look into the matter and make sure that Welbilt got "fair treatment or a fair hearing."

The following week, Wallach dictated an update on the situation to Meese and Edwin Thomas, a Meese assistant who had loaned $15,000 in January 1981 to Meese's wife, Ursula. Thomas in turn passed the Welbilt material along to another White House aide, Craig L. Fuller, director of the Office of Cabinet Affairs. In a covering memo, Thomas made sure Fuller knew exactly who Wallach was: "Bob Wallach, even though he uses low case, is an extremely close friend of Ed Meese."

Yet for all the notes passing back and forth among White House staffers, Welbilt's position was deteriorating rapidly. The army was continuing its efforts to remove the contract from the pilot program and offer it for competitive bidding. SBA officials expressed a willingness to allow the army to withdraw the small engine contract—but then threw in a new wrinkle: that the army agree to reconsider Welbilt if a competitive solicitation didn't produce any bids within 10 percent of the army's fair-market price calculation.

Exactly where this idea originated is unclear. It may have surfaced in a meeting between Welbilt officials and an Addabbo aide on the House Small Business Committee. Whatever the origin, it was Welbilt's way of asserting that nobody could build the engine for the army's asking price or even for 110 percent of that price.

From a legal point of view, "the 10 percent solution" was unprecedented and bizarre, totally outside the realm of competitive procurement regulations. Army officials—sensing the uproar that would ensue if the army invited competitive bids and then tried to call off the solicitation—viewed the whole concept as unworkable.

On further reflection, the Welbilt gang didn't think much of the idea either. At best, it might divert attention from the real issues and buy the company more time. At worst, the army might take them up on the idea, and they'd probably lose the contract to a low-ball bidder.

In early July, David Epstein wrote to Wallach urging him to kill the SBA's 10 percent idea. Epstein left no doubt what Welbilt expected. "I hesitate to tell you what you certainly know—that a single phone call from and to an appropriate person would do it," Epstein wrote.

Now Wallach was really feeling the pressure. The fate of the engine contract seemed to be on his shoulders. He sent yet another memo to Meese—by express mail, to both his office and his home.

> Dear Ed: There appears to be more urgency involved than I realized when we last spoke about this project . . . Some course of action more aggressive than the one we discussed, even if less definitive than your personal intervention, is in order to avoid what may well be, and probably is, a substantial miscarriage . . .

After receiving this latest plea, Meese discussed the matter with his assistant, Ken Cribb. He told Cribb to stay on top of the situation and report back in mid-August.

The situation was still critical for Welbilt. The army might at any moment decide to accept the 10 percent solution, leaving Welbilt with only slim hopes of ever getting the engine contract. On July 20, the army responded to the SBA in a letter from small-business director Juanita Watts, who explained that the 10 percent idea would violate procurement regulations. In a tactical move, she said the army accepted the SBA's offer to withdraw the contract, and suggested immediate action to get rid of the impermissible 10 percent stipulation.

The SBA didn't fall for the ploy. It refused to approve the withdrawal on the army's terms, instead urging the army to proceed with an audit and negotiations with Welbilt.

By the summer of 1981, the battle lines were clear. Welbilt had assembled an impressive set of allies—the SBA, various members of Congress, private lobbyists, and two well-connected entrées to the Reagan administration. Facing this formidable group were only a mid-level bureaucrat stationed in St. Louis and his colleagues.

Although the scales of power seemed tipped in Welbilt's direction, the problem was that the army had the regulations and the facts on its side. The army was not supposed to award a noncompetitive contract to a firm that lacked the capability to perform under the terms of that contract. Nor was the army supposed to award a contract far in excess of the fair market price, or to do an audit of a bid if the bid price was not "sufficiently competitive."

So long as these facts were undisputed, the army's position was impregnable. To prevail, Welbilt had to obscure the facts and generate sufficient political pressure to cause the regulations to be "interpreted" differently.

Welbilt's executives circulated half-truths and misrepresentations that came to be accepted as gospel by the SBA and the White House staff. The company, they asserted, had "acquired a 112,000 square foot production facility," had "outstanding banking institutions ready to support us financially," and, "in short, [had] all the factors of production . . . in place."

In fact, Welbilt hadn't yet acquired a facility, and the company was desperately short of both investment and working capital. Keenan and his colleagues either knew or strongly suspected all this. They had, after all, sent knowledgeable specialists to inspect Welbilt's capabilities. But the company's increasingly strident supporters had, for a variety of reasons, bought the company snow job.

Washington, D.C. usually shuts down during August. To escape the stultifying heat and humidity, Congress goes into recess, the president leaves town, and the bureaucrats head for the beaches of the Delmarva peninsula. In August 1981, however, with the fate of the engine contract still hanging in the balance, Welbilt's supporters couldn't afford to go off on vacation.

Wallach continued to blitz Meese with memoranda. Addabbo wrote to Marsh, urging the army to agree to an audit. And in a contact that turned out to be particularly fruitful, Denlinger raised the Welbilt matter with Pier Talenti, a Michigan businessman serving as an unpaid volunteer in the White House Office of Political Affairs.

In late August, Talenti visited the Welbilt plant in the South Bronx. His tour guide was Mario Biaggi. Talenti, a bright, heavyset Italian-American, was impressed with the modern machinery in Welbilt's basement and the company's apparent capabilities.

"Let's drop the party lines," Biaggi told the Republican visitor. "From one paisan to another, let's do something here."

When Talenti returned to Washington, he convened a Friday meeting in his White House office with three Army officials—Juanita Watts, Col. Albert R. Spaulding, and Robert J. Stohlman—involved in the Welbilt controversy.

Just before the meeting, the army procurement office had made final plans to release the engine contract for competitive bidding. Such action, however, still required authorization from above to remove the contract from the pilot program.

Stohlman and his boss, George E. Dausman, were the army officials with the authority to order the audit and technical review the Welbilt supporters had been demanding. Stohlman knew that the company, the SBA, and various members of Congress were pressing for the audit. He had resisted that pressure. The meeting with Talenti, however, was his first indication that the White House was interested in the matter.

Learning of that interest, Stohlman and Dausman caved in. They decided to order the audit and technical review. Welbilt was one step closer to victory.

Keenan and his colleagues at TSARCOM had been circumvented. As the military expression goes, the decision was now "above their pay grade." They had been directed by their superiors to audit Welbilt's proposal. As disagreeable as this was, they had no choice but to salute and comply.

# Life at Welbilt

**H**ad any of Welbilt's outside supporters spent more than a few hours inside the company in the early 1980s, even they might have questioned the wisdom of awarding an important army contract to the company.

On the surface, Welbilt seemed to be the exemplar of the federal government's 8(a) set-aside program: a prospering, minority-owned company providing scores of jobs for minority workers. "Welbilt is a shining exception" in the scandal-ridden program, *Forbes* magazine declared in a feature story in August 1981.

Beneath the shiny surface, however, were some dirty little secrets. As a melting pot of employees, Welbilt was actually rather successful. With its blue-collar work force drawn from the immediate neighborhood and its white-collar staff consisting largely of anyone willing to work in that neighborhood, the company was an ethnic amalgam. It was almost as though Hollywood had assembled one of those multiracial situation comedy casts designed to appeal to the widest possible audience.

A family atmosphere reigned at 595 Gerard Avenue. Every day, it seemed, was some sort of ethnic holiday. Among the factory workers, Mariotta was an almost mythic figure, a man they viewed with awe and affection. It was a source of pride that he was Puerto

Rican like most of them. John and Jennie Mariotta were childless, and he treated his workers like his children. He trained the unskilled to operate sophisticated machinery. In small ways, he was generous almost to a fault. At Thanksgiving, everyone received a twenty-pound frozen turkey. He gave employees $100 when they got married or had a baby. If there was an illness or death in a worker's family, no matter how far away the family, Mariotta would provide the worker with time off and enough money to take a plane back home. Once, observing a porter being unusually diligent in cleaning a rug, Mariotta gave the man $200 out of his pocket. These gestures seemed impulsive and genuine. And they helped Mariotta inspire a great deal of personal loyalty and enthusiasm.

Mariotta was also popular with the white-collar employees. Many were receiving salaries far above what their talents could have commanded elsewhere in the private sector. The company provided the office workers with coffee, tea, and pastries every morning, and a lunch allowance of $25 a week.

The office workers benefitted from individual acts of generosity as well. Late in 1980, Mariotta spotted Ed McCarthy, the contracts administrator, painting his new office on a Saturday. Impressed with McCarthy's efforts, Mariotta presented him with a new briefcase. McCarthy didn't need the valise, so he gave it, unopened, to one of his young nephews for Christmas. The nephew, pleased with the gift, was doubly excited when he opened the briefcase and found five $100 bills inside.

Many of the workers on the shop floor were born-again Christians, and at lunchtime dozens would crowd into the "Capilla Evangelica"—Room #14, on the main floor of the Gerard Avenue headquarters building—for Pentecostal services led by a punch press operator named Mario Rosado. From 12:15 P.M. to 12:30 P.M. each weekday, the hallways would resonate with amens and hallelujahs.

Workers of other faiths considered the religious services bizarre, but after a while the thunderous prayer sessions became accepted as a normal part of life at Welbilt. When Ed McCarthy suggested it might be illegal for a federal contractor to sanction such services, he saw the darker side of John Mariotta's personality. "What the fuck am I listening to you for?" Mariotta told the young contracts administrator who had twice failed the bar exam. "You're not a real lawyer."

41

Unfortunately, Welbilt's success in fostering high morale and ethnic harmony was not matched in the areas of finance and operational efficiency. The rudimentary management systems that did exist were largely carryovers from Welbilt's days as a small machine shop. The company had a problem performing basic business functions, such as submitting bids.

On one memorable occasion, bids on a relatively small commercial contract—worth about $50,000—were due at an office in the Empire State Building. A few hours before the deadline, Mariotta summoned two Hispanic workers off the factory floor. The pair was given manila envelopes containing Welbilt's bid and told to deliver them promptly.

A couple of hours passed. Neuberger called the office to which the bid was to be delivered. Welbilt's messengers hadn't arrived, he was told. A short time later, Neuberger called again. Still no bid. And so it went throughout the afternoon, Neuberger calling and cursing and pacing. The deadline came and went. Welbilt's bid had not been received.

At the end of the day, the workers slunk back to the plant. Mariotta and Neuberger confronted them.

"Why didn't you deliver the documents?" Neuberger demanded.

The workers looked sheepish.

"We got lost," one stammered. "We couldn't find the Empire State Building."

Neuberger nearly gagged on his cigar.

"Jesus fucking Christ!" he screamed. "You guys couldn't find the Empire State Building? Even King Kong found the Empire State Building!"

Welbilt was only marginally more successful in performing such routine financial functions as meeting its payroll. Employees quickly learned that getting their paychecks was only half the battle; turning them into cash was the real challenge.

Welbilt would often hand out paychecks without depositing enough money to cover them at the check-cashing establishment on 149th Street. As a result, each Friday, when the checks were distributed between 2:30 and 3:00 P.M., a stampede to the check cashier would ensue. It was not uncommon for people at the back of the line to see the cashier's window slam shut long before they reached it.

Eventually the company would always find a way to cover its payroll, but the bouncing checks help illuminate the dark side of what was happening at Welbilt in the early 1980s. One reason Welbilt was having trouble meeting its payroll—and the reason that John Mariotta could afford to be so generous—was that its top officers had increased the amount they were stealing from the company.

The way they were stealing was not very sophisticated. When Mariotta or Neuberger wanted to supplement their salaries, they would have Ceil Lewis write a company check to F.H.J. Associates. Lewis would deposit these checks, in amounts ranging from $24,000 to $80,000, in the F.H.J. account at Banco Popular. Lewis would then remove cash from the F.H.J. account and give it to the executives. As later events would prove, stealing directly from the company was risky because it was easy to detect. But for unsophisticated thieves, Mariotta and Neuberger weren't doing badly. In 1981, they deposited about $363,000 of Welbilt money in the F.H.J. account; that same year they withdrew some $293,000.

The F.H.J. account was also the source of monthly $5,000 payments to the leaders of Teamsters Local 875, which represented Welbilt's production workers. The payments were aimed at guaranteeing labor peace and contracts favorable to management. As a result, the factory workers who thought they were being treated so paternalistically were actually victims of labor racketeering.

That factory owners operating amid the lawlessness of the South Bronx were skimming from the company treasury or making payoffs to leaders of a potentially militant union is hardly startling. Welbilt's officers, however, were also getting involved in criminal conduct involving the United States government.

Since Welbilt had been certified as an 8(a) contractor, most of its contracts had been for various upgrade kits for the army's "battle taxi"—the M–113 armored personnel carrier. Designed to enable an infantryman to keep up with fast-moving columns of tanks and provide him with some protection from artillery fire, the M–113 had been in the fleet for twenty years. The army, unable to replace the vast inventory, was constantly trying to prolong the usefulness of the aging vehicles. Upgrading the suspension and cooling systems, as well as adding a smoke-grenade launcher to enable the vehicle to provide its own smoke screen, were viewed as necessary stopgaps.

On the assumption that what worked in the Bronx would work elsewhere, Mariotta and Moreno had begun to wine and dine Gordon Osgood, an industrial specialist at the army's procurement office in Warren, Michigan. Osgood happened to be the person assigned to review Welbilt's capabilities to produce the cooling kits for the M–113 armored personnel carrier. According to Moreno, after dinners at such expensive Manhattan restaurants as Inagiku at the Waldorf-Astoria, The Palm, and Windows on the World, Osgood felt sufficiently friendly to ask Welbilt to pay some legal bills he had incurred in a side venture. In return, Osgood allegedly used his influence to get a contract for M–113 suspension kits set aside for Welbilt in 1981 under the 8(a) program. Payments to Osgood and his company would continue for the next several years, eventually totalling $467,143. (Osgood has described the allegations as "inaccurate" and denies any wrongdoing).

Even more seriously, Welbilt began cheating on its progress payments from the government. Progress payments are given to a contractor before delivery of the product to reimburse start-up costs the contractor has incurred. The system is designed to alleviate the burden that would be imposed if businesses couldn't recover fully their start-up costs until the end of the contract, which, in the case of government contracts, is often a long time. Properly used and administered, the progress payment system is a reasonable one, particularly for small businesses. In the wrong hands, it can be used to defraud the government.

Welbilt's hands were certainly the wrong ones. By mid–1980, the company had exhausted most of the money it had received from the Economic Development Administration. It was teetering on bankruptcy when Moreno stumbled on a novel way to improve cash flow.

In a conversation with an employee responsible for preparing the progress payment requests, Moreno learned that Welbilt had made mistakes in previous requests. Further, Defense Department auditors hadn't caught the mistakes, so Welbilt was paid more than it was due. Although these past mistakes were characterized as innocent, Moreno immediately saw the possibility of using deliberate "mistakes" as a way to obtain needed cash.

The story was repeated to Mariotta and Neuberger. Mariotta expressed some reluctance at defrauding the company's biggest customer, the U.S. government. As Mariotta liked to say, "A customer is a customer. In manufacturing, you don't take a customer for a one-time Charlie. You don't sell him a suit that if he walks out in the rain will shrivel up and choke him to death."

Neuberger had no such compunctions. Without some cash coming into the company, there wouldn't be a next-time Charlie. It would be Welbilt that would shrivel up and die.

As was his habit in disputes like these, Moreno held his counsel until he could determine which side was going to prevail. In this case, the meeting broke up without a decision.

The indecision couldn't last; the financial situation was deteriorating too rapidly. When the same group got together a short time later, Moreno was blunt.

"We are running out of time," he warned. "Are we going to do it, or are we not going to it?"

This time, Mariotta assented. An employee was told to do whatever he had to do to speed up payments from the government.

What had to be done was to forge some invoices. At first, actual invoices from suppliers were copied, all of the information except the letterhead was whited-out, phony billing data was typed in, and the forged invoice was copied again. Later, the operation became more sophisticated. On the assumption that printed invoices would be more convincing, Welbilt had blank invoice forms printed with the names of various vendors. The forged forms were attached to the progress payment requests to back up the claimed expenses. The ploys worked, and Welbilt stayed afloat.

By the summer of 1981, Moreno decided that as long as he was participating in multiple felonies, he ought at least to have a full-time job and an equity position with the company. Moreno went to Mariotta and Neuberger and asked for an ownership interest. If he didn't get it, he warned, he would quit. Moreno had the two partners over a barrel.

Moreno's sad eyes and tentative smile gave his rather olive-skinned face a wistful quality, suggesting a degree of self-awareness lacking in his partners. If Moreno did occasionally engage in soul-searching, however, it did not result in moral scruples triumphing over greed. He had been an ideal addition to the Welbilt management team; his modest financial skills complemented the modest manufacturing and marketing skills of Mariotta and Neuberger. With Welbilt, the 8(a) program, and the South Bronx, the trio had found the ingredients for fraud on a scale even they were only beginning to appreciate.

A deal was struck giving Moreno 9 percent ownership, leaving Mariotta and Neuberger with 45.5 percent each. Implicit in this agreement was an understanding that Moreno would get 9 percent of the F.H.J. funds as well. A lawyer was needed to formalize the accord, but the trio didn't want to go to Biaggi & Ehrlich. Mariotta had promised stock in the company to the congressman and his partner, and the Welbilt executives didn't want them to know that Moreno was getting a piece of the action first. Moreover, Biaggi & Ehrlich was Welbilt's link to the Small Business Administration. If the SBA found out that Mariotta didn't have a majority interest, the company would have to be ousted from the 8(a) program—ruining its chances of getting the engine contract.

The legal work for Moreno's deal was handled instead by the firm of Delson & Gordon. (Max Delson, the firm's founding member, was a noted Socialist Party leader and labor union attorney. For a time, Welbilt paid $1,000 a month to a Delson company for unspecified "consulting and business advisory services.") The agreement giving Moreno 9 percent ownership was, of course, kept secret from the SBA.

In addition to getting stock in the company, Moreno received an $80,000 salary and arranged a no-show job for his companion, Caridad Vazquez. Vazquez, known to friends as Conchita, received about $30,000 for a period of a little more than a year. (Moreno later tried to justify Vazquez's salary by contending she was required to attend a lot of "boring banquets." This led the New York tabloids to dub her the company's "$30G Party Girl.") Even though Moreno had been living openly with Vazquez for some time, his devoutly religious wife, Luz, refused to divorce him.

Fred Neuberger, meanwhile, was tying the knot for the third time. On this occasion, his bride was the former Eileen Vanora. An attractive, raven-haired, $25,000-a-year employee of the New York City Board of Education, she was nearly twenty years younger than her new husband. Like Neuberger's previous wife, she had a history of mental problems. After a ceremony in Neuberger's apartment on Eighty-Fifth Street, the newlyweds celebrated their marriage with a reception at Tavern on the Green on the evening of August 23, 1981.

With his increasing prosperity, Neuberger decided it was time to upgrade both his physical appearance and his public image. He ditched his toupee in favor of expensive hair transplants. He told a reporter for *Inc.* magazine that he had become "more relaxed, more patient, more public-spirited" and had reached a stage where he had "the time and the ability to give something back." As part of his effort to buy respectability, Neuberger received the 1982 Humanitarian Award from the Albert Einstein College of Medicine "in recognition of his outstanding community leadership, his creative efforts to help those in need, and his commitment to improve the quality of life for all people." It's not clear what Neuberger did to earn the encomium, but the plaque was prominently displayed on the wall of his office.

John Mariotta was also doing his share to benefit humanity. The Welbilt founder donated generously to various religious causes, quickly acquiring a reputation as a soft touch who had trouble saying no when pressed for a contribution. It wasn't unusual to see clergymen roaming the halls of Welbilt on yet another solicitation mission.

Mariotta was not, however, as generous as he liked to appear. He had the company reimburse him for some of his contributions, and many were made using funds stolen and laundered through the F.H.J. account. In fact, in a rare moment of candor, he once told Ceil Lewis that he donated so much because the money was dirty and giving some away helped to clean it.

By the early 1980s, Mariotta had become more ostentatious and unusual in his religious practices. He was attending not only the Sunday morning Catholic mass at Our Lady of Good Counsel Church in Manhattan, but also Protestant services on Sunday afternoons and occasionally Jewish services on Saturdays. "It's against my three religions," he would tell people by way of explaining why he was not going to do something.

The more he learned about Judaism, the more Mariotta began to sound Jewish himself. His speech became sprinkled with Yiddish expressions—*nudnik, tateleh, mensch, chutzpah,* and *tsorris* (which he pronounced "zoo-rees"). If he was impressed with someone's head for business, he would tell them they had a "Yiddishe kup."

Mariotta was an ultra-competitive man who hated to lose. When he gambled at Atlantic City, he would stack chips on every number of the roulette table so he'd always get money back. By practicing more than one religion, John Mariotta was covering all the squares with God. Through his charitable donations, he may well have been trying to buy his way into heaven. "I give to the rabbi, the minister, and the priest, because this way I cover my bets [with] whoever is up there," he would tell Ed McCarthy.

The more Mariotta stole, of course, the easier it was for him to be charitable. For a while, he put his wife, Jennie, on the books of Bronx Borough Security Corp., a company Moreno owned that provided security service for Welbilt. Jennie received about $400 a week for the no-show job.

The money Mariotta stole helped him fulfill the American

47

dream, a house in the suburbs. In December of 1981, he and Jennie moved from the four-room apartment in the Bronx where they had lived since 1966 to a $260,000 ranch-style home in the pricey Westchester County community of Scarsdale. The home had a two-car garage, a large white brick chimney, birch trees on the lawn, and a swimming pool in the backyard. The interior was comfortable but not showy. A stone foyer led to an airy family room with a white brick fireplace and wood beams running along a vaulted ceiling.

Life in the suburbs was not entirely serene for the Mariottas, however. As they told the story, a short time after they settled in, John took a business trip to Italy. Jennie was alone in the house for the first time. At about 1:30 A.M., Jennie was putting away clothes in a closet that had just been painted. Suddenly, she heard a tremendous thud on the roof, and a voice exclaimed, "Oh, my God!"

Jennie called the police. The police checked to see if she was all right, then walked around to the back of the house.

"Lady, you are not going to believe this . . ." said one of the officers. Dangling from the roof was a man dressed in a black jacket and black pants, strapped to a black parachute.

"He claimed he was dropping in on his grandparents who lived in Hartsdale, but that the wind shifted and he landed over here," Jennie recalled. "That was his story."

John Mariotta, returning from his business trip, quickly concluded that the young man must have been on a CIA training mission and flunked the parachute-jumping test. People to whom Mariotta told the story didn't quite know what to make of it. Some thought it was funny. Others chalked the whole thing up to paranoia.

"I come from the South Bronx. I never had a problem like this," said John Mariotta. "I come to Scarsdale. And look what happens!"

# 6

# Chauncey the Gardener

**T**he army's audit of Welbilt's engine contract proposal was completed in November 1981. The conclusions were predictable.

The army's manufacturing specialists reported that Welbilt had at least one engineer who knew how to produce engines, but the company had no building or equipment. As a result, Welbilt would have great difficulty establishing an engine production line. Nevertheless, the TSARCOM officials concluded that the company would ultimately be able to produce engines.

The army's financial auditors were hampered because Welbilt's cost and pricing data were incomplete. Despite these limitations, the auditors were able to conclude that at least $6.2 million of Welbilt's proposed $38.9 million price was invalid.

When the audit results were passed to the company, the Welbilt team immediately interpreted them to mean that the correct price for the contract should be $32.7 million—Welbilt's proposed $38.9 million less the $6.2 million in invalid costs. Welbilt's managers believed the army could now be pressured into giving them the contract at that price.

While the audit was going on, the army had been reviewing its own price estimates. By now it was clear this procurement was not going to be handled through normal channels. The army was going to have to defend any decision not to award the contract to Welbilt at Welbilt's price. The bureaucrats at TSARCOM and army headquarters wanted to be sure they were on solid ground. In December, after three separate reviews, the army adjusted its fair market price upward by about $4 million to $23.7 million.

The Welbilt team took the adjustment as a sign the army was willing to dicker over the final contract price. The difference between the army's price and Welbilt's price was now "only" about $10 million. TSARCOM officials, however, believed they had a completely defensible price estimate and were prepared to stand fast. At Welbilt, winning the engine contract had taken on the aura of a crusade.

To break the stalemate, Welbilt's hired guns took direct aim at Thomas Keenan.

Ambassador Sanchez wrote to Lyn Nofziger at the White House, suggesting that Keenan be cut out of the negotiations and replaced with someone "more in tune with the stated objectives of this administration."

Denlinger reported to Welbilt that Keenan had said the audit was forced on him by the White House, but the outcome would remain unchanged and Welbilt would not receive the contract. "Dr. Keenan should be removed from this case given his antagonistic and prejudicial attitude," the LAMA lobbyist wrote in a memo to Henry Zuniga, the White House liaison with Hispanic groups. What business Denlinger, a lobbyist representing private interests, had to demand that the White House discipline and transfer a member of the executive branch was never explained.

Wallach also weighed in with an October 7 memo to Meese about Welbilt, his third in as many days. The memo quoted Keenan as telling Denlinger that he had "developed great skill in dealing with and countering White House pressure." Wallach, a private citizen, went on to express concern that Army Secretary Marsh might be advised on the engine contract by Keenan, an army employee whose job it was to do just that.

With the new year the situation was still looking bleak for Welbilt. A summit meeting of representatives from the army, Small Business Administration, and the White House was scheduled for Friday, January 15, 1982.

Two days before the meeting, an Air Florida jet taking off from

National Airport in a snowstorm crashed into the Fourteenth Street bridge, then plunged into the icy Potomac River, killing seventy-eight persons. At nearly the same time, three Metro passengers died in the worst accident in the history of the city's subway system. Washington was a city in shock. When the army, White House, and SBA officials gathered at the SBA, it was just beginning to be possible to concentrate on more mundane matters such as the Welbilt engine contract.

As the meeting began, the army representatives reiterated that the army's revised price was not negotiable. Talenti and Zuniga, representing the White House, argued strenuously on Welbilt's behalf. The SBA officials—Administrator Michael Cardenas; his special assistant, David V. Gonzales; and Deputy Administrator Donald R. Templeman—took the position that their agency shouldn't try to force the army into a contract with Welbilt unless the army could negotiate a price it found acceptable. The meeting ended inconclusively.

The failure to bow to White House demands may have cost two of the SBA officials their jobs. Less than a month after the meeting, Cardenas was forced to resign, and Gonzales—active in California G.O.P. politics since 1965—was fired. Templeman was appointed acting administrator and James Sanders, a California businessman who'd gotten a position at SBA through his friendship with top White House aide Michael Deaver, was nominated to replace Cardenas at the top of the agency.

(Cardenas would later maintain his firing was a "direct result" of his failure to bend to White House pressure on the Welbilt contract. According to Sanders, however, Cardenas was removed because he had embarrassed the administration by failing to show up for scheduled speaking engagements. Templeman said there were strong management reasons for Cardenas's dismissal, but the Welbilt matter "might have hastened" his departure.)

The following Monday, Talenti called in Mariotta and Moreno to tell them about the meeting the previous Friday. A sense of gloom pervaded Talenti's office. The army was still demanding that the SBA either withdraw the contract from the set-aside program or make up the cost differential between the Welbilt price and the army's price. Mariotta's and Moreno's spirits sank even lower when Talenti mentioned that Nofziger was going to be leaving the White House in a matter of days to form his own consulting firm.

51

The Welbilt executives believed Nofziger's departure would rob them of one of their most powerful supporters, although events would soon prove them wrong.

On January 19, Wallach wrote again to Meese, quoting Talenti as saying "it would be nice if [Nofziger] could go out with a bang and get this contract . . ." for Welbilt.

Two days later, apparently through the intervention of Nofziger's office, John Mariotta, the high school dropout, walked into the White House to participate in a conference on urban enterprise zones.

Enterprise zones were the Reagan administration's answer to the crisis of the American cities. As envisioned by supporters, such zones would be designated areas in which the federal government would offer major tax incentives for job creation and small-business growth. The leading congressional champions of the concept were a political odd couple from New York: Robert Garcia, the liberal Democrat whose Bronx district included Welbilt's headquarters, and Jack Kemp, the conservative Republican and former professional football player from the Buffalo area.

In February 1981, at the urging of David Epstein, Mariotta had gone to a national conference on enterprise zones in Atlanta sponsored by the Heritage Foundation, a conservative think tank. When they got to Atlanta, Epstein informed Mariotta that the Welbilt founder would have to make a speech. Epstein handed him a pencil and paper to jot down some thoughts. Mariotta, terrified that Epstein would discover his inability to write, pushed the pencil and paper away.

"I'm going to shoot from the hips," said Mariotta.

"You're crazy, you can't do things like that," said Epstein. Epstein underestimated Mariotta's abilities as a showman. Without a prepared text, Mariotta got up at the Atlanta meeting and preached his gospel of resurrection in the South Bronx. With his intensity of conviction, his "how you say?" pauses as he knitted his brow and seemed to search for the right word in English, Mariotta struck his audience as the real thing, the ghetto entrepreneur struggling against all odds to fulfill the American dream.

It was basically the same spiel he used with newspaper reporters, with Wallach, with anyone who would listen. Coming from Mariotta, commonplace ideas sounded profound and foolishness went unchallenged. Mostly, he was telling people what they wanted to hear and believe. He had been giving a version of the spiel for several years; it had been honed and refined through numerous presentations. In his delivery, Mariotta radiated sincerity and ingenuousness. Shooting from the hips in Atlanta, he was interrupted seven times by applause and received a standing ovation.

The shtick had passed its out-of-town tryout. Now it was ready for the big time: 1600 Pennsylvania Avenue.

Entering the White House on Thursday, January 21, 1982, John Mariotta felt like Chauncey the gardener, the childlike man played by Peter Sellers in the 1979 movie, *Being There*. In the movie, Chauncey meets important, powerful people who interpret his bewildered silence and banal utterances as brilliance. Mariotta had become fascinated with the movie and played it repeatedly on a video cassette recorder in his office.

Mariotta passed through security, then into a lobby where the other participants in the meeting were greeting each other like long-lost friends. Mariotta just felt lost. And nervous. He stared at a picture of George Washington crossing the Delaware.

After a while, Mariotta and the other participants were ushered into the Cabinet Room, with its olive green drapes and brass lighting fixtures. As Mariotta recalled it, he spotted his nameplate at the long wooden table and made a beeline for his seat. Everyone else was still standing and talking. Sitting alone at the table, Mariotta felt foolish. Adding to his discomfort were the pad and paper in front of him. He was afraid he'd be asked to write something, and his inability to write would be exposed.

After an awkwardly long period, Sen. John Heinz, a Pennsylvania Republican, sat down to the right of Mariotta, and Sen. John Chaffee, a Rhode Island Republican, sat down to the left of the Welbilt founder. Among the others taking places at the table were Vice-President Bush, Treasury Secretary Donald Regan, and a dozen presidential aides, elected officials, and business leaders. Mariotta had no idea who most of them were.

After an extended discussion on the merits of the enterprise zone program and who would bear the costs, Mariotta could restrain himself no longer. The Spiel was welling up in him. Finally it erupted.

"Can I have the floor?" he asked plaintively in his high-pitched voice.

Heads turned.

"Gentlemen and ladies, my name is John Mariotta. I'm president of Welbilt Electronics. I'm a New York Rican. For those who don't know what a New York Rican is, it's an individual that cannot speak English and cannot speak Spanish. I'm in the Twilight Zone."

Laughter.

"I'm in Fort Apache. No, it's not in Texas. It's in the South Bronx. But let me tell you what my company is all about."

Mariotta proceeded to discuss Welbilt's product line, its "seventeen years without one rejection" from the Defense Department, its "partnership in craftsmanship" award from General Electric's jet engine division.

He trotted out the math purporting to show how much money Welbilt was saving the government by employing former welfare recipients.

"Gentlemen, I am no bookkeeper. I'm just a simple tinsmith . . . If youse people spend twenty-five million dollars on welfare, you are minus twenty-five million. Gentlemen, but Welbilt came into the picture, and put all these people to work . . . We produce fifty million dollars in government defense parts . . . I'm no mathematician, but coming from minus twenty-five to above fifty is seventy-five million dollars we have saved the taxpayers of this country. Gentlemen, bring ten more companies into the South Bronx and you will save SEVEN HUNDRED AND FIFTY MILLION DOLLARS!"

Mariotta was just getting warmed up. He waved his arms animatedly.

"Gentlemen, spread this penicillin from the city of decay to Watts area, Chicago—"

"Don't forget Paterson, New Jersey," interjected Lawrence "Pat" Kramer, the Republican mayor of Paterson, who was seated across the table from Mariotta.

"And you are on there, sir," Mariotta responded. He picked up where he had left off.

"I was talking with the dope pusher . . ."

A gasp.

"I see some people sighing in here. It's normal to talk in the South Bronx to the local pusher."

Suddenly, Mariotta realized everyone was looking not at him, but behind him. President Reagan had entered the room and was waiting for him to pause. Everyone but Mariotta stood up. The president walked around the table and settled into the empty chair between aide Rich Williamson and Margaret Hance, the mayor of Phoenix. A jar of jelly beans was within easy reach of Reagan's left hand. Everyone sat down, except for Mariotta, who in a nervous reaction stood up.

"Mr. President, I'm sorry," Mariotta stammered.

Reagan smiled and told Mariotta to sit down and continue with the dope pusher.

Mariotta took his seat and plowed ahead.

"It's a common thing to talk with the dope pusher. I don't go into the dope business. He doesn't go into the machining business. We have a mutual respect."

More laughter. They thought he was a comedian. He had them.

"One day the dope pusher passed by my garage door. And he said, '*Hola*, babe, I like what you're doing with our people.' And I said, 'Yeah, but I don't like what you're doing with our people.'

"And he jumped back about three feet and said, Bug out, John. What I'm doing with our people is not any worse than what this society is doing with our people. This society is killing our people by giving them opium or welfare . . .'

"Mr. President, not only are you killing my people, but you're killing the taxpayer by strapping a welfare on the back of the tax-payer. Don't misunderstand me. Welfare is good if you're down and out in the hospital. If the provider of the family is out or dead, by all means give welfare. But not as a cop-out because we ain't got no jobs . . .

"Mr. President, when youse people give me a contract for one hundred million dollars, don't take it away from Boeing, Sikorski, Lockheed, Western Electric. We don't need a revolution on our hands. When you give me a contract for one hundred million dollars, don't increase the defense budget. We're broke. Youse people give out in opium or welfare sixty billion dollars a year. And these poor people when they look at the apple pie on television, they go out and mug somebody to have a few minutes of party timing, and they land in jail. And the jail is twenty billion dollars a year. That comes out to eighty billion dollars a year. Mr. President, what we have to do is reduce that and create a surplus. What you do with that surplus, that's your problem!"

Flabbergasted silence.

"I'm sorry," said the heavily perspiring Mariotta. "I'm talking too much. But that's what it is all about."

The president, always a soft touch for stories that confirmed his long-held beliefs, even if the stories didn't make a whole lot of sense, seemed taken with the intense little machinist with the high forehead, wavy dark hair, and long sideburns.

That is what this thing is all about, Reagan responded.

At the end of the Cabinet Room discussion, the participants adjourned for lunch. Mariotta sought out Elizabeth Dole, then head of the White House Office of Public Liaison, and tried to tell her about his three-year war with Keenan.

At lunch, he was seated near Mayor Jane Byrne ("the redhead woman from Chee-CAH-go," as Mariotta called her). She told him his little speech was terrific. Then everyone in the room stood up. This time, Mariotta knew it was the president entering the room. Reagan made the rounds of the luncheon tables.

If he had ten people like him, yes, he could balance the budget, Reagan told Mariotta, whose company would ultimately leave Uncle Sam $101 million in the hole.

The Spiel was winning rave reviews. *That was terrific, John. Terrific. Just terrific.*

To John Mariotta, the praise was barely audible. He was staring intently through his gold-framed glasses at the luncheon menu. He was terrified he was going to have to order from it, and he could barely read the selections.

Despite John Mariotta's virtuoso performance at the White House, Welbilt's chances of getting the engine contract remained remote. The army still had the facts, and logic, on its side. But as word of Mariotta's tête-à-tête with Ronald Reagan filtered out, Keenan and the political appointees in the secretary of the army's office could be forgiven if they began to feel a bit overmatched.

To Mariotta, Neuberger, and Moreno, the problem couldn't have been that the army was right. The problem was that the Welbilt stable of consultants was not influential enough. They needed more powerful support.

The day after Mariotta's power lunch, Lyn Nofziger left the White House to form a consulting firm with a fellow Californian, Mark Bragg. Nofziger was known as a shrewd political strategist, blunt and profane, with a wisecracking sense of humor. Portly, bearded, and mostly bald, the fifty-seven-year-old Nofziger went way back with Ronald Reagan. In 1966, he left a job as Washington correspondent for the Copley newspaper chain to become press secretary for Reagan's gubernatorial campaign. He served as communications director when Reagan was in the statehouse, and again when he became a presidential candidate.

After the 1980 election, Nofziger was named assistant to the president for political affairs. He was probably best known to Americans for his cool-under-pressure briefing of the press in 1981 amid the chaos that followed the shooting of Reagan and White House press secretary James Brady. After toiling at government wages for many years, Nofziger was anxious to cash in on his connections.

Nofziger's partner, Bragg, was twenty years younger. Part of the California contingent that accompanied Reagan to Washington, he had worked as news director at radio stations in San Francisco and Los Angeles, and later as president of a private company that distributed radio and television documentaries.

No sooner did Nofziger and Bragg hang out their shingle than they were retained to assist Welbilt in its efforts to obtain the small-engine contract. On March 1, 1982, the company issued a $3,000 check to Nofziger & Bragg. Welbilt had another powerful, and expensive, ally.

In mid-March, the SBA rejected the army's latest request to withdraw the engine contract from the set-aside program. The SBA also refused to provide the $10 million to cover the gap between the army's price and Welbilt's offer, noting that the average business development grant was about $100,000. Once again, the SBA urged the army to negotiate with Welbilt.

In this truth-is-stranger-than-fiction turn of events, the army now found itself forced to defend both the price it was willing to pay for the engines and its lack of confidence in a particular company. To add insult to injury, the army's adversaries were primarily other government employees, many of whom had no business being involved in a procurement decision and wouldn't know a six-horsepower engine if they tripped over one.

The whole game now was to step up pressure on the army. Nofziger and Bragg quickly began to exert their influence on behalf of their new client. Bragg cultivated Delbert Spurlock, the general counsel of the Department of the Army, and James Jenkins, Meese's top deputy. Nofziger called Army Secretary Marsh; he didn't arm-twist, but he made it clear there was White House interest in the engine contract.

Nofziger then went to Meese, whom he had known since 1966, when both were members of Governor-elect Reagan's staff. On

57

April 5, 1982, the two old colleagues met and briefly discussed the Welbilt matter, despite the existence of a federal ethics law that prohibited former high-ranking administration officials from lobbying their old agencies for at least a year after leaving office. Nofziger had left the White House less than three months earlier.

Three days after their meeting, Nofziger followed up with a letter to Meese stating:

> Welbilt appears to be well qualified to do the work, but is having some problems with the Army. . . . Awarding the contract to Welbilt would be a major first step in the president's commitment to revitalize the South Bronx . . . I am sure [Army Secretary Marsh] would listen carefully to [Deputy Defense Secretary] Carlucci or [Defense Secretary] Weinberger, or Meese or even Reagan.
>
> Ed, I really think it would be a blunder not to award that contract to Welbilt. The symbolism either way is very great here.

Not only did Meese listen to Nofziger's overtures on behalf of Welbilt, he authorized his deputy, Jenkins, to follow up on the matter. He did so despite a 1981 memo from White House counsel Fred F. Fielding that admonished employees about getting involved in any federal contracts in which they or friends had a financial interest. Both Meese and Jenkins said later they didn't know Nofziger had been retained by Welbilt.

One of the things Jenkins did was summon the new SBA administrator, James Sanders, to his office. At the meeting, Jenkins emphasized to Sanders the president's commitment to providing employment in the South Bronx. Giving Welbilt the engine contract, they agreed, would be a nice joining of an opportunity and a commitment.

It was beginning to look, however, like the game was over. The engine contract decision had finally percolated to the highest levels of the army. At a meeting on April 16, Marsh and other top army officials decided it was not in the best interest of the U.S. government to award the contract to Welbilt. Marsh determined that steps should be taken to release the contract for competitive bidding.

The "final" decision was conveyed to Sanders, Representative Addabbo, Senator D'Amato, and Denlinger. Denlinger, very dejected, called Bragg. Don't despair, Bragg told him. Other things were happening that might be cause for optimism.

At the White House, Jenkins, a gravelly voiced former naval officer and veteran of bureaucratic wars, knew that in Washington things can happen to provoke the reconsideration of "final" decisions. Before proceeding, however, he sought guidance from Craig Fuller. Fuller, a model of caution who clearly understood the ethics policy on procurement matters, wrote back: "Jim Jenkins—I strongly recommend that no White House action be taken."

This was not the advice Jenkins wanted to hear, so he ignored it. Fuller "wasn't my boss, so he couldn't tell me not to," Jenkins explained later. Jenkins set up a meeting for May 19, at the White House, for all the interested parties.

Learning what Jenkins had done, Fuller wrote to White House counsel Fielding, asking for specific legal guidance. One of Fielding's assistants wrote back, saying the White House should not get involved in a procurement matter, and "J. J. should not call meeting." Jenkins again ignored the advice.

On May 19, Jenkins convened the meeting in the "Ward Room" adjacent to the mess in the White House basement. While meetings to discuss procurement policy, or the needs of a particular industry, are not unusual in the White House, a meeting to discuss a particular contract for a particular contractor, one that represented .01 percent of the military budget, was extraordinary. Sanders later recalled that this was the only instance in his four-year tenure at the SBA in which the White House took interest in a particular 8(a) contract.

Jenkins fifty eight, gray haired, overweight, with jowls hang ing from his ruddy face—was no neophyte. A public affairs officer to four secretaries of the navy, he had worked as a Washington lobbyist and cabinet officer for Gov. Ronald Reagan. After Reagan left office, Jenkins capitalized on his contacts, founding a Sacramento-based government relations and economic development consulting firm. He returned to Washington to join the Reagan administration as Meese's deputy in October of 1981.

An experienced survivor of the bureaucratic wars, Jenkins could be abrasive and arrogant to people with less influence or power than himself. But he was shrewd in calculating whom he could or could not afford to alienate. Jenkins took a seat at one end of the table, close to the bureaucrats from three federal agencies involved in the controversy. Mariotta, Moreno, and Bragg sat at the other end.

Jenkins got right to the point. He reminded the group about Reagan's promise to revitalize the Bronx, then announced that he had lots of experience with the nuts and bolts of these programs, and he wasn't going to tolerate any delaying tactics or fogging of the issue. Glaring at the army representatives, he said if he ran into any evidence of foot-dragging, he would be talking to them directly, or to their bosses. Jenkins then laid his general feelings about the matter on the line.

"I am not going to stand for any bullshit," he declared.

The Welbilt representatives were ecstatic. They interpreted Jenkins's remarks as tantamount to an order to the army to give the contract to Welbilt—and an order to the SBA to come up with the funding to bridge the gap between the army's price and Welbilt's proposal. At the meeting, Moreno committed Welbilt to providing a revised proposal, based on promises of federal financial assistance.

For all intents and purposes, the battle was over. The issue had been decided. All that was left was to go through the motions of making a formal award.

To Moreno, the army representative at the meeting, Assistant Secretary J. R. Sculley, looked as if he had been dragged into the meeting like a little dog on a leash. Sculley no doubt concluded that further resistance by the army would be regarded as disloyal and was, in any case, futile. Factoring in two years' worth of inflation, the army raised its fair market price to almost $28 million.

The SBA came through on its end. It chipped in a Business Development Expense grant of $3 million—more than one-half of the agency's BDE expenditures for the entire fiscal year. The SBA also committed $2 million for advance payment loans. The commitments were made on June 18, 1982—ten days *before* Welbilt formally asked for them.

The deal being all but done, politicians and political appointees of all stripes scrambled to climb aboard the Welbilt bandwagon. James Sanders, having heard so much about the company, decided to take a look for himself. Accompanied by Mario Biaggi, the SBA chief visited the Welbilt headquarters on September 1 and declared it to be a "great example of success" with "a very bright future." Mariotta and Neuberger, he continued, "are a great example for others to follow. They have the faith in hard work and thrift and all those kind of virtues you don't hear about anymore."

On September 13, 1982, Welbilt accepted the army's price of

$27.7 million. The SBA came through with the $5 million in financial assistance. On September 28, the contract to build 13,100 small engines was finally awarded to Welbilt. The first engine was to be delivered in February 1984.

Everyone, it seemed, wanted to take credit for trampling ethical and economic considerations and steering the engine contract to Welbilt. In a note to Meese, Jenkins wrote, ". . . your personal 'go-ahead' to me saved this project." This apparently referred to a conversation between the two the previous spring after Meese had met with Nofziger and Jenkins with Bragg.

Politicians showed up in droves for the October 4 signing ceremony for the engine contract. Jockeying for credit was so intense, in fact, that the SBA regional administrator, Peter Neglia, urged David Epstein to disinvite all the local New York City politicians. Epstein agreed it should be a Reagan administration show. But Mariotta was furious when he found out Epstein was putting a stop to certain invitations, and Epstein's days as a Welbilt consultant came to an end.

The signing ceremony began at 10:30 A.M. at Welbilt headquarters. Mariotta introduced SBA regional administrator Peter Neglia, who in turn introduced SBA chief Jim Sanders.

"Welbilt—and John—it's one of our best investments, one of America's best investments," Sanders intoned for the television cameras. Senator D'Amato and Housing Secretary Samuel Pierce followed Sanders at the podium. The euphoria was widespread.

Winning the engine contract put Welbilt a giant step toward the big time. The company was on a roll. Now all it had to do was produce. Welbilt took steps to acquire a subsidiary in Carmiel, Israel, that would produce the casting components of the six-horsepower engines.

More importantly, the executives had learned some valuable lessons. When it came to getting contracts in the 8(a) program, it was political clout that made the difference, not capability or competence. Money talked in Washington, just as it did in the Bronx. The company had assembled a stable of allies—to whom facts and ethics were far less important than money—leading all the way into the White House. Mariotta was personally acquainted with the Leader of the Free World.

In fact, on October 27, 1982, Mariotta invited Reagan to visit Welbilt. Plans were made to have the president go to the Bronx in December to present the company with a Defense Department quality control award. (Although Welbilt had trouble producing profitably or on time, its products to this point were generally of high quality.) In preparation for Reagan's visit, White House advance men and security personnel descended on the Welbilt plant, installing a bank of phones for the news media and special telecommunications equipment. Light poles were removed from the parking lot so they wouldn't interfere with the presidential helicopter. The loudspeaker system was cut to prevent unauthorized announcements. A White House advance man told the plant manager to cover up the nameplates on certain Japanese machines on the shop floor, because he didn't want the president photographed praising a contractor with a plant full of foreign-made equipment. Cutting the metal plates to accomplish this task was, of course, right up Welbilt's alley.

The day before Reagan was to arrive, however, Welbilt got word that the president had changed his plans, apparently because of a budget crisis, and wasn't coming. In retrospect, the decision would prove to be the best his administration would make with respect to Welbilt.

# 7

## Going Public

**W**ith the signing of the six-horsepower engine contract, Fred Neuberger began to campaign in earnest to take Welbilt public. Neuberger had always been fascinated with playing the stock market; his work day usually ended when the closing prices came in. All his investments were in other people's companies; a public offering of Welbilt stock would allow others to invest in his company—and make him a very wealthy man.

Since Mariotta and Neuberger could rarely agree, it wasn't surprising that Mariotta resisted the idea at first. He didn't want to sell "his" company to the public. Neuberger, however, was resourceful and persistent. During the latter half of 1982, he ran into Mariotta's wife at a party given by Congressman Garcia at the Club A in the Bronx. Jennie, like her husband, had risen far in just a few years. During the early days of her marriage, she had been a sewing machine operator in a garment factory. Now she was adjusting to a more comfortable life as a Scarsdale matron. Neuberger had calculated shrewdly where the power was in the Mariotta marriage. He approached Jennie and warned that she might have to go back to operating sewing machines unless her husband agreed to take Welbilt public. His message had the desired effect. A short time later, Mariotta dropped his opposition to Neuberger's proposal.

Taking private companies public (or, in the case of leveraged buyouts, taking public companies private) was the wellspring of American business during the bull market years of the Reagan presidency. Once men dreamed of striking it rich through discovering gold or oil or uranium. Or they developed an invention that created or revolutionized an industry. By the 1980s, however, huge conglomerates controlled mineral rights and the cutting-edge research and development labs. The surest way to become wealthy to the point of financial independence was via Wall Street—starting or buying a company, making it profitable and, as quickly as possible, taking the company public through a sale of its stock.

This method of capitalizing a business is old and honorable. Most of the companies that have become part of the fabric of American life—General Motors, International Business Machines, etc.—have raised the money to enable them to grow via public equity offerings.

Welbilt Electronic Die Corp., of course, was no GM or IBM. Taking even a well-run company public isn't easy. The process is complex, expensive, and time-consuming. Factors such as interest rates and investment climate are beyond the control of the company and its underwriter. Taking Welbilt public would be a large challenge.

As with any public sale of securities through a regulated exchange, initial public offerings are regulated by the Securities and Exchange Commission. To protect investors from being defrauded by con men offering worthless or overvalued stock, the SEC has developed an extensive set of rules with which a company must comply before it can issue publicly traded securities. These regulations require full public disclosure of all relevant information about a company—its assets, liabilities, operations, management—so investors can make fully informed investment decisions.

These regulations loomed as a major obstacle to a successful public offering by Welbilt. As Neuberger knew only too well, if Welbilt were to disclose the truth, the offering would never get off the ground. The company had too many skeletons in its closets. Therefore, it had to fabricate or sugar-coat much of the information it was going to make public.

Hiding the skeletons and falsifying information wouldn't have been particularly tough had Welbilt been able to submit the required information directly to the SEC. Mariotta, Neuberger, and Moreno had already demonstrated that truth was not a major consideration when personal gain was at stake. The problem was that the SEC required the financial statements to be audited by a firm of certified public accountants. In addition, the disclosure statement would be carefully prepared and scrutinized with "due diligence" by lawyers representing both the corporation and the underwriter. Getting falsified data past a top-notch accounting firm and two law firms was going to be tricky. So tricky that fainter hearts than Mariotta, Neuberger, and Moreno wouldn't even have tried.

As a small, private company, Welbilt had no reason to retain a prestigious accounting firm. Although audited financial statements were needed for such things as bank loans and SBA financing, the imprimatur of an unqualified opinion from a "Big Eight" firm was something Welbilt didn't need and couldn't afford. Besides, the bigger the accounting firm, the more likely that the auditors would discover the financial sleights-of-hand that Welbilt had been pulling. With the award of the engine contract and the decision to go public, however, there was no getting around Welbilt's need for a prestigious auditing firm.

The man charged with selecting the firm was Welbilt's new financial consultant, Lawrence Shorten. Shorten was the newest star on the Welbilt management team. Neuberger, always susceptible to get-rich-quick schemes, had run into Shorten at a meeting for prospective investors in a small genetics company. Shorten was involved in preparing the prospectus for the company and was introduced at the meeting as a banker. In fact, his banking career had been something short of illustrious. He had spent twelve years in mid-level positions in small banks. While employed at Bergen State Bank in New Jersey, he finished his undergraduate degree at Fairleigh Dickinson University.

In 1980, Shorten took a job as a financial officer for a computer software company. By the following year, he was self-employed as a "consultant," supposedly providing mid-sized companies with assistance on banking matters.

Something about the balding, mustachioed Shorten must have impressed Neuberger, because they struck up a conversation as the meeting was ending. On the ride down in the elevator, Shorten, who seemed to be constantly smirking at some joke that only he appreciated, confided that he didn't think much of the genetics company and advised Neuberger to save his money. Neuberger, knowing that Welbilt could use all the financial help it could get,

asked Shorten if he really was a banker. If so, would he be interested in working with a company in the Bronx?

Evidently Neuberger was one of the few people to have been impressed by Shorten, whose consulting business was struggling.
Shorten's taxable income for 1981 was just $6,390. He was glad to
accept Neuberger's offer to visit Welbilt.

Meeting with Mariotta, Moreno, and Neuberger at the Welbilt
headquarters on Gerard Avenue, Shorten learned of the difficulties
that Welbilt was having raising capital. Astonishingly, Shorten
also learned at this introductory meeting that Welbilt had lied to
the SBA about its ownership in order to qualify for the 8(a) program. So far as the SBA knew, John Mariotta owned two-thirds of
the company and Fred Neuberger one-third. In fact, Shorten was
informed, Mariotta and Neuberger each owned 45.5 percent, and
Moreno the remaining 9 percent.

Shorten didn't bat an eye at this revelation that his prospective
partners were defrauding the government. Then thirty-five years
old, he seemed to realize his chances of making it big in the world
of honest commerce were growing remote. He had a wife with expensive tastes and an eight-year-old daughter. He didn't want any
more lean years. For the time being, the Welbilt officials had
equated his stylish appearance and glib charm with cleverness and
sophistication. Offered a salary of $45,000, Shorten jumped
aboard.

The accounting firm Larry Shorten found for Welbilt was KMG
Main Hurdman. Originally a German company, Main Hurdman
was a solid, well-respected member of the Big Eight, and its clients
included a number of Fortune 500 companies. It recruited its junior accountants from the best schools; its partners were among
the most highly paid in the accounting profession. All in all, Welbilt could not have found a more reputable auditing firm.

In late 1982, Main Hurdman began auditing Welbilt's books. The
relationship between an auditing firm and its client is called an
"engagement." Typically, an "engagement partner"—a senior
member of the auditing firm—oversees each audit. The actual details of the audit, including the day-to-day work at the company
being audited, are supervised by the "audit manager." The manager in turn has a number of "juniors" working for him, performing various reviews. Typical steps include checking inventory, accounts payable, cash disbursements, and assets and liabilities.

Richard Bluestine of Main Hurdman became the engagement

partner. His audit manager was Anthony Guariglia. Their point of contact at the company was to be Larry Shorten.

Unfortunately, Welbilt's managers were as poor at hiding their crimes as they were at running the business. Disaster occurred almost immediately. The Main Hurdman auditors discovered the progress payment fraud—the dummy invoices that Welbilt had submitted to the government to get advance reimbursements.

By this time some $4 million in premature progress payments had been obtained from the government. The auditors didn't have to be brilliant detectives to spot the forgeries, dated from 1980 to January 1983. For certain companies, the computer-generated invoices in Welbilt's files were genuine and the typewritten ones were phonies. The audit manager, Guariglia, laid the evidence on the table in the conference room and called in his point of contact, Shorten.

Shorten was taken aback. He knew about the SBA fraud, but this . . . this could be disastrous for Welbilt, and he had no explanation. All he could do was urge Guariglia not to do anything rash.

As Mario Moreno was then Welbilt's chief financial officer, Shorten and Guariglia scurried to his office, bringing with them examples of the phony invoices. Moreno was caught virtually red-handed. He admitted that invoices had been forged but, he insisted, no harm had been done. The money received from the falsified progress payments would have been owed to Welbilt eventually. The fraud only accelerated the payments. (In essence, Welbilt was getting interest-free loans from the government that ended up saving the company about $1 million.) Mariotta and Neuberger spouted the same line.

Guariglia knew he had discovered a major irregularity in the company's finances, one that would probably prove fatal to any planned public offering. It was what was known in the profession as a "defalcation," or misuse of funds, and it was the biggest defalcation Guariglia had found in his career. He knew he had no choice but to report it to his superiors at Main Hurdman. He did so, informing both Richard Bluestine and Alan Ackerman, the independent review partner at Main Hurdman. Ackerman directed Guariglia to suspend the audit—to "disengage."

Shorten went to Mariotta and Neuberger to make sure they understood the seriousness of the situation. Disengagement was one step removed from resigning the account—a step that would have ended Welbilt's hopes of going public and, quite possibly, its exis-

67

tence. Mariotta, seeing his dreams evaporate because of a scheme he had been reluctant to approve in the first place, took his frustration out on Moreno.

"Every job that I give you, you always fuck it up!" Mariotta shrieked.

Shorten interceded, explaining it was just possible they could survive the discovery without mortal damage. To do so, he continued, Moreno was going to have to take the fall. Moreno would be portrayed as a well-meaning but overzealous employee who made some mistakes in judgment without the knowledge of Mariotta and Neuberger. It was possible, Shorten added, that Main Hurdman would insist that Moreno be fired as the price of resuming the audit.

Mariotta, who just moments earlier had been tearing into Moreno, now leapt to his defense. Moreno had been like a savior when he came to the company four years earlier. He was too valuable to sacrifice. He shouldn't be thrown to the wolves.

Shorten shrugged. That might be, he explained, but they really had no control over the matter. Moreno's dismissal might be the price Main Hurdman would demand.

Once everybody had his story straight, it was time to get the engagement partner, Richard Bluestine, involved. Shorten ran the story by Bluestine. Overzealous employee. Mariotta and Neuberger knew nothing. Government payments simply accelerated. Surprisingly, Bluestine didn't reject Shorten's explanation out of hand. In fact, he agreed with Shorten that nothing drastic ought to be done, but he believed his superiors would probably demand Moreno's resignation.

To resolve the issue, a meeting was held in Alan Ackerman's office at Main Hurdman. Mariotta, Neuberger, Shorten, and Bernard Ehrlich, acting as corporate counsel, attended for Welbilt. Ackerman, Bluestine, and Guariglia attended for Main Hurdman. The Welbilt executives stuck to their stories.

Ackerman was noncommittal about Main Hurdman's final decision. But he did say that if Main Hurdman resumed the audit, some stringent conditions would be imposed. Moreno could have nothing to do with the financial controls of the company. The scope of the audit would be expanded. And full disclosure of the progress payment fraud would have to be made to the government.

To hear that Main Hurdman was willing to stay on the job at all was a major victory; resignation from the account had seemed a more likely outcome.

The only condition imposed by Main Hurdman that could cause any significant problems was the requirement for full disclosure to the government. Ehrlich, Biaggi's law partner who had become close to Moreno, took on the responsibility of handling that delicate issue.

Ehrlich knew he couldn't possibly disclose everything that had taken place and expect the Small Business Administration to overlook it. The size of the fraud was too large, and no government agency would be able to give a written statement that essentially promised forgiveness for a criminal act. The only way to finesse the problem would be to find a sympathetic ear and understate the extent of the fraud.

The sympathetic ear was that of Peter Neglia, the regional administrator for the Small Business Administration. Neglia's father, Joseph, was a Republican district leader from the Bensonhurst section of Brooklyn. Peter Neglia had been appointed to his position in the SBA in 1981 after George Clark, the Brooklyn Republican chairman, had recommended him to Lyn Nofziger.

Ehrlich told Neglia that there was a problem with the Defense Department progress payments, that the situation was being investigated by the Defense Department and Main Hurdman, that the government hadn't lost any money, and that Welbilt would take care of the matter. He was able to convince the thirty-four-year-old administrator to treat the company gingerly. In fact, Neglia did not even require Welbilt to make an official report of the fraud, much less launch a full-scale investigation or impose any sanctions. For these and other favors, Neglia would later be rewarded handsomely.

After talking to Neglia, Ehrlich turned around and told Main Hurdman he had made full disclosure, which, of course, Main Hurdman took to mean disclosure of the full $4 million fraud. In fact, the firm of Biaggi & Ehrlich wrote a letter to Main Hurdman that said, in part:

> Mr. Ehrlich has discussed the matter extensively with the SBA and that matter has been resolved. The SBA has indicated that they will be satisfied so long as significant inventory and shipments exist to cover the advance payments and progress payments . . .

Main Hurdman was being asked to believe that a federal agency had forgiven a fraud against the government. Mariotta and his cro-

69

nies probably understood that the chances of the auditors accepting such a flimsy story were slim. They also knew there were other skeletons in the company's closet that Main Hurdman had not yet discovered. If they were going to pull off the offering, they were going to need friends on the inside at Main Hurdman.

In late January 1983, Bluestine joined Mariotta on a trip to Japan, ostensibly to conclude a licensing agreement with Kawasaki Steel under which the Japanese company would use a new patented coating process Welbilt was developing. The trip was not a great success; at one point Mariotta told his Japanese hosts that they should act more decisively . . ."like the samurai."

While in Japan, Mariotta bought some pearls for Bluestine to give to his wife. On the trip back, Japan Air Lines Flight 006, Mariotta offered Bluestine stock and long-term employment with Welbilt.

Bluestine's complicity did not come cheap. Having worked out the terms on the flight from Japan, Mariotta decided that the details would be more palatable to his partners if delivered over a nice lunch. So shortly after his return, Mariotta invited Neuberger and Moreno to join him at Rikyu, a Japanese restaurant on Manhattan's Upper West Side. Piling into Mariotta's Lincoln, the trio headed south toward the Columbus Avenue destination. On the way, Mariotta disclosed that he had almost finalized the agreement with Bluestine.

"How much?" Neuberger wanted to know.

Nine percent of the company's stock, Mariotta replied.

"Are you crazy?" Neuberger yelled. "You continue to give stock away like the stock was limitless, like a bottomless pit!"

Mariotta began to scream back. Moreno and Neuberger didn't understand. They were cheapskates. Without Bluestine, the company couldn't go public.

As the argument escalated, the car accelerated. Soon both Mariotta and the Lincoln were out of control, with Mariotta speeding through a red light as the shouting match continued.

When they arrived at the restaurant, no sooner did they step inside than Mariotta, still in high dudgeon, turned on his heels and stalked out. Neuberger and Moreno decided to stay and have lunch.

Ultimately, Mariotta prevailed. Bluestine was to get his stock and would officially remain the Main Hurdman engagement partner. Bluestine's task was to get Main Hurdman to resume the audit

70

and provide the necessary "clean" opinion. He coached the Welbilt executives on how to present their case and what to expect from Main Hurdman. Bluestine helped get Biaggi & Ehrlich's flimsy explanation of the progress payment fraud accepted by Main Hurdman and, as Main Hurdman's audit partner, remained in position to defuse any further bombshells that might burst during the rest of the process.

It didn't take long for the next explosion. Frank Musso, a Main Hurdman auditor who later became the Bronx company's controller, discovered the F.H.J. Associates account.

Musso had been conducting routine checks of the cash disbursements when he noticed that some of the disbursements were incorrect. In the journal, these disbursements were listed as checks written to suppliers such as Alcoa or Bauer, but when the actual checks were produced, they turned out to have been written to F.H.J. Associates. Musso reported his discovery to Guariglia.

Guariglia showed the cancelled checks to Mariotta, Neuberger, and Moreno and asked for an explanation. The officers replied lamely that a restrictive covenant in the financing agreement with the Economic Development Administration capped their salaries at $50,000. They had used the F.H.J. account to supplement what they considered to be their unreasonably low salaries. In other words, they were stealing from the company.

The Main Hurdman auditors understood that very clearly. The memo they wrote to their superiors at the accounting firm was quite explicit:

> When we examined cancelled checks we noted that the payee was F.H.J., a related party . . . owned by John Mariotta and Fred Neuberger. This entity was used by Welbilt to divert money out of the company to the personal use of the officers.

So again Welbilt was in trouble. And once again Bluestine rode to the rescue. This time his brainstorm was to pretend that the money siphoned into the F.H.J. account was actually a loan to Fred Neuberger. A promissory note for $185,000 was created and backdated to December 31, 1981. In the spring of 1983, as final documents were being assembled for the public offering, Neuberger signed the note. Presumably with a straight face, Bluestine asserted that the company would be repaid the full amount that was stolen. Thus, he suggested, the company was not damaged by the theft, so the theft itself was not a material fact that had to be reported to the public in the prospectus. (What no one seemed to notice was that the note still represented only about one-third of the amount that had actually been siphoned off. Mariotta, Neuberger, and Moreno had taken some $511,000 out of the F.H.J. account.) As farfetched as this rationalization sounded, Bluestine was able to sell it. The memo from Musso documenting the theft went into Main Hurdman's files, and the audit continued.

Having compromised Bluestine, the engagement partner, Welbilt next turned to Guariglia, the audit manager. Guariglia was then thirty-two years old. Married, with one daughter, he had both his bachelor's and master of accounting degrees from Adelphi University. His technical accounting skills were held in high regard by his associates—he had been selected to serve on the government contracting committee of the New York State Society of Certified Public Accountants.

But despite his professional status and upward mobility, Guariglia had the aura of a wise guy—a smart punk, but a punk nonetheless. About average height, stocky, with his dark hair blow-dried and combed forward in a Napoleonic sweep, Guariglia always seemed to be swaggering, even when seated. He was constantly working the angles, looking for the edge. His speech, style and demeanor seemed calculated to ensure that no one missed that fact.

On a Sunday morning in early May, Guariglia and the Welbilt executives were in the conference room at 595 Gerard Avenue. Mariotta said he felt the company needed a financial officer and he asked Guariglia to join. At the time, Guariglia was making about $65,000 a year, including bonuses. But he was also on the verge of becoming a partner at Main Hurdman, which would have put him into the $100,000 to $125,000 bracket. To walk away from that kind of money, security, and prestige, Guariglia would need a lot of incentive . . . say, 3 percent of the Welbilt stock. At the time, it was being assumed that each one percent would be worth around $1 million.

Mariotta offered one percent; they settled at 1.5 percent. The Brooklyn-born Guariglia saw an opportunity to be an entrepreneur instead of an accountant, to join a fast-growing company with lucrative government contracts and a potentially exciting

72

coating process. Still, Guariglia wondered about giving up a lifetime of security. He consulted with his colleagues at Main Hurdman. Go for it, they advised. If it doesn't work out, you can always come back. What Guariglia knew, but his colleagues didn't, was that he was walking into a den of thieves.

# 8

## Biaggi's Bite

With Bluestine and Guariglia in their pockets, Welbilt's executives felt confident they could keep a lid on any further audit problems that might arise. But accountants weren't the only outside professionals necessary for a successful public offering. A law firm experienced in securities work would also be needed to prepare the prospectus, and an investment banking firm would be needed to sell the shares to the public.

Finding an investment banker fell to Tony Guariglia. Guariglia contracted a friend, Roger Rowe, at the firm of Moseley Hallgarten, Estabrook & Weeden Inc. Guariglia said Welbilt was looking for a firm that was big enough to command respect but small enough to provide the personalized service and hand-holding that Welbilt would require. Moseley, a venerable Boston-based firm, fit the bill nicely.

On May 5, 1983, Moseley sent Welbilt a letter of intent to underwrite the initial public offering of 1,750,000 shares of common stock in the company. Based on an expected offering price of $16 to $18 per share, the offering would raise approximately $29 million: $25 million from the sale of shares to be issued by the company, and $4 million from the sale of shares to be sold separately by Mariotta, Neuberger, and Moreno. Moseley's fee would be about $2.2 million; Rowe would get a $66,000 finder's fee for bringing in the new business.

Lining up the law firm wasn't as easy. From the outset, it was clear that a firm more sophisticated than Biaggi & Ehrlich would be needed to handle the legal work. Biaggi & Ehrlich's practice was based on power brokering, not on knowledge of the nation's corporate securities laws.

Bob Wallach, whose star with the Welbilt crowd had risen with the engine contract victory, took it upon himself to find new legal representation for Welbilt. Wallach might have told himself and others that his initial interest in Welbilt stemmed from his empathy with these struggling entrepreneurs in the Bronx, but then Wallach already had a history of wanting to do well in addition to doing good.

At least two cases Wallach handled in California produced allegations that he tried to do too well. In the first case, Wallach and a partner negotiated a $2.2 million settlement for a child who had been severely brain damaged at birth. The payout structure was unusual—$1.1 million to fund a trust for the child and the other half as a lump sum payment to the parents. While California court rules limited attorney fees in children's cases to 25 percent of the settlement, there were no such limits for adult settlements. So Wallach and his partner waived their fee with regard to the child's settlement but kept $862,000 from the parents' settlement. That was $300,000 more than they would have been entitled to if the entire settlement had gone to the child. The presiding judge was latter quoted as saying he was shocked by the arrangement.

In the other case, Wallach and his partner represented two little girls who had been severely burned in a tent fire. The judge in the case, State Superior Court Judge Eugene Lynch, was seeking Wallach's assistance in obtaining a presidential appointment to the federal bench. In August 1981, Wallach wrote his old friend Edwin Meese about Lynch and the appointment. The following month, Lynch granted Wallach and his partner $1 million in fees on the girls' case, an unusually high 57 percent of the $1.74 million settlement. Wallach wrote to Meese again in January 1982, and later that month President Reagan nominated Lynch to the U.S. District Court. Unfortunately for Wallach, another judge reduced the legal fees in the case to $322,000 after objections by the children's parents.

By December 1982, Wallach was taking steps to ensure that he receive tangible rewards for his assistance to Welbilt. He prepared a "legal and policy advisor" agreement between himself and the company. Under this agreement, he would receive $30,000 for "advisory services" he had provided in October through December of 1982. For 1983, he would receive a $50,000 retainer and $10,000 per month. Thus, Wallach was proposing that this struggling minority enterprise pay him $200,000 for fifteen months of part-time work. In addition, Wallach was to receive 1 percent of the sales of the coating process and 5 percent of any coating sales that he generated. The agreement was never signed, apparently because the company didn't have the money to make the payments it called for. Mariotta and Moreno promised Wallach, however, that when Welbilt could afford it, they would compensate him generously.

Also in December of 1982, Wallach asked to get together with Bernie Ehrlich to pave the way for Welbilt to retain new legal counsel. Mariotta and Moreno set up the meeting.

The law offices of Biaggi & Ehrlich were in an old office building at 299 Broadway in lower Manhattan. It was a long way from the congressman's district in the Bronx, but it was also conveniently close to many of the federal bureaucrats with whom the firm was peddling its influence. Because of congressional restrictions on outside income and activities, Mario Biaggi was no longer a name partner at the firm. The Biaggi in the firm's name now was the congressman's eldest son, Richard. But, lest anyone miss the point, Mario Biaggi continued to be listed as "of counsel" on the firm's letterhead. The congressman also continued to draw a salary, consulting fees, and payments from the firm.

Mariotta, Moreno, and Wallach were greeted by a receptionist who ushered them into the law offices to see Ehrlich. Despite his status as a name partner in the firm, Bernie Ehrlich was actually little more than a front man for the congressman. Born in Bermuda in 1928, Ehrlich had been deserted by his father and was brought to the United states at an early age by his mother. After growing up on Manhattan's Lower East Side, he received undergraduate and law degrees from New York University and served in the army during the Korean War. Before he met Mario Biaggi, he had been one of hundreds of New York's small-time lawyers hustling any clients they could buttonhole.

After joining Biaggi, Ehrlich continued his association with the

76

military through the New York National Guard, rising to the rank of colonel. An insecure man, he revelled in the authority implied by the title. He seemed to believe that the uniform, which he invariably wore at inappropriate times, masked his unprepossessing appearance—a bald pate fringed with bushy gray hair over weak eyes blinking owlishly behind thick glasses.

After some general conversation with Ehrlich about Welbilt's growth, Wallach got to the point. Although Biaggi & Ehrlich had done a lot for the company, Welbilt was entering a new national stage and needed new legal representation. Biaggi & Ehrlich, Wallach continued, didn't have what it took to prepare for the public offering or to function as corporate counsel in the future.

Ehrlich was practically speechless. He turned beet red, but after Wallach's patronizing remarks there wasn't much more to be said.

Back in the car, Wallach announced that he was already making plans to bring in the firm of Squadron, Ellenoff, Pleasant & Lehrer as the new corporate counsel. The firm, although not large, had a good deal of experience taking companies public and doing corporate legal work.

Wallach had met Howard Squadron, the firm's senior partner, in 1981 at a meeting of the Northern California chapter of the American Jewish Congress. The introduction was made by Hal Lipset, the San Francisco private eye Welbilt had asked to investigate Keenan. At the time, Squadron was national president of the American Jewish Congress, and he was interested to learn that Wallach was quite friendly with Meese. The ever-helpful Wallach introduced Squadron to Meese. In late summer of 1982, Wallach introduced Squadron to Welbilt. Welbilt was looking for financing from Bank Leumi, and Squadron had good contacts at the Israeli-owned bank. Now Wallach was looking to bring Welbilt to Squadron's firm as a new corporate client.

After dropping Wallach off in midtown Manhattan, Mariotta and Moreno returned to the Bronx. By the time they arrived at Welbilt headquarters, Congressman Biaggi had already called twice. The secretary who took the calls told Moreno that Biaggi sounded very upset; he wanted to be called back immediately.

Moreno, realizing that Ehrlich had reported to Biaggi on the meeting with Wallach, was not anxious to return the call. A few moments later, however, Biaggi made a third call. Moreno had no choice but to take it.

Biaggi was direct. In his rage at Wallach, he apparently forgot about the thousands of Jewish votes that helped get him re-elected every two years.

"What do you people do? Why do you take that fucking Jew bastard over there?" Biaggi said. "Why do you let him do that to poor Bernie? If I had been there, I would have knocked him down flat on the floor."

Moreno tried to smooth Biaggi's ruffled feathers.

"Congressman, we didn't know that Wallach was going to be saying these things over there. It probably was a mistake to have brought him there at this time, but don't be concerned with the situation. We will not let it happen anymore."

Even Biaggi recognized, however, that Welbilt would need legal help more sophisticated than his firm could provide. The congressman began pushing the high-powered Manhattan firm of Shea & Gould (Shea Stadium, home of the New York Mets, is named after the firm's William Shea), where Biaggi knew one of the senior partners.

Biaggi set up a meeting at Shea & Gould and continued to disparage the capabilities of Squadron Ellenoff. He maintained that Squadron Ellenoff was disliked by various government agencies, and that the congressman's firm could work more effectively with Shea & Gould. Ehrlich took a different tack: Picking Squadron Ellenoff, he told the Welbilt executives, would be a direct slap in the face to the congressman.

Welbilt's executives faced a dilemma. On the one hand, they wanted to use Squadron Ellenoff to keep Wallach happy and retain his influence in Washington. On the other hand, they couldn't afford to offend Biaggi because of his influence with the local politicians. In the end, after much internal argument and debate, national beat local. Welbilt chose Squadron Ellenoff to handle the public offering.

Squadron Ellenoff was a medium-sized firm—it had about thirty lawyers—that had been formed in 1970. Its offices were in the landmark Fred W. French building on Fifth Avenue in midtown Manhattan. Howard Squadron was the firm's great white father and chief "rainmaker," or source of business. As a Jewish leader, Squadron was becoming increasingly prominent on the national stage.

The firm's largest client by far was Rupert Murdoch, the media magnate from Australia with whom Squadron had developed a close personal relationship. The rest of the firm's billings were divided among many smaller clients. A new account like Welbilt would be welcomed. As a minority company in the South Bronx, Welbilt offered an unusual challenge. It remained to be seen, however, whether the fledgling new client would survive long enough to produce any legal fees.

Wallach's insistence that Welbilt use Squadron Ellenoff wasn't based entirely on his friendship with Howard Squadron or his regard for the firm's capabilities. Later in 1983, Wallach requested a 20 percent "referral fee" for bringing the new client to the law firm. Squadron initially balked, because referral fees as such are considered unethical. The parties finally worked out an arrangement under which the law firm would pay Wallach $2,500 from Welbilt's $12,500 monthly retainer; Squadron Ellenoff's invoices to Welbilt would characterize Wallach's "co-counsel" fee as compensation for the hours he spent on Welbilt business. Later, the arrangement was changed to provide Wallach with 10 percent of Squadron Ellenoff's fees. Wallach apparently never submitted any time records to substantiate the fees he was paid. But then Welbilt proved to be a more lucrative client than anyone at Squadron Ellenoff had initially imagined, and these arrangements would net Wallach some $157,000 over the next three years.

Welbilt's decision to retain Squadron Ellenoff relegated Biaggi & Ehrlich to handling the company's contacts with the SBA and other government agencies. Mario Biaggi and Bernard Ehrlich didn't exactly walk away empty-handed, however. As early as 1981, Mariotta had begun promising that Biaggi and Ehrlich would receive stock in Welbilt "when the time is right." Since Welbilt was chronically behind in its retainer payments, it seemed a good way to get the law firm off its back.

The promise had become a lot more specific in the summer of 1982, when Biaggi met with Mariotta in the backyard of Mariotta's recently acquired home in Scarsdale. It was a hot day, and they were lounging around the pool. The congressman had already begun taking a proprietary interest in Welbilt. When another Bronx politician tried to place two cronies on Welbilt's payroll, Biaggi interceded. He didn't want "his" company paying for "no-shows." But now, Biaggi wanted his interest in the company formalized. He pressed Mariotta for a commitment.

Mariotta said he'd have to check with his partners, but that Biaggi shouldn't worry.

"I'll make you a millionaire," Mariotta promised. In fact, Mariotta continued, he would make Biaggi a millionaire five times over.

Mariotta, whose concept of large amounts of money was tenuous at best, fervently believed he could deliver. Whether Biaggi, a tough-minded survivor of New York City's asphalt jungles, believed what he was hearing from this semiliterate machinist is doubtful. Nevertheless, this semiliterate machinist was already making more money than a member of Congress, already had a home in Scarsdale, with a swimming pool in the backyard and a Lincoln in the driveway . . . so maybe anything was possible.

Biaggi's immediate goal, of course, was to get this grandiose promise, uttered in a relaxed and informal atmosphere, committed to writing as quickly as possible. He told Mariotta that he wanted to meet with Neuberger and have him confirm the promise of $5 million in stock. A dinner was scheduled for Joe Nina's, an Italian restaurant on Westchester Avenue, not far from Biaggi's congressional office.

Neuberger, naturally, was less than pleased when he heard that his partner had promises Biaggi $5 million in stock. "It is insane!" he bellowed. "What are you giving such crazy promises for?" Mariotta, who considered himself a man of his word, replied that he had committed himself. Neuberger, no doubt thinking that his partner ought to be committed to an institution, replied that he would negotiate with the congressman and bring the figure down to a more reasonable level. For the time being, however, he wasn't going to have dinner with a cop with his hand out.

When Mariotta and Moreno arrived by themselves at Joe Nina's, the perceptive Biaggi immediately noticed that someone was missing.

"Where is Neuberger?" demanded the congressman, whose rugged good looks and impeccable tailoring didn't quite mask the rough edges.

Mariotta and Moreno tried to cover by saying Neuberger had a previous meeting and wouldn't be able to attend. Biaggi wasn't fooled. His carefully cultivated air of polished urbanity vanished.

"That cheap bastard Jew," he muttered.

Mariotta assured the angry congressman that he would talk to Neuberger and bring him around. Trying to change the subject, he provided the congressman with a glowing report on the company's progress.

This, however, merely served to whet Biaggi's appetite. In addition to the $5 million in stock, he announced, he wanted 5 percent of every contract he helped bring to the company.

Mariotta and Moreno were stunned by Biaggi's escalating demands. First a retainer, then a bigger retainer, then stock, now this. If Welbilt ever got as big as they hoped, 5 percent of revenues could mean millions of dollars.

Moreno, hoping to talk some sense into Biaggi, explained that the profit margin on government contracts was only about 10 percent, and there was no way the company could afford to give away half its profits. But Moreno, never wishing to offend his politically powerful friends, added helpfully that subcontracts were not monitored as carefully as direct contracts. Perhaps Biaggi and Ehrlich could get a 5 percent commission on any subcontracts they brought in.

By the end of the $185 dinner, the parties had informally agreed that Biaggi and Ehrlich would get 5 percent of the company's stock, no commission on direct government contracts, and possibly 5 percent on subcontracts. The only hurdle, they reminded Biaggi, was that they still had to get Fred Neuberger's approval. Another meeting was arranged, this one at corporate headquarters.

After being briefed on the dinner meeting, Neuberger again questioned his partner's sanity. Neuberger, who claimed to be fluent in eight languages, normally spoke English with only a trace of an accent. When he got excited, however, his accent thickened and grammar deteriorated to the point that he would sometimes sound like a character out of *Fiddler on the Roof*.

"If we keep giving the stock away, one of these days you and me are going to end up with nothing!" he stormed.

The showdown with Biaggi came a few days later at 595 Gerard. Biaggi and Ehrlich went straight to Mariotta's office. Neuberger went straight to the point:

He had heard about the discussions with Mariotta and Moreno, and he thought 5 percent was too much. It was promised by his partner in a rash moment and was totally outrageous. As a reasonable person, Biaggi should understand that. Two percent, worth $2 million dollars, was more money than the congressman had ever seen, and he ought to be happy with that. Five percent was simply out of the question, unless Mariotta wanted to give it to Biaggi from his own shares.

Biaggi was having none of it. He recited everything he and Ehrlich had done for the company. He had made the company, and he

81

could destroy it. He was unhappy Welbilt wouldn't keep a commitment from its chairman of the board. It would affect his future attitude toward the company. He resented Neuberger's suggestion that he was like a cop with his hand out.

"I don't think that you," he said, indicating Neuberger, "are going to go to businessman's heaven."

Neuberger was not swayed. He prided himself on being a tough bargainer. "Well," he said, "this is all you are going to get." He walked through the connecting bathroom into his own office.

The tension in Mariotta's office was palpable. Everyone knew the stakes were high. The difference between the 5 percent the congressman was demanding and the 2 percent that Neuberger was offering could be worth as much as $3 million.

As the standoff continued, Mariotta joined Neuberger in his partner's office. Mariotta argued that he had given his word to the congressman. With all the problems in the company, they couldn't afford to make an enemy of someone as powerful as Biaggi. We should show a united front, Mariotta argued. Partners should back each other. It was embarrassing that his commitment was not being met. People would think John Mariotta didn't keep his word.

Neuberger realized the game was over. He could count, and it was two against one. By himself, he wasn't going to get Biaggi to back down.

Neuberger went back into Mariotta's office. "All right, Mr. Biaggi, you got your 5 percent," he said. "Just because John gave his word, I will go along with the agreement."

Biaggi smiled, and everyone shook hands.

Neuberger was hardly graceful in defeat, however. Storming out of the meeting, he ran into Shorten in the hallway. Neuberger began ranting. He could have negotiated Biaggi down to 2 percent or 2.5 percent but Mariotta—that moron!—turned around and insisted on giving him the 5 percent he'd originally promised.

Mariotta, meanwhile, was only slightly more gracious in victory. A short time after the big meeting, he complained to Shorten that Neuberger was always trying to sell him to the lowest bidder. Fred, Mariotta complained, just didn't understand how badly Welbilt needed Mario Biaggi's friendship.

Now that the deal was done, the only remaining problem was how to convey the stock. Giving it directly to a member of Congress was out of the question on legal and public relations grounds. The initial plan was that all of the promised shares would go to the law firm of Biaggi & Ehrlich. After further discussion, it was decided to give half the shares to Bernard Ehrlich and the other half to Representative Biaggi's son, Richard.

Richard, then thirty-four, was just three years out of law school and had only recently been admitted to the bar. Physically, Richard resembled a younger version of his father; emotionally, he was gentler and less driven. After graduating from Manhattan College in 1970, he served in the New York Army National Guard and the U.S. Army Reserves during the final years of the Vietnam War. He eventually got his law degree in 1980 from the University of Baltimore School of Law, the third law school he had attended. Joining his father's law firm was the path of least resistance.

Richard Biaggi did little work on the Welbilt account. There was one Sunday, while others at the firm were dealing with a Welbilt crisis, that Richard spent moving the office furniture and watching a basketball game on TV. For his father, however, Richard had one priceless qualification. Mario Biaggi knew that Richard would never double-cross him.

# 9

# A Suitcase Full of Cash

In the months leading up to the public offering, the audit discoveries weren't the only matters demanding attention from Welbilt's executives. In fact, the most urgent problem was that the company was once again out of money. Without a quick infusion of cash, Welbilt might not survive long enough to go public.

Of course this was nothing new. There'd been few times in the company's history when it wasn't short of cash. Sometimes the problem was manageable; other times it was a crisis. Part of the problem was attributable to the normal growing pains of a start-up, capital-intensive business. Certainly the company's South Bronx location made it more difficult to obtain capital and credit, a theme the Welbilt officers trumpeted often. But they conveniently overlooked the degree to which their own theft, high living, and incompetence exacerbated the problem.

To deal with the latest cash crunch, Mariotta and Moreno decided to ask the Bronx-based New York National Bank for a larger loan. Since both owned shares in the bank and the company had an account there, they hoped bank officials would be receptive to their overture.

In the fall of 1982, they met with Serafin Mariel, the bank president, and Ivan Irizarry, the vice-president (and former regional director of the SBA), at a cafeteria in Hunts Point, a section of the

Bronx where food processing and used auto parts seem to be the leading industries. The cafeteria was a block and a half from the bank's headquarters, which was located above a Blimpie Restaurant at the corner of Southern Boulevard and East 163rd Street.

Like Mariotta, Serafin Mariel was born to Puerto Rican parents in New York City. Mariel, thirty-nine, had started out as a teller at Banker's Trust, rising through the ranks to became a branch manager. In early 1982, he and Irizarry had helped found New York National, which targeted its loans to small and medium-sized businesses.

Moreno explained the situation and asked for a loan of $500,000. Mariel demurred, noting that Welbilt was already at the limit—$150,000—of what the bank could lend to a single company.

The soft-spoken, round-faced banker did have a suggestion, however. He knew someone who would be willing to consider the request for financing. Moreover the financing could be arranged quickly, without a lot of paperwork, and could be provided in cash. The bad news was that the interest rate would be a tad high—approximately 100 percent a year.

Mariotta and Moreno looked at each other and nodded. The Welbilt executives weren't astute businessmen, but they knew enough to realize they were about to become involved with a loan shark. That meant dirty money, usurious rates, and nasty collection techniques. After consulting with Neuberger, they decided they had no alternative. They were desperate. Check with the unnamed lender, they told Mariel, and let us know the answer.

A short time later, Mariel called Moreno and told him that his contact would lend them the money. The loan would be for three months; the interest rate would be 100 percent. In other words, in three months they would have to pay the lender the $500,000 principal and roughly $150,000 interest, with no excuses accepted for late payment. Mariel told Moreno to bring Mariotta and Neuberger to the bank office around noon on a Friday.

As Moreno recalled it, they were at Mariel's office at the appointed hour. Mariel wasn't. The Wedtech executives, joined by Neuberger's brother-in-law, Elias Gutter, a diamond dealer from Belgium, waited for the banker, fidgeting as time passed.

Shortly before 2 P.M., Mariel walked in carrying a briefcase. He ushered Mariotta, Neuberger, Moreno, and Irizarry into his office and closed the door.

85

Mariel opened the briefcase, revealing neatly packed stacks of $50 and $100 bills. Even Neuberger, who generally affected an I've-seen-it-all demeanor, was impressed.

"Wow!" he whistled.

Before the loan could be transacted, the money had to be counted. Unfortunately, the bank's counting machine was broken. So it fell to Mariel and Irizarry to count the half a million dollars by hand, while the senior executives of the Welbilt Electronic Die Corp. retreated to the waiting room. The count revealed that the briefcase held only $485,000, so a check made out to cash was issued for the missing $15,000.

It was now nearly three o'clock on a Friday afternoon, and the Welbilt executives had a problem. They were about to be handed a very large amount of cash. What would they do with it over the weekend? In the South Bronx, where you can get rolled for pocket change, trying to protect $500,000 was too great a risk to take.

Mariel had no intention of depositing the money at New York National. That would create a paper trail, because federal law requires that banks report all their cash transactions of $10,000 or more.

So Moreno made a hasty call to an acquaintance at European American Bank, Alice Kennedy. She agreed to stay late at her bank, near the United Nations, to do what she could for the Welbilt officials.

The group took the briefcase and piled into Mariotta's car, along with a New York National Bank security guard dispatched by Mariel. No loan documents had been signed, but everyone understood the terms of the agreement and the consequences of violating them. Everyone also understood that enforcement of those terms would not be left to the courts.

As the group sped away, anxious to get to Manhattan before Kennedy had to close the bank, a crisis arose almost immediately. A policeman pulled the car over for a traffic violation.

There they were, an odd-looking collection of middle-aged men crowded into a car in the South Bronx with a briefcase full of cash. At best, it seemed, they would be delayed and have to try to protect the money over the weekend. At worst, well, they didn't even want to think about that. If the cop made them open the briefcase, they were going to have a lot of explaining to do. Even worse, the lender, whoever he was, was not going to be pleased.

Fortune smiled on the Welbilt group. The cop's suspicions were not aroused. Maybe because it was a Friday afternoon, maybe—who knew? In any event, the cop gave them a stern lecture about making illegal turns and let them go with a warning. They were off the hook.

The incident, however, had spooked Moreno. It seemed like an omen, and he was getting very cold feet. Because he didn't want the security guard to know what was going on, Moreno began talking to Neuberger in French. They were still in the Bronx, driving under the elevated Bruckner Expressway, the area made famous as the scene of the auto accident in Tom Wolfe's novel *The Bonfire of the Vanities.*

Moreno tried to convince Neuberger that they ought to turn back and return the cash. He focused on one point in particular: *"Si nous ne pouvons pas les rendre d'argent, nous pouvons probablement être executé"*—if they couldn't pay back the money, they could be executed very easily.

Moreno's French must have been eloquent, because for five or six blocks they hesitated. If they turned back now, they could probably just return the cash and forget the whole thing. Perhaps there was another way of raising money ... but then the moment of doubt passed. There wasn't any other way. If they didn't go ahead with the transaction, the company would collapse in less than a week.

Now they were in a hurry to get the money secured. Moving as fast as traffic and potholes would permit, they sped past blocks of grimy industrial buildings, across the Willis Avenue Bridge, down the humpy FDR Drive, past Harlem and the Upper East Side to midtown. Pulling up in front of the United Nations plaza, they scrambled out of the car and raced to the bank entrance, clutching the briefcase. A security guard called Kennedy, the branch manager, who arrived to escort them inside.

When the officials explained to her what they wanted to do, her response was simple. No, she said.

After the dash to Manhattan, the brush with the law, and the fears of execution, this news was devastating. Why wouldn't the bank accept their perfectly good cash? they bleated.

Kennedy patiently went over what the president of New York National Bank had already tried to explain to them. If they made a lump sum deposit that large, the bank would have to notify the government, and she had a feeling nobody was anxious to call attention to this particular transaction. The only one whose deposit

87

wouldn't raise any eyebrows was Gutter, the Antwerp diamond merchant who frequently made large cash deposits when he came to the U.S.

After kicking around various ideas, the group decided to let Neuberger's brother-in-law deposit about $80,000 and to launder the rest of the money through various friends and relatives. That is, they would give the cash to these relatives, who would deposit it in their personal accounts, then write checks to the company for the amount of cash they were given. These checks would be deposited into Welbilt's account and carried on the books as loans by these individuals to Welbilt. In that way, Welbilt would receive $500,000 and it would show loans payable of $500,000 plus interest.

Kennedy arranged for them to get a safe deposit box in which to stash the cash until they set up the various sham loans. Over the next few days, Mariotta, Neuberger, and Moreno were busy swapping cash for an equivalent amount in checks from friends and relatives. Although rather untidy, it all seemed very clever, and the Welbilt officers were pleased they'd been able to pull it off.

By early 1983, however, the satisfaction was fading fast, replaced by a feeling of concern about their physical well-being. The loan had come due, and all they had were excuses. Checks from the government were in the mail, or at least were going to be soon. The $3 million grant from the SBA was untouchable; it could be used only to buy machinery. To angry creditors, these excuses sounded pretty good. The executives weren't looking forward to trying them out on a loan shark.

Having no choice, Mariotta and Moreno went back to Mariel. Without much conviction, they ran through all the excuses. They asked whether the lender would be willing to grant an extension. Mariel hedged. He'd try, he said, but it was going to be difficult.

Mariel called the next day. They could have another three months. It would cost them another $150,000. The lender wanted the full $800,000, principal and interest, by early April. No more extensions, no more excuses.

Although Mariel had never told them the name of the loan shark, Neuberger had noticed a name embossed on the briefcase in which they were given the original $500,000. SIMONE. Neuberger recognized the name. Pat Simone owned a huge auto parts business in the Hunts Point area as well as a lot of real estate in the Bronx.

Although he had a clean record, Welbilt's executives assumed he was somehow connected with the Mafia. What they didn't know was that Simone and his son, Joseph, were major shareholders of New York National Bank.

The three months passed quickly, and once again it became obvious that Welbilt would be unable to come up with the cash to pay off the loan. Plans for the initial public offering were well underway, and under normal circumstance this would have been management's first priority. But these were not normal circumstances—or normal managers, for that matter. Their first priority was staying alive long enough to enjoy the fruits of the public offering.

Mariotta and Moreno went back to Mariel with the bad news. Mariel told them to meet him at the construction site of a Jehovah's Witnesses church in which he was active. There Mariel confirmed the Welbilt executives' fears. The lender (still unidentified) wouldn't give them an extension. They had to come up with the money from whatever source they could. Mariel told them he was very distressed.

Mariel's concern was mild compared to Mariotta's and Moreno's. As they headed back to their offices after the meeting, Moreno turned to Mariotta.

"John, I am really very worried," he said. "These people may be very dangerous individuals, and we don't know what may happen to us."

Sleeping on the problem didn't seem to help. The next day, Ehrlich stopped by Moreno's office at Welbilt headquarters. He quickly picked up on Moreno's anxious demeanor.

When Ehrlich asked what was happening, Moreno unburdened himself with the history of the loan and the meeting the previous day with Mariel. Ehrlich, as always, claimed he knew someone who could fix the problem.

"Simone, if it is Simone—my partner knows him very well," the lawyer volunteered. "Let's see if he can do something for you there." By his partner, Ehrlich was referring, of course, to Congressman Mario Biaggi.

Not long after leaving 595 Gerard, Ehrlich phoned Moreno to say that Biaggi would be attending a Democratic Party function at Marina Del Ray in the Bronx that night. Moreno should meet him there to discuss the problem.

Moreno arrived before the congressman. After a few minutes, Bi-

89

aggi strode into the reception hall, dragging the left leg he had injured decades earlier. Ehrlich intercepted him.

Biaggi, on his way into the men's room to change into his tuxedo, told Moreno to join him inside while Ehrlich waited outside. As the congressman dressed, Moreno went through the history of the transaction, mentioning that the loan shark appeared to be Pat Simone. Biaggi said simply that he would speak to Simone and see what he could do about another extension.

A few days later, Ehrlich called Moreno. The congressman had spoken to Simone, Ehrlich reported, and Simone was willing to extend the loan. But—there were going to be some new conditions. Ehrlich told Moreno somebody representing Simone would be getting in touch with him.

That somebody was John Tartaglia, Simone's nephew and personal attorney. Tartaglia had begun his professional career in the Bronx district attorney's office. Now in his thirties, he was working for his uncle as an adviser, attorney, and confidant. Like his uncle, he was a big man, and he used his size to advantage. When talking with someone, Tartaglia would constantly edge closer; the other party would be forced to keep retreating or, if he stood his ground, would find Tartaglia looming over him. Often, Simone's nephew would clutch the arm or shoulder of his interlocutor.

Tartaglia's style ran from bluff to domineering, depending on how the conversation was going and the reactions of the other party. In the final analysis, his stock in trade was intimidation. Not overt or explicit, but intimidation nonetheless. With the reputation of his uncle, his skillful use of his size, and the rumor that he wore a pistol strapped to his ankle, Tartaglia was not to be trifled with.

According to Moreno, Tartaglia's first proposal was a request that Biaggi and Ehrlich give personal assurances that Welbilt would make good on the loan. Ehrlich demurred.

Mariotta, Moreno, and Ehrlich then met with Tartaglia to present their counterproposal. They told him Welbilt was about to go public. Perhaps the loan could be paid off the day of the public offering. Perhaps the loan shark could make a little extra money if he would agree to wait.

A complex deal was struck under which Mariotta, Neuberger, and Moreno sold Belenguer N.V., a Netherlands Antilles company, 40,000 shares of their personal Welbilt stock at $12.50 a share. (Belenguer was represented by Tartaglia, and the Welbilt executives believed it was controlled by Simone.) Then the officers loaned the resulting $500,000 to the corporation. Welbilt used that money to pay off the loans from the friends and relatives that had been concocted to launder the original loan. The friends and relatives immediately cashed their checks, returned the money to the Welbilt officers, who then repaid the original loan.

At the end of all these machinations, Belenguer was left with 40,000 shares of Welbilt stock, and Welbilt still owed interest to the loan shark. It had taken quite a bit of doing, but the loan shark had been pacified for the time being. Their kneecaps intact, the Welbilt executives resumed their march toward the initial public offering.

# 10

# Dividing the Spoils

The suitcase full of cash had been helpful, but it wouldn't be enough to keep Welbilt afloat until the public offering. The company had a huge accounts payable balance and was delinquent on its long-term debts. Creditors were clamoring louder than usual for their money; many refused to ship Welbilt raw materials or supplies without cash in advance. To stave off bankruptcy, the company was trying to negotiate a bridge loan from Bank Leumi.

Before the bank would agree to the loan, it wanted to see a signed labor agreement to replace the three-year accord that was expiring in 1983. The labor talks had gotten off to a rocky start. At a meeting in January, the union representatives noted they'd been getting a large number of complaints about the activities of Mario Rosado, the "pastor" of Welbilt's chapel. It seemed as though Rosado's requests for contributions had become rather aggressive; several workers complained of extortion. According to one executive, Rosado controlled access to Mariotta. If a worker wanted a loan, he would have to make the request to Rosado. Often, if the worker were not part of the Pentecostal clique, Rosado would inform him that Mariotta had refused the request. A couple of hours later, Rosado or one of his cronies would approach the worker and offer to lend him the money, only the rates would be usurious and the period of the loan very short.

The union representatives, Richard Stolfi and Frank Casalino, urged Mariotta to get rid of Rosado. Mariotta, furious, said he'd rather get rid of the union. Stolfi, a squat man with square shoulders and beady eyes, called Mariotta "an idiot." The meeting ended unproductively.

On March 14, Welbilt received the union's demands for the new contract. Neuberger thought the terms—raises of $3 an hour for each of the three years—were excessive; he arranged a meeting with Stolfi. The two quickly reached a deal: for $25,000, Stolfi would do what he could to avert a strike (which could have sunk the planned public offering) and make sure the contract was more to the company's liking. Stolfi helpfully suggested a labor lawyer, Sanford Pollack, for Welbilt to use in the negotiations. Pollack also happened to be the attorney for the union's welfare fund.

As the bargaining began, a newly rehired tool- and die-maker, Horace Jung, approached Neuberger. Jung, a hulking, bearded Austrian, asked Neuberger whether he ought to join the union. Jung explained that he wouldn't be able to afford a strike.

"Don't be a schmuck," replied Neuberger, never terribly discreet. "We have the union like this," he added, pointing into his pocket.

After a charade of intense negotiations, the tentative new contract was put to a vote of the union workers. The contract provided for raises of seventy-five cents an hour the first year and fifty cents the following two years. The workers were given two choices: accept the contract or go on strike.

The first vote, taken on the loading dock, ended in chaos when dissident union members broke the ballot box, tore up ballots, and threw them in the air. A second vote was scheduled for the following week in the parking lot. This time Neuberger stood near the ballot box with a big cigar, glaring at the workers as they cast their votes. Moreno watched the farce from his office window and laughed. The contract was approved.

The day after the public offering, Neuberger fired Mario Rosado. Mariotta, in retaliation, fired Julio Rivera, an abrasive security captain and former street-gang leader who had asked Neuberger to be best man at his wedding.

With the new labor agreement in place, Bank Leumi approved a loan package totaling $5.1 million for Welbilt—a $3.2 million line of credit and the assumption by Bank Leumi of $1.9 million in old Citibank loans to Welbilt that had been guaranteed by two government agencies, the EDA and the SBA.

There was just one catch: before Welbilt could get its hands on the money, the government agencies would have to agree to subordinate their interests to Bank Leumi. In other words, if Welbilt went bankrupt, Bank Leumi would get to seize the assets first to recoup its money; Uncle Sam would be second in line.

Neglia, the SBA regional administrator in New York, was now firmly in Welbilt's camp and could be counted on to take care of SBA's subordination. The problem was going to be the EDA, an arm of the U.S. Department of Commerce.

By now the Welbilt gang had almost abandoned any pretense of dealing through normal channels on the more substantive aspects of their problems. When confronted with the challenge of obtaining EDA subordination, Ehrlich's reflexive response was that it shouldn't be too difficult because one of Representative Biaggi's aides was cozy with a key official at the EDA's regional office in Philadelphia.

This time, however, Ehrlich and his connections couldn't deliver. Decision-making power on issues like the Welbilt loan subordination had been moved from Philadelphia to Washington. Only Carlos C. Campbell, the assistant secretary of commerce in charge of the EDA, could make the decision.

Carlos Campbell was no patsy. A forty-six-year-old Harlem native, he was one of the highest ranking black appointees in the Reagan administration. Campbell was heavy-set, with brown eyes behind round glasses, a broad nose, bushy mustache, and crooked lower teeth. A former naval aviator and intelligence analyst, he had a master's degree in city and regional planning from Catholic University. He also had a keen understanding of finance and accounting, which is more than could be said for the top two officers of the Welbilt Electronic Die Corp. His mission at EDA, as he understood it, was to clean up the agency's horrendous loan portfolio—42 percent of the loans were delinquent—and protect the taxpayers' money.

With his blunt and frequently profane manner, Campbell had alienated those on Capitol Hill who had regarded the agency as a sort of private pork barrel. But Campbell felt he had marching orders from President Ronald Reagan, and he wasn't about to be intimidated—not by members of Congress, and certainly not by private lobbyists.

Predictably, given this kind of attitude, Carlos Campbell replaced Keenan at the top of Welbilt's enemies list.

What Welbilt thought would be a simple political fix was turning into a full-blown crisis. The corporation needed money to survive; it couldn't get its hands on the money without the EDA subordination. And the man in charge at EDA saw no good reason why a government agency should make an exception to normal procedures and guidelines.

Employing lessons learned in winning the engine contract, the Welbilt gang began appealing to its political allies in an effort to force Campbell to make the "right" decision, or force someone else to make the decision for him.

After efforts by the New York group—Biaggi, Ehrlich, and D'Amato—failed to sway Campbell, the Washington group—Nofziger, Bragg, and Wallach—was enlisted in the battle.

Wallach quickly called Jenkins, who had done such a fine job on the engine contract, and sent the White House aide a memo about Welbilt's latest crisis. Meanwhile, Bragg and then Nofziger started calling Campbell to urge quick action on the loan subordination.

According to notes taken by Meese, the Welbilt situation was discussed at an early morning White House staff meeting on Tuesday, June 7. Later that day, probably as a follow-up to the staff meeting, Jenkins asked Craig Fuller whether any action could be taken on Welbilt's behalf. Jenkins urged that the White House contact the Department of Commerce to suggest the Welbilt proposal be reviewed on an expedited basis.

As with the engine contract, Fuller again had ethical qualms and sought guidance from White House counsel Fielding. Fielding responded the next day, making it plain he believed White House intervention would be inappropriate:

> . . . Any communication from the White House could . . . be misinterpreted by EDA and/or misperceived by the public as untoward and inappropriate interference, either on the loan decision or the decision to expedite, both of which are EDA's to make.

Fuller adhered to the advice, and his office of Cabinet Affairs did not contact the Commerce Department on the Welbilt matter.

While memos were passing back and forth in the White House, Welbilt was telling its consultants that bankruptcy was imminent.

Wallach called Jenkins on June 9. "He is in a state of panic," Jenkins noted in his telephone log.

A week later, a meeting of all the interested parties took place in New York. John Geraghty, the EDA project manager in Philadelphia responsible for Welbilt, came to the meeting expecting that EDA and the SBA would present a united front. Geraghty had visited Welbilt's plant in March and had concluded that the company had management problems and knew it was delinquent in its loan payments. He was surprised, therefore, to hear Neglia, New York regional director of the SBA, strongly urge the EDA to approve the subordination agreement. At the meeting, the outline of a deal began to take shape under which Welbilt would promise to pay off its loan early in return for EDA agreeing to the subordination.

The deal percolated through the bureaucracy while Campbell was out of the country on official business. On July 14, the plan was approved by the EDA regional office in Philadelphia and forwarded to Campbell for his signature.

The papers had barely landed on Campbell's desk when Bragg called to request quick approval. Campbell said he wasn't going to rubber stamp a soft deal. Bragg couldn't understand why Campbell would refuse to approve a deal that would result in the EDA loans being paid off. Campbell said Welbilt's financial viability was far from certain, the success of the planned public offering could not be assured, and repayment of the EDA loans was therefore questionable. He wanted to run the proposal past the legal department and financial staff before signing off on it.

That was not what Bragg wanted to hear. He began to grow frantic.

"Goddamn it!" he shouted. "Just do it! Do it!"

Campbell had heard enough. He wasn't going to take orders from some pissant lobbyist.

"Go fuck yourself!" Campbell shouted back, slamming down the phone.

Back at Welbilt headquarters, the company officers were celebrating Fred Neuberger's fifty-sixth birthday with a little party in the office courtyard. The merriment was interrupted, however, by word from Washington that Campbell had refused to approve the subordination agreement and had, in fact, hung up on Bragg.

This was terrible news. A crisis of the first order. If Campbell wouldn't listen to the vast array of consultants Welbilt had retained, perhaps only a White House order would change his mind—or remove him from the decision-making process.

96

The birthday party quickly turned into an emergency strategy session. The group decided that Moreno would fly to Washington at once to arrange for White House pressure on the Commerce Department. The matter was deemed sufficiently urgent for Moreno to forego going home for a change of clothes. He borrowed $500 and some credit cards from Tony Guariglia and headed straight for La Guardia Airport.

Within a few hours, Moreno had checked into the Hay-Adams Hotel in downtown Washington and made arrangements to meet Wallach early the next morning. He telephoned back to corporate headquarters that night and reported, somewhat cryptically, that arrangements had been made to "get into the White House." Guariglia was greatly relieved.

July 15 was an especially hazy and humid summer day in the nation's capital. The temperature was already in the mid-seventies when Wallach and Moreno met around 6:30 A.M. in the hotel lobby, before walking to Lafayette Park, between the hotel and the White House. Again they spoke of the urgent need for the EDA loan subordination and Campbell's obstinacy. After a few minutes, they walked through the park toward the White House. Wallach instructed Moreno to wait for him, then security guards waved the dapper lawyer through the White House gates. Moreno, greatly impressed, waited outside with the derelicts and peace activists who had come to be as much a part of the park as the pigeons and the benches.

Wallach and Meese sat down to breakfast at 7:15 A.M. Nearly two hours later, Wallach returned to the park. The news he brought was worth the wait. He told Moreno he had seen his friend and explained the problem to him. Meese had picked up the phone and called Malcolm Baldrige, the secretary of commerce and Carlos Campbell's boss. Baldrige was in the shower when Meese called. As Wallach related the story to Moreno, Meese had asked the dripping commerce secretary whether he could sign off on the EDA loan subordination for Welbilt. Baldrige indicated that such a move would be too political for himself, but perhaps an assistant secretary other than Campbell could approve the agreement.

Later that day, at 5:05 P.M., Baldrige called Meese back to say that a meeting on the issue was scheduled for the following week, that there was support for the subordination, but there were some lingering questions about whether Welbilt's purchase of Carmo Industries in Israel violated terms of the EDA loan agreement. Baldrige may also have told Meese that Campbell was the only appro-

97

priate official to decide the issue and, accordingly, Baldrige would not reassign the matter or handle it himself.

Discouraged by the afternoon's developments, Moreno decided to call for reinforcements from the Bronx—Mariotta, Neuberger, Shorten, and Bluestine. Ehrlich, whose work on the subordination issue was seen as more hinderance than help, was not invited. Biaggi's law partner, by now a general in the state national guard, found out where the group was staying, however. He called Moreno's hotel room, interrupting a strategy session.

Shorten answered the phone. "It's the general," he told Moreno. "He needs to talk to you."

"How are you?" Ehrlich opened.

"I'm okay," Moreno responded.

"What's happening?"

"A few things are happening."

"You are a fucking liar!" Ehrlich exploded. "Like all the other guys at the room over there." The general went on to remind Moreno that the company couldn't function in New York without his and Biaggi's assistance, and they should be treated as full-fledged members of the team. They shouldn't think they could do everything with the Washington people.

Moreno hung up the phone. Wallach asked what Ehrlich had said.

"He sends his regards to all of you," Moreno responded, and the meeting returned to its main subject: a confrontation with Campbell.

Tuesday, July 19, was Carlos Campbell's forty-sixth birthday. The crowd that gathered in his conference room on the seventh floor of the main Commerce Department building was not bearing gifts, however.

Before the meeting started, Lyn Nofziger came into Campbell's office to feel out the situation. Campbell explained he was just trying to uphold the president's mandate to make EDA more efficient. "I understand where you are coming from," Nofziger replied.

As the meeting began, Campbell took a seat with his back to a large window overlooking the Mall as it stretched down Independence Avenue toward the Lincoln Memorial. Mariotta sat across the table to Campbell's left, Howard Squadron was directly across the way. To Squadron's left were Nofziger and Mark Bragg.

Mariotta gave his usual pitch. It had worked with Reagan. Maybe he could sway Campbell with his religious fervor . . .

The Spiel ended, and Campbell wasn't impressed. ("It's hard to mau-mau a brother from Harlem," he would say later.) Mariotta had showed no substantive understanding of the economic issues at stake.

Fortunately for Welbilt, Squadron presented a more coherent argument as to why the loan agreement should be approved. He said Carmo was a great opportunity for Welbilt, the Bank Leumi package would carry the company through March 1984, and the EDA would be better secured under the proposed deal than it had been in 1980.

Campbell held his ground. Welbilt, he noted, was undercapitalized on the army contract (which it was) and had no cost control system that made any sense (also true). He said the company needed to establish an independent board of directors to strengthen its management expertise (a good suggestion). Some observers at the meeting thought that Campbell's approach was reasonable; the Welbilt crowd thought he was being an obstructionist.

Campbell made no final commitment at the meeting, but the pressure was getting to him. He had dealt with a lot of hot potatoes, but this had become the hottest of them all. He was working ninety hours a week, his marriage was falling apart, his phone was ringing off the hook, and Welbilt's lobbyists were pounding him over the head.

Campbell weighed three options: turning down the request and sending Welbilt down the tubes, giving Welbilt exactly what it wanted, or coming up with a valid quid pro quo in return for subordinating the loan.

The third option carried the day. Campbell agreed to sign off on the subordination on the condition that Welbilt use some of the proceeds of the Bank Leumi financing and the public offering to pay off the EDA loans. With time growing short, Welbilt was only too happy to oblige. By the end of July, the deal was cut.

Welbilt's allies, however, weren't done with Carlos Campbell. On August 4, Meese and Jenkins met with thirteen Republican members of Congress who'd been critical of the way Campbell was handling his job. After several months of behind-the-scenes maneuvering, John Herrington, then White House personnel director, telephoned Campbell three days before Christmas and asked for his resignation. A promised presidential appointment never came through, and Campbell was forced out of the Reagan administration.

With the EDA issue resolved, the path toward the initial public offering seemed clear. There was just one minor roadblock. When management attempted to register the stock under the name Welbilt Electronic Die Corp., the Welbilt Corp., a New York-based appliance maker, took exception and filed a suit charging trademark infringement.

At first, Mariotta was furious and wanted to fight the suit. He retained Shea & Gould, which had been the runner-up as new corporate counsel. Attorneys there persuaded him that it was a senseless struggle. So Mariotta agreed to use the initials of *Welbilt Electronic Die* as the basis for the company's new name, Wedtech.

To promote the Wedtech stock sale, the underwriter, Moseley Hallgarten, Estabrook & Weeden, organized a "road show" for the Wedtech executives. The purpose of such shows is to familiarize potential investors and investment analysts with the new company. Under strict SEC regulations, however, the executives were not allowed to tout the stock or disclose any information or projections not included in the prospectus, which was prepared by Squadron Ellenoff and by Shearman & Sterling as counsel for the underwriter. The Wedtech road show took the executives to Boston and Chicago on July 25.

Given John Mariotta's performance, it's a miracle any stock was sold. The same pitch that was a hit with Ronald Reagan and his cabinet was less effective with a group of blue-blooded, bottom-line-oriented financial analysts gathered in Boston. When Mariotta launched into the Spiel—"I am a New York Rican. I don't speak English or Spanish . . . You probably think we're all a bunch of spearchuckers and machete swingers . . ."—the analysts just shook their heads and laughed. In Chicago, an analyst mistook Mariotta for a waiter and asked the Wedtech chairman and chief executive to fetch him a drink.

Despite Mariotta's performance on what he called the "pony and dog" show, Moseley was able to place all the Wedtech shares with individual and institutional investors. This was, after all, the Reagan bull market, and any stock with a "story" was an easy sell. Wedtech's story was better than most.

The investing public, of course, never got the *full* story. The prospectus said nothing about management integrity, nothing about the progress payment fraud, nothing about the F.H.J. account, nothing about loan sharks, and nothing about payoffs to union leaders and contracting officers.

Now all that remained was to divide the spoils. As a small company in the Bronx with limited capital and small contracts, Welbilt had attracted little interest. With a market capitalization of nearly $100 million, however, Wedtech Corporation was already creating a feeding frenzy.

First in line were the corporate insiders. In one part of the offering, Mariotta, Neuberger, and Moreno sold some of their personal shares. Moreno received two checks totalling $534, 240; Neuberger received one check for $2.7 million. Mariotta received two checks, one for $2.5 million and one for $227,500. The officers used some of this money to settle up with Belenguer N.V.

In connection with the main part of the public offering, Mariotta and Neuberger would each end up with some 1.56 million shares, worth, at the offering price of $16 a share, nearly $25 million. Moreno would retain about 308,000 shares, worth nearly $5 million. Slightly more than 153,000 shares, worth $2.5 million, were reserved for Bluestine when he joined the company in the fall. Guariglia and Shorten would each get 67,500 shares, about $1.1 million worth. Ceil Lewis got 11,700 shares.

Then all the "consultants" and "advisers" had to be taken care of. In advance of the offering, Ehrlich and Richard Biaggi, as the nominee for his father, were issued 112,500 shares apiece. Squadron Ellenoff got 45,000 shares—giving the firm a vested interest in keeping the company afloat. Bob Wallach received 45,000 shares and, not long afterward, a $125,000 check for which he submitted an invoice citing the money as "my fee for consultation relative to the registration and public offering." (Guariglia has testified that the invoice was a fiction designed to allow Wedtech to "cook the books" by giving a more favorable accounting treatment to the payment.) Nofziger and Bragg got 22,500 shares each, worth about $360,000 apiece at the offering price. Another 15,000 shares went to companies controlled by Arthur Lipper III. Lipper, chairman of *Venture* ("The Magazine for Entrepreneurs"), had helped Welbilt secure an important loan prior to the public offering.

Cashing in on the spoils, however, would require propping up the share price over an extended period of time. Under Rule 144 of the federal securities laws, these shares were "restricted" and generally couldn't be sold for two years after the public offering. Two years was a long time for the sharks to wait, however. Many of the shares issued to insiders were backdated to January 1, 1983, chopping some six months off the waiting period.

Of the 5.86 million shares of Wedtech common stock issued as part of the initial public offering, some 3.56 million, or 70 percent, went to management and its cronies. Neuberger and Mariotta were now very rich. Their cronies were also wealthy, at least on paper. Euphoria reigned.

The offering was settled the morning of September 1, whereupon everybody went to a luncheon hosted by the underwriter at Delmonico's restaurant. By the time the lunch ended, it was already late in the afternoon, and no one felt like going back to the office. Someone suggested that it was time for John Mariotta, now the chairman of the board of a public company, to get a new car. The old Lincoln he was driving was getting shabby.

The whole gang traipsed into the Mercedes-Benz showroom at the corner of Park Avenue and Fifty-sixth Street. After checking out the various floor models, Mariotta selected the car he liked, a model costing about $50,000. Neuberger, whose philosophy of life included never paying retail, began bargaining with the salesman.

The Mercedes dealership on Park Avenue, designed by Frank Lloyd Wright, was not like a Chevy dealership in the Bronx, however. The salesman, perhaps sensing the aroma of new money in the air, tersely informed Neuberger that there were no "discounts" on the purchase of a single car. At that point, Mariotta interceded. They were not buying one car, he informed the salesman. Actually they were leasing—he paused to count those present—himself . . . Neuberger . . . Moreno . . . Guariglia . . . Shorten . . . Bluestine—that made six. That's right. They were leasing six new Mercedes!

(After a few months, Mariotta decided he didn't like the Mercedes that much. "Mercedes, they are nice, if you want prestige, if you want to show off," he told his colleagues. "Me, I am for riding comfort. I am always picking people up at the airport and driving people around. So I need a large car . . . If a car is going to hit me, I don't want to come out like toothpaste." So Mariotta gave the Mercedes to his wife, and the company bought him a Lincoln Continental.)

# 11

# Wedtech Joins the Navy

**B**efore the public offering, Wedtech's managers and lawyers had assumed that the biggest disadvantage of going public would be having to give up the company's eligibility for the Section 8(a) set-aside program. No 8(a) company had ever gone public; it seemed inherently contradictory that a company could be both publicly owned and "minority-owned" at the same time. Further, the public offering would reduce John Mariotta's ownership interest to 26 percent, well below the 51 percent threshold required by law.

As a result, the initial prospectus for the public offering—known as a "red herring" because of warnings about its preliminary nature printed in red on the cover—had stated that after the public offering Wedtech "will" no longer be qualified for the 8(a) program.

At the time the red herring was prepared, leaving the 8(a) program didn't seem critical because no contracts comparable to the engine contract were on the horizon. Certainly the jackpot at the end of the public offering seemed to outweigh any benefits of remaining in the 8(a) program. Neuberger even looked forward to getting out of 8(a) so the company wouldn't have to continue to deal with "the idiots" at the SBA who administered the program. But Ehrlich, Moreno, and Guariglia—perhaps with a more prag-

103

matic view of Wedtech's ability to compete in the real world—urged that the company leave its options open. As a result, in the final prospectus for the public offering, the company hedged on its future in the 8(a) program, saying that after the completion of the offering, the company "may" no longer be qualified for the 8(a) program.

The decision to hedge was fortuitous. Within two months of the stock sale, Moreno learned of a contract that made the engine contract seem like small potatoes. Moreno and Richard Bluestine had gone to Washington to try to drum up business (Bluestine having left Main Hurdman after the public offering and joined Wedtech as vice-president of corporate planning and development). They met with Denlinger, the president of the Latin American Manufacturers Association.

Denlinger had some interesting news: He had heard that the navy was considering the idea of putting a huge pontoon purchase into the 8(a) program. The program, Denlinger continued, might be worth up to $1 billion over the next several years.

That was all Moreno and Bluestine needed to hear. A meeting was quickly convened in New York so Denlinger could brief the full Wedtech team on this exciting new business opportunity.

The pontoons the navy needed were essentially large steel boxes designed to get men and material from ship to shore. Each was to be about ninety feet long, twenty-one feet wide and five feet high, and would weigh between sixty-five and one hundred tons.

The navy considered the pontoons to be essential to the mission of the Rapid Deployment Force. Supporting this force involved stationing huge ships—loaded with ammunition, gas, rations, and other vital supplies—near the world's trouble spots. Under normal circumstances, these ships could be unloaded at established ports using piers, cranes, and other amenities. But the Rapid Deployment Force might well have to operate under abnormal conditions. Therefore, each supply ship was to be outfitted with pontoons—small craft designed to ferry supplies to an undeveloped shore. Some of the pontoons were to be motorized, so they could act as tugs; the other, non-powered pontoons would serve as barges.

There was nothing terribly new or high-tech about the pontoons. The technology for the non-motorized units hadn't changed since World War II.

Given the potential size of the pontoon program, it didn't take long for Wedtech's managers to decide this was a contract they wanted to pursue. It was a golden opportunity to get a large stream of government cash flowing through the company.

The decision, of course, had nothing to do with the company's expertise or capabilities. Wedtech had never built any naval vessels, had no naval architects on its staff, had no facilities in which to build or test the pontoons, and had no work force with the necessary skills.

No matter. If the Wedtech team had learned anything from the engine contract experience, it was that in the 8(a) program the issue of capabilities was largely irrelevant. The decisions on whether the pontoons would be set aside, and which company they would be set aside for, would be political ones. Therefore, Wedtech's chances of getting the contract would depend on the success of its political strategy.

Wedtech wasn't the only company that understood this. Denlinger told the group that behind-the-scenes political jockeying had already begun. Companies in California, Texas, New Mexico, Pennsylvania and Puerto Rico were eyeing the pontoon contract and had begun lining up political allies.

To outfox the opposition, Wedtech was going to need some inside help. Denlinger knew just the man: Richard Ramirez, director of the navy's small business program.

A native of the Washington, D.C. area, the dark-haired, mustachioed Ramirez had a glistening resume—two tours of duty in Vietnam with the army, service as a military sky marshall during the skyjacking epidemic of the early 1970s, a member of the federal government's senior executive service at an unusually young age, two national awards of excellence from the U.S. Small Business Administration, and a meritorious civilian service medal from the secretary of the navy. So far as Wedtech was concerned, however, Ramirez had one attribute more valuable than all the rest: he was on the take.

Moreno flew to Washington, where he was met by Denlinger. The LAMA lobbyist drove Moreno to Ramirez's suburban home. (Ramirez had worked briefly for LAMA himself during the 1970s.) After introductions and small talk, Denlinger suggested to Moreno that he and Ramirez might be more comfortable talking in private. Moreno, taking the hint, went with Ramirez to another room.

Once alone with Moreno, Ramirez got to the point. Wedtech was going to have a lot of problems trying to get the pontoon contract. Several well-connected companies were interested in it. But he could be of help. He worked directly with the assistant secretary of the navy for procurement. He was invited to all the meetings regarding the pontoon contract. But if Wedtech wanted his assistance, he would need some financial aid.

Moreno was no rookie at this game. He didn't beat around the bush."How much?" he asked.

"Sixty thousand dollars in green."

Moreno protested, but only mildly. He seemed to operate under the premise that anyone who demanded a bribe must be important enough to get one.

"That is a lot of money," he said. "It's very difficult to get all that money in cash. But maybe we can make installment payments after I check with the other people at the company. And if they agree, then we will give the money to you."

Ramirez, understanding that a tentative bargain had just been struck, turned his attention to the mechanics of the bribe. He told Moreno he wouldn't be picking up the money personally, but would assign that task to someone whose identity he would disclose to Moreno once the deal was finalized.

That was it. In less time than it takes to buy a new washing machine, a very senior navy official and the executive vice-president of a public company had negotiated a bribe involving a contract that would ultimately be worth more than $100 million. In a serene suburban setting, two college-educated, upwardly mobile strangers had agreed to commit a felony.

The next day, Moreno reported back to the other executives. Neuberger, as usual, growled his dissent, not for any ethical or legal considerations, but because he thought Ramirez couldn't deliver. Moreno urged the others to authorize the payment to Ramirez. The navy official, he argued, could be a very important "mole." Moreno carried the day.

Moreno called Ramirez with the good news. Wedtech would pay the $60,000, but it would have to be in three installments. A few days later, Moreno took the Eastern Shuttle to Washington with the first installment—$30,000 in cash in the inside pocket of his coat.

On the ground at National Airport, Moreno met Ramirez's courier at a cocktail lounge. Like well-acquainted businessmen, Moreno and the courier found a table and ordered screwdrivers.

"Did you bring what you are supposed to bring?" the courier asked.

Moreno nodded and reached inside his coat for the envelope. The courier took the envelope and, without even glancing inside, stashed it in his briefcase. Business having been concluded, the two men finished their drinks.

The final two installments were paid in New York City. Once Moreno took the courier to lunch at a restaurant near Rockefeller Center; the other time the two dined at an Italian eatery on the Upper East Side.

In return for the money, Ramirez kept Moreno informed of the internal discussions the navy was having regarding the pontoon contract. His access allowed him to supply Wedtech with the latest information on the thinking of senior navy personnel and on the negotiations between the navy and the SBA. To Fred Neuberger's surprise, Ramirez turned out to be a valuable ally.

Even with Ramirez as its paid "mole" within the navy, Wedtech had no chance of getting the pontoon contract unless it could find a way to stay in the 8(a) program. That was going to be difficult.

The 51 percent ownership threshold required for eligibility was meant to apply to socially and economically disadvantaged individuals who ran the company's day-to-day operations. Under the regulations, blacks, Hispanics, native Americans and Asian Americans were presumed to be socially disadvantaged. Economic disadvantage was to be determined by various calculations of net worth and access to capital. Further, each company in the 8(a) program had a "fixed program participation term" during which it was eligible to receive set-aside contracts. Once this term ended, the company was assumed to be ready for free market competition and was "graduated" from the 8(a) program.

Shortly after the public offering, Wedtech received a letter from the SBA's district office terminating the company from the 8(a) program because it was in technical default. With its eye on the pontoon contract, the company made its first priority to deal with the termination notice.

The SBA district office certainly had solid grounds for its letter. First, the company had all but conceded in its prospectus that it would no longer be eligible. Second, Mariotta no longer controlled 51 percent of the stock. Third, Wedtech hadn't bothered to notify

107

the SBA in advance of the change in ownership, despite regulations requiring such prior notification.

In any event, Wedtech's "fixed program participation term" was scheduled to expire October 12, 1983. The SBA really didn't have to kick Wedtech out of the program; it could simply let the company "graduate" in accordance with normal policies and procedures.

Again, Wedtech was up against a bureaucracy armed with facts, reason, and law. But again, Wedtech had ways of at least evening the odds.

Ehrlich and Moreno immediately began a campaign with the officials at the SBA. Despite his perceived ineffectiveness on the engine contract and EDA loan subordination, Ehrlich was still regarded as a useful conduit to the SBA, particularly to Peter Neglia, the regional administrator. As with the engine contract, the Wedtech campaign was designed to buy enough time to get the company's political allies into the fray. The Wedtech representatives asserted they would be able to respond to the points raised in the SBA's termination letter, but they needed more time to do so.

The campaign was successful. On September 27, the SBA issued a "bridge letter" providing Wedtech with an indefinite but temporary extension of its 8(a) eligibility. The letter was signed by then-SBA Deputy Associate Administrator Robert Saldivar. At the time, according to Saldivar, such extensions were almost automatic while the SBA considered the merits of the request. The bridge letter paid off: Neglia immediately notified the army that it provided the basis for Wedtech to receive a $5 million option on a contract for the M–113 armored personnel courier. The bridge letter was soon followed by another from the SBA extending Wedtech's 8(a) status until January 16 while the company's appeal was considered.

Wedtech's management now had some breathing room in which to devise a scheme to stay in the program. The major issue, of course, was Mariotta's lack of 51 percent ownership.

Moreno and Ehrlich met with Neglia at Villa Pensa, a restaurant in Little Italy. They explained that Wedtech management had been kicking around various ways to keep the company in the set-aside program. The one that looked the most feasible, Moreno told Neglia, was for the company to give Mariotta options to buy enough shares to give him majority ownership. To make sure Mariotta didn't double-cross his partners and actually exercise the options, they would be priced at some ridiculously high number, like $100 a share. Neglia promised to run this dubious proposal past the lawyers at the SBA and report back.

Not surprisingly, the SBA lawyers told Neglia this wasn't going to fly. Options could not be counted in determining percentage of ownership.

In late October, Neglia learned exactly why the Wedtech crowd was so intent on finding a way to stay in the 8(a) program. The occasion was "New York's Salute to George and Barbara Bush," a $500-a-plate, black tie dinner in the ballroom of the Grand Hyatt Hotel. At Ehrlich's request, Wedtech had purchased a number of tickets. Just before dinner, Moreno went up to Neglia.

"Pete, I need to talk to you about something very important," he said. "We have found a contract in Washington that seems like it can be obtained for Wedtech."

At this, Moreno pulled out some information Denlinger had supplied about the pontoon contract. Neglia scanned the literature.

"You people are crazy," he commented.

As the group sat down, Ehrlich whispered to Moreno, reminding him that Neglia's regional jurisdiction also included Puerto Rico and that he had already had discussions with "certain people" about bringing the pontoon contract to Puerto Rico, the option said to be favored by Bush and ex-governor Luis A. Ferre.

"Let's see where Peter's alliances really are," Ehrlich concluded.

Alliances were irrelevant, however, unless Wedtech could find some way to stay in the 8(a) program. Moreno, being Hispanic, presumably could have been certified as socially disadvantaged. This, however, would take more time than the company had—and would have precipitated a tremendous row with Mariotta. The only practical solution was to have the lawyers figure out some way to give Mariotta the appearance of control, preferably without having to actually give him any more stock.

Arthur Siskind was co-chairman of the corporate department at Squadron Ellenoff and the partner directly responsible for the Wedtech account. Stocky, soft-spoken, with short dark hair and a gap between his front teeth, the forty-five-year-old lawyer was smart, hardworking, and detail oriented. Given his serious and demanding personality, Siskind had a reputation of being difficult to work for.

At a firm like Squadron Ellenoff that specializes in corporate law, the attorneys try to respond to the client's instructions, regardless of their merits, within the limits of the law. In his efforts to help Wedtech obtain its goals, Siskind may have crossed the fuzzy line from counsel to co-conspirator.

Siskind and Guariglia weighed several imaginative ideas for keeping Wedtech in the set-aside program. After much thrashing about, however, it became clear the SBA would not go along with any plan that did not involve the actual transfer of shares to Mariotta.

Concocting such a plan was going to be tough. Even if the normally fractious insiders could actually reach an agreement, there was still no guarantee the accord would get past the SBA. But with the clock ticking on the extension, there was no time to lose.

A new plan quickly took shape: the insiders would surrender enough of their shares to give Mariotta a majority. It would have all the appearances of a sale. The shares would go through the transfer agent and be held in escrow by Squadron Ellenoff. Only no money would change hands. Starting in two years, Mariotta would pay for the shares with a promissory note that was to be redeemed over ten years. Then came the kicker: the note would have default provisions that would trigger the return of the stock to the original owners.

The only apparent drawback to the plan was how the IRS would regard a default that transferred shares from Mariotta to the other insiders: almost certainly they would owe taxes on the value of the shares when the default occurred. The tax impact would be most severe for Neuberger, who would be transferring the most shares.

The Wedtech executives asked the lawyers at Squadron Ellenoff whether they could get Mariotta to sign a side agreement committing him to default. No, the lawyers replied, that wouldn't be proper.

Mariotta apparently decided that honor among thieves was an operable concept. He made a solemn declaration: "You can trust me to default." Then Mariotta shook hands with his fellow executives as if to seal the conspiracy.

Neuberger still had his doubts. Wasn't there some way to limit his tax exposure? Told that there wasn't, he shrugged and said he'd worry about it in two years when Mariotta defaulted. (It wasn't in Neuberger's nature to concern himself with such matters. "Since I was nineteen, everything's been kind of anticlimactic," he once said. "I'm going to worry about the IRS? What can they do to me?")

No, Neuberger wasn't going to worry about something as minor as tax consequences. His main concern was Mariotta's mental condition. Like his father, Mariotta had something of a volatile personality. One moment he could be kind and generous, the next in a blind and cruel rage. Yet for all his tantrums, Mariotta had never reneged on his word.

Using the affectionate Yiddish expression for a male, Neuberger told his long-time business partner, *"Tateleh,* we are going to go through with it—but don't go crazy with me."

Having reached agreement among themselves, the insiders now had to sell the scam to other major shareholders and to the SBA. The other shareholders were brought into the picture at a November 7 luncheon in a private room on the mezzanine level of the ornate Helmsley Palace Hotel in midtown Manhattan. Bob Wallach, Howard Squadron, Richard Biaggi, and Bernie Ehrlich were all asked to participate in the transfer (collectively, they or their firms held 315,00 shares).

Squadron and Wallach demurred. But Squadron's firm and Wallach owned only a total of 90,000 shares, so their participation wasn't essential. The cooperation of Biaggi and Ehrlich, with their 225,000 shares, was far more critical.

A follow-up meeting was convened at the law firm of Biaggi & Ehrlich. Mariotta, Moreno, and Guariglia came representing Wedtech. They were met by Mario Biaggi, Richard Biaggi, and Ehrlich. After Guariglia explained the proposed transaction, the congressman asked Mariotta point blank if he was going to default. Mariotta assured him that he would. Since Mariotta had delivered on his earlier promises, the congressman seemed reassured. But his trust would extend only so far. He told the anxious Wedtech executives he would allow his shares (the shares technically owned by his son) to be transferred to Mariotta, but only if the period before the default occurred were shortened from two years to one. He also objected to placing his shares in escrow with Squadron Ellenoff.

The first version of a transfer agreement submitted to Neglia didn't pass muster. The default provisions were so transparent, Neglia said, it would be obvious to anyone that Mariotta was planning to default. So a new version was prepared, narrowing the default provisions. Under this version, the stock would revert only if Mariotta died, left Wedtech's employ, or failed to make the promissory note payments.

The agreements between Mariotta and the other executives—Neuberger, Moreno, Guariglia, and Shorten—were final-

111

ized in December 1983. As the agreements were signed, Mariotta again reassured his cronies that he would return their shares. Evidently feeling very avuncular, Mariotta patted Shorten on the head and told him, "Don't worry, *tateleh*, you'll get your stock back when it's due."

By the time Moreno brought the separate agreements to Biaggi and Ehrlich for signing, it was late in December. Mariotta had departed for his annual Christmas trip to Puerto Rico before the final agreement had been drafted and could be signed. Wedtech was anxious to get all the documents to the SBA, but couldn't without Mariotta's signature.

"He should not be on vacation now," Representative Biaggi complained.

Moreno tried to explain that Mariotta always went to Puerto Rico at Christmastime.

"This time he should not have gone there," the congressman repeated.

Grousing about Mariotta's vacation habits wasn't going to get the document signed, however. Moreno, deciding that one more transgression wasn't going to make a difference, volunteered to forge Mariotta's signature on the documents. No one objected, so he signed.

With the stock transfer in place, the company had one last thorny issue to address. Under SBA rules, a firm is only eligible for the 8(a) program if it and its minority owner are "economically disadvantaged." As Wedtech had just received more than $20 million from the public offering and had established a $20 million line of credit, it was going to be tough to argue that the firm was still disadvantaged. And making the case that *the owner* was economically disadvantaged was going to be even tougher. Mariotta had received some $2.7 million in cash at the public offering, had another $25 million in restricted stock, the house in Scarsdale . . . Perhaps only in relation to Donald Trump was John Mariotta still economically disadvantaged.

Biaggi & Ehrlich, nothing if not imaginative, was up to the challenge. In their argument to the SBA, they asserted that Wedtech was in the defense contracting business competing against such giants as Grumman, Rockwell, and General Dynamics. Compared to these multibillion-dollar companies, Wedtech was still *relatively* disadvantaged. (In reality, Wedtech was not competing against the giants of the military-industrial complex; virtually all its contracts

112

were on a no-bid basis, and its competition for those contracts was other small businesses.)

As for Mariotta, it was asserted that his wealth was "illiquid" because it was largely in the form of Wedtech stock which he could not yet sell. Since this truth had the potential to cause problems, the assertion was supported by documention that reverted to the tried and true tactic of lying. Guariglia falsified Mariotta's financial disclosure forms by neglecting to report almost $1 million of Mariotta's cash and assigning no value to his Wedtech shares.

With time running out, the various documents—including two stock purchase agreements, two escrow agreements, and three legal memoranda—were submitted to Neglia for approval on January 4, 1984.

It should have been obvious to anyone at SBA, not just Neglia, that the transfer agreement was a sham. There was no penalty attached to Mariotta's failure to make the payments; the stock merely reverted to its original owners. At best, the agreement gave Mariotta an option to buy the shares in question. To consider it a sale that gave Mariotta majority interest in Wedtech was absurd.

Each annual payment would have cost Mariotta more than $3 million, assuming the stock price remained where it was. If Mariotta could afford the payments, he couldn't possibly be "economically disadvantaged." If he couldn't afford the payments, then he wouldn't have control of the company. Either way, Wedtech should have been out of the program.

Moreover, legitimate or not, the transfer did nothing to erase the company's violation of SBA regulations that occurred when it failed to notify the SBA of ownership changes. And it had no bearing on the fact that Wedtech should have "graduated" from the 8(a) program the previous October.

The Wedtech executives were unconcerned. They took the attitude that the SBA bureaucracy could be ignored, deceived, bullied, or paid off. They were right.

Despite the complex legal issues involved, the stock transfer was approved in record time. The national leadership of the SBA was aware that the decision set a precedent. The regional office in New York was directed to forward the application to Washington for review. Neglia started to get cold feet at the last moment; he told Ehrlich that he'd better be right on the stock transfer because he was going to sign and send it to Washington. Neglia need not have worried: on January 30, 1984, Robert Webber, the SBA's general counsel in Washington, took the path of least resistance and signed an opinion upholding the sham stock transaction, an opinion he later conceded should not have been signed: "The facts were not clearly expressed, the issues were not stated, the legal analysis was not there, and the opinion is not a good opinion in itself."

Now the question became how long Wedtech's eligibility should be extended. The regulations identified specific reasons for limiting a firm's participation in the program: substantial 8(a) awards, substantial SBA grants and loans, failure to decrease reliance on the 8(a) program, and long-term participation in the program. By any of these standards, Wedtech should have been out of the program well before now, let alone eligible to continue in it. The company had already received more than $50 million in 8(a) contracts, more than $3 million in SBA grants, and more than $8 million in SBA loans. It was 95 percent dependent on 8(a) contracts, and had been in the program for seven years.

But Wedtech was a favored, well-connected company, and the facts were immaterial. Neglia endorsed a three-year extension and passed the recommendation to Washington. James Sanders, the SBA administrator, concurred with the policy decision not to boot Wedtech out.

"Nobody had gone public before with an IPO. And I reasoned that if you wanted this program to be a success, once someone began to achieve success, you shouldn't cut them off," he eventually explained. (At the time of his Wedtech ruling, however, Sanders was in the middle of ousting, effective February 14, 1984, some of the 8(a) companies that had been in the program the longest. The protesting companies—mostly owned by blacks—were calling the action the St. Valentine's Day Massacre.)

In late January, Deputy Associate Administrator Robert Saldivar signed a letter in which he granted the requested extension. With all the failures in the 8(a) program, Saldivar was reluctant to cause trouble for what appeared to be the big success story. He signed the letter the very day the SBA informed the navy that Wedtech was its candidate for the pontoon contract. (Wedtech, taking the attitude that no favor should go unrewarded, authorized Denlinger to give Saldivar a $10,000 cash gift. Saldivar, perhaps uniquely in Wedtech's experience, refused to take the money. But he never reported the offer, and in time he would ask Moreno to help find financing for a Mexican restaurant at which his son was employed; Wedtech loaned the establishment $25,000. Denlinger, unexpectedly finding himself with the $10,000 meant for Saldivar, did the predictable thing—he kept the money.)

To celebrate its continuance as a small, disadvantaged business, Wedtech threw a party for itself on February 28 at Tavern on the Green. The open-bar reception and dinner were billed as a fundraiser for an organization called "Save Russian Jewry." The two hundred or so guests dined on Nova Scotia Salmon, poached salmon, artichoke hearts, chateaubriand, and cornish hen. The caterers' tab came to $20,823. Awardees of the event were to include (presumably on behalf of "Russian Jewry") Serafin Mariel and Ivan Irizarry of New York National Bank.

Wedtech's struggle to remain in the 8(a) program had succeeded. That, however, was just the preliminary bout. Getting the pontoon contract would be the main event.

As with the engine contract, the first step was to ensure that the contract was set aside for an 8(a) firm. The navy, understandably, had reservations about placing a contract for a crucial project with a small and inexperienced firm—especially at a time when many of the finest shipyards in America were idle or underutilized. The navy, however, had never had to contend with Wedtech.

Ramirez was not the only one working on getting the contract set aside for Wedtech. The company unleashed its full complement of attorneys, consultants, and political supporters on the new mission.

At first, the navy opposed setting aside the pontoon contract. Everett A. Pyatt, acting assistant secretary of the navy for shipbuilding and logistics, had some very good reasons. The project was urgent, massive, and complex. A competitive procurement would produce a better price. A previous attempt to award a pontoon contract to a small business had been a flop.

None of this appears to have mattered to Wedtech's supporters. On November 8, 1983, Sanders, under pressure to meet ambitious contracting goals set by President Reagan, appealed the navy's decision. He argued it would be a good idea to establish a disadvantaged company in the "metal fabrication" business.

There is also evidence that Nofziger and Bragg began to cultivate Pyatt during this period. Although Pyatt testified that he didn't discuss the pontoon contract with Nofziger or Bragg before

January 1984, a calendar maintained by Pyatt's secretary indicates he met with Nofziger at least three times in September and October 1983.

Bob Wallach evidently had a good pipeline into the behind-the-scenes maneuvering. On December 7, he wrote a remarkably prescient memo to Wedtech's executives:

> I am advised of the following information: Secretary Piot's [sic] office from the Navy with Richard Ramirez writing the letter will issue a letter which will set out qualifications that really apply only to Wedtech. Delivery will be to the east coast first and will include elements of the propulsion as well as the non-propulsion portions of the contract. In other words, it should be terrific.
>
> The answer then is to get a letter back to the SBA specifying Wedtech and apparently Sanders has already decided to do that. If it goes as scheduled, we should have the contract by the end of the year. We will see.

The very next day, as Wallach had foretold, Pyatt reversed himself and agreed to set aside the less sophisticated, non-powered pontoon portion of the contract for a minority business. This constituted about one-fifth of the first $25 million portion of the contract.

Wedtech, however, was not willing to settle for half a loaf. The company's allies stepped up the pressure to have the entire contract set aside. On December 16, Nofziger met with Pyatt's boss, Navy Secretary John Lehman, to discuss the contract. Within the navy, meanwhile, the uniformed officers in charge of the pontoon program were urging Pyatt to keep the pontoons out of the set-aside program.

The naval officers, however, were no match for Wedtech's powerful allies. On January 6, 1984, Pyatt caved in. In a letter to SBA Administrator Sanders, he formally agreed to "entertain" setting aside the entire contract. In an extraordinary departure from the navy's bureaucratic procedures, Pyatt provided no written rationale for his decision. As a result of his letter, the navy's procurement officers shelved plans to put the pontoon contracts out for competitive bids.

Pyatt didn't immediately inform officials at NAVFAC—the navy

command responsible for procuring the pontoons—of his decision.
At a meeting on January 19, Capt. David de Vicq, the pontoon program manager, presented a detailed point paper showing there
was no way an 8(a) firm could tool up and meet the delivery schedules. Other navy officers seconded de Vicq's comments, but nothing they said seemed to sway Pyatt. After the meeting, they would
learn the decision had already been made.

The company had managed to remain eligible for the 8(a) program, and now it had succeeded in making sure the pontoon contract was taken out of competitive bidding and put into the 8(a)
program. All that remained was to ensure that Wedtech, and not
some other 8(a) company, managed to get most if not all of the
action.

Wedtech wasn't the only, or even the first, eligible firm to pursue
the pontoon contract. As early as mid-June of 1983, a West Coast
company, Univox Corp., had expressed an interest through Nevada
senators Paul Laxalt and Chic Hecht. Lee Engineering of San Francisco, Medley Tool and Die of Philadelphia, and Universal Canvas
of Corpus Christi, Texas, soon joined the hunt. Others, including a
Texas joint venture and several Puerto Rican companies, were also
in the running.

If the SBA had followed normal procedures, the first company
to express interest in the pontoon contract, Univox, would have
been the SBA's choice. But the SBA's associate administrator,
Henry Wilfong, wasn't allowed to award the contract to Univox.
He was told that regional administrators had decided the contract
was too big for any one company. He was also advised to tell Univox not to make waves because a second phase of the pontoon production would be made available to a West Coast contractor.

Lee Engineering's efforts were also fruitless. The California firm,
owned by a Chinese-American entrepreneur, Frank Lee, had been
led to believe it was a strong candidate to receive at least a portion
of the contract. In fact, some of the encouragement came from
Richard Ramirez at the navy. The company went so far as to set
up joint ventures in San Francisco and Puerto Rico to ensure it
would have adequate facilities and expertise. Then, abruptly, SBA
officials in San Francisco were told by the Washington headquarters that Lee Engineering had been dropped from consideration.
"That's the way it goes sometimes," Sanders reportedly told Irene

117

Castillo, the regional administrator, by way of explanation. (Sanders does not recall saying this. He has a "vague recollection" that Lee was found deficient in its economic capabilities.)

Frank Lee was devastated. Not long afterward, his naval engineering company, which had 200 employees at its peak, collapsed into bankruptcy, and his thirty-five-year marriage ended in divorce. Lee, then in his mid-fifties, became so depressed he sought psychiatric care.

The Texas and New Mexico companies were taken care of with promises that Wedtech would subcontract part of the pontoon contract to them. Wedtech also hired away from a Texas company the company's leading consultant and political contact.

To deal with the Puerto Rican contenders, rumored to have the support of Vice-President Bush and former Governor Ferre, Wedtech retained Ines Capo, the wife of former Bush aide Rafael Capo. Mrs. Capo's influence did not come cheap. The arrangement was to be $8,000 up front, $3,500 per month, and $25,000 in stock in a new company to be set up in Puerto Rico. Through Rafael Capo, Wedtech arranged to have Ferre visit New York to see the company. Ferre never endorsed Wedtech but apparently was sufficiently impressed to soften his support for other companies.

Thus, one by one, the other companies fell by the wayside. Wedtech had too much influence and acted too quickly for them to respond. Wedtech simply out-maneuvered and overwhelmed its competitors.

The only other firm left in the running was Medley Tool and Die, the Pennsylvania company. Getting rid of Medley would be tough. The Philadelphia office of the SBA had a lot of clout in Washington, and Medley had the backing of Senator Heinz and Rep. Bill Gray. On January 30, 1984, Sanders wrote to Pyatt, officially designating Wedtech and Medley as the SBA's contractors for the pontoon program. It appeared that Wedtech had run into another company with its own strong political contacts and, like it or not, was going to have to share the pontoon contract.

Having lost the battle to put the pontoon contract out for competitive bidding, Captain de Vicq, the navy's officer in charge of the pontoon program, was responsible for briefing the SBA's nominees on exactly what the program entailed. Representatives of Wedtech and Medley gathered in a conference room at the SBA to hear the navy's presentation.

Captain de Vicq had joined the navy in 1957 and had built a reputation as a dedicated, hardworking officer. A forty-nine-year-old native of Newton, Massachusetts, he had a slightly raspy smoker's voice that bore traces of his New England upbringing. With his receding, close-cropped blond hair and steely blue eyes behind wire-rimmed glasses, de Vicq projected a firm, no-nonsense image—a marked contrast to the political hacks and glad-handers the Wedtech crowd was accustomed to dealing with.

Using slides, de Vicq made a lengthy presentation on the purpose of the program. He wanted the contractors to understand this was no simple undertaking. He covered the detailed engineering and software requirements. He emphasized the tight timetable.

Moreno thought de Vicq made the project sound like sending someone to the moon—perhaps to try to dissuade Wedtech from pursuing the contract. As for Mariotta, when de Vicq concluded his presentation, the Wedtech chairman launched into the Spiel, indicating that Wedtech was ready, willing, and able to go. The Medley people didn't say much of anything.

Listening to Mariotta's Spiel, it struck de Vicq that he was going to be dealing with a very unusual individual. Mariotta's discourse sounded like a tape recording. It was inappropriate to the occasion. The navy didn't want patriotic speeches. It wanted pontoons—built to specifications and built on time.

The next step in the process was to visit the sites at which Medley and Wedtech proposed to manufacture the pontoons. This was the last chance for the uniformed navy officers in charge of this procurement to reverse Pyatt's decision. To do so, however, they would have to prove a negative assumption: that it was impossible for the minority contractors nominated by the SBA to do the job.

At Medley, that was clearly the case. The company was in the hills outside Philadelphia, landlocked, with not nearly enough real estate to handle the project. The company itself was also too small. It had never done anything remotely like the pontoon project. The contract was obviously beyond its capabilities.

At Wedtech, the issue wasn't quite as clear cut. The first stop was Mariotta's office at 595 Gerard—a room the navy team quickly took to calling the "trophy hall" because of the photographs on the wall showing Mariotta with President Reagan and lesser politicians. Mariotta was his typically flamboyant self as he guided the navy visitors through corporate headquarters.

119

"There are two kinds of mechanics in the South Bronx," he gushed. "There are guys who take things apart and guys who put things together. My guys can put anything together!"

Given the neighborhood in which it was located, 595 Gerard was indeed an impressive facility. However, the pontoons were not to be built at 595 Gerard. When de Vicq and the other navy visitors were finally led to the proposed pontoon fabrication plant, what they saw was the shell of a building. The building had no roof, no heat, no lights, and no plumbing. And it wasn't on the water. When the navy officers asked where sea trials would be conducted, they were led over railroad tracks, along a road owned by a trucking company, then onto a private junkyard to look at a waterfront site on the East River. The Wedtech officials explained they would negotiate a right of way to the site and install a concrete pad on which to place pontoons.

To de Vicq, the man responsible for supplying the fleet with pontoons, the sight was frightening. A lot had to happen to that building very quickly in order to meet the schedule. Wedtech would be starting a long climb at the bottom of a very steep hill. But it was not a demonstrably impossible undertaking. De Vicq had been involved in construction most of his adult life. He'd seen some amazing accomplishments. As a battalion commander in Diego Garcia, he'd watched a military base sprout amid the jungle. Who was to say absolutely that it couldn't happen again amid the concrete jungles of New York City?

On the basis of the trip report—which concluded that Wedtech could develop the technical capability to build the pontoons, though probably not on time—Pyatt approved Wedtech for the pontoon contract.

Medley, meanwhile, dropped out of picture. It may have been because of the navy team's findings, it may have been because SBA's inspector general suddenly reopened an investigation into alleged misconduct by Medley. (Curiously, Mark Bragg had somehow found out about this internal investigation and passed the word on to Wedtech.) Whatever the reason, Wedtech found itself where it hoped to be from the start—all alone with the pontoon contract.

Once again, through bribery, lies, and political muscle, the Wedtech gang had victory in its grasp. Now it was just a matter of quibbling over the price.

Here Wedtech was on familiar ground. Its initial price was almost $36 million; the navy's fair market price was slightly more than $24 million. Over the next three weeks, Wedtech reduced its price twice, first to $33.2 million and then to $30.5 million.

With both sides at an impasse, the uniformed navy saw one last chance to take the pontoon contract away from Wedtech. A NAVFAC officer sent Pyatt a memo stating that "prompt termination of the Section 8(a) consideration seems necessary to preserve any opportunity to meet delivery dates required."

Pyatt was not about to let the deal fall apart. He directed Ramirez to call together the SBA and Wedtech to attempt to reach a resolution. Wedtech was now in the enviable position of having the negotiations handled by its paid "mole" within the navy. Ramirez could provide timely progress reports and make sure Wedtech told the navy exactly what it wanted to hear.

Unfortunately for Wedtech, this time the SBA refused to sweeten the pot. It would not come up with any grants or loans to cover the difference between Wedtech's price and the navy's.

On March 19, Wedtech submitted a revised cost proposal of $29.6 million. Even this was a bluff. The company's illusion of success had been created as a classic Ponzi scheme, and to perpetuate it the Wedtech executives needed a stream of cash passing through the company just to keep it afloat and, not so incidentally, from which they could steal. By the spring of 1984, the company had used up the $23 million provided by the initial public offering; it desperately needed to lock up the pontoon contract so it could bring off another $40 million public offering of securities.

Unknown to the navy, therefore, Wedtech was negotiating from a position of weakness. It would have been willing to accept almost any price the navy offered. The Wedtech officers hoped, however, that rather than delay the urgent pontoon program, the navy would meet the company's price.

Both sides held firm until March 28, when Wedtech agreed to accept the navy's $24.2 million price. In return, the navy agreed to include options, potentially worth tens of millions more, for 1985 and 1986.

No one was under any illusions that Wedtech could build the pontoons for $24.2 million. Wedtech had "bought in" to the contract. Even if it performed as efficiently as possible, it would lose at least $4 million on the first portion. The company would make up the loss, presumably, on the options.

121

The pontoon contract was signed during a ceremony and press conference at Wedtech headquarters on April 23, 1984. Again the politicians flocked to take credit. D'Amato, Garcia, Bragg, and Neglia attended to bask in the limelight and the glow of victory. And there were the usual disputes as to who would speak at the press conference and in what order. Spying Bragg in the hallway, Senator D'Amato snapped, "Tell Mr. Nofziger that we control the government, not him. Make sure you tell him that."

In front of the assembled press corps, D'Amato was all smiles. "Wedtech is living proof that if you work hard, are dedicated and willing to compete, you can succeed," he declared.

Mario Biaggi was also seated prominently at the head table. The day before, Moreno had questioned Ehrlich about whether Biaggi's attendance was a good idea; Wedtech, after all, wasn't even in his congressional district. "I tried to persuade him not to come," Ehrlich responded, "but he wants to be in the newspapers."

# 12

## Buying the Bronx

The pontoon contract presented Wedtech's management team with new problems and new opportunities. Problems in the sense that the company had to find places to build and test the pontoons. Opportunities in the sense that each construction project, each machinery purchase, could generate kickbacks into the F.H.J. account.

The F.H.J. slush fund had been revived in late 1983, a few months after the initial stock offering. At a meeting in the head quarters building, Mariotta informed the rest of the gang that he and Neuberger were tired of using personal funds to make political contributions and monthly payoffs to the union. Moreover, they still owed some interest—the "vig"—to the loan shark. It was time to put some more money "en la bolsa," Mariotta said, tugging at his pocket for emphasis.

A businessman who never quite grasped the concept of a public company and the various legal responsibilities involved, Mariotta announced that he wanted a new salary of at least $300,000 a year. You can't do that, Guariglia protested. It'll kill the stock price. The shareholders won't stand for it.

"Fuck the shareholders," Reagan's hero for the eighties replied. "This is my company and I'll take what I want to take."

Guariglia again tried to reason with Mariotta. He said he'd talk to Fred Moss of Moseley Hallgarten, the only member of the board of directors who was not a Wedtech employee. He'd look into alternate forms of compensation such as bonuses and stock options.

"You're nothing but an accountant!" Mariotta screamed at Guariglia. "I'm an entrepreneur. As long as you work for me, you have to fill my pockets!"

Neuberger and Moreno had been down this path with Mariotta many times. Once things degenerated into a screaming match, there was no reasoning with him. Yet Guariglia's comments about alternate forms of compensation had triggered an idea. What about reactivating the F.H.J. account, dormant since early in the year?

Bluestine, Shorten, and Guariglia balked at the proposal, not because it was illegal, but because they might get caught. They knew how easily Main Hurdman had discovered the F.H.J. shenanigans in its initial audit; no doubt it could happen again.

Bluestine, the most experienced and knowledgeable accountant in the group, made a counterproposal. What if he went to Switzerland to set up a dummy sales agency that would overcharge Wedtech and kickback the excess into a secret bank account?

To Neuberger, this sounded too convoluted. The F.H.J. account was already in existence. It was down the block, at Banco Popular, not somewhere halfway around the world. He'd been able to open the account without using a Social Security number or a federal tax identification number. He could keep it hidden.

Moreno and Mariotta agreed. "Don't worry," Mariotta assured Shorten. "We are all one big, happy family. Nobody is going to know about it unless we talk about it."

With that, the gang agreed to bring the F.H.J. account out of dormancy. Guariglia would oversee the account; Ceil Lewis would handle the checkbook. Mariotta and Neuberger would each get 25 percent of the proceeds.

That left Moreno, Guariglia, Shorten, and Bluestine to decide how to divide the remaining 50 percent. It was a somewhat ticklish issue because Moreno had been at the company significantly longer than the others. Moreno solemnly announced that he didn't want to be greedy. In the spirit of "one for all and all for one," he suggested they each take an equal cut of 12.5 percent. The others agreed.

With the decision to revive the F.H.J. slush fund, the task was to fill it. The old-fashioned way—stealing money directly from Wedtech's corporate coffers—was too risky. Construction and equipment kickbacks seemed to be the most promising approach.

One of the first things the Wedtech group did was get in touch with Henry Zeisel, the owner of several New Jersey machinery companies. They told Zeisel to substitute used equipment for the new equipment they had ordered, but to bill the price of the new equipment on the invoice. They would share the difference in the price of the new equipment and the cost of the used.

Zeisel complied, and by October 21 he had kicked back $192,500 to the F.H.J. account. Over the years, the machinery kickback scam would become a reliable source of cash; in total, Zeisel kicked back almost $600,000 into the F.H.J. account.

(In 1985, Zeisel was tried in federal court on arson charges. One of his character witnesses was Mario Moreno, who testified that Zeisel was "an honorable man." Zeisel was acquitted. One of the jurors, ABC News Vice-President Av Westin, later wrote Zeisel to say he was pleased that "justice was done, and your name cleared and your reputation restored to an unblemished state.")

Because Mariotta, Neuberger, and Moreno had incurred so many expenses for various payoffs, everyone agreed those three should get first pickings from the new and improved slush fund.

Within a few months, however, a rift developed within the big happy family. Bluestine had received an enormous amount of money and stock to join Wedtech, so there was the normal jealousy to begin with. Bluestine made matters worse by seeming to spend more time on the golf course than in the office. When he was in the office, he seemed to contribute little of value.

The last straw was the discovery that Bluestine hadn't used a $900,000 company-backed loan to pay his taxes—word had it that he'd bought an apartment in Florida, another in Westchester Country, and his wife was seen wearing an expensive diamond necklace. It didn't bother the other executives that Bluestine had, in their minds, participated in a fraud and accepted a bribe. But pulling a scam on *them* was an intolerable breach of conduct.

Mariotta called in Neuberger, Moreno, Guariglia, and Shorten to discuss the situation. Guariglia was particularly enthusiastic about punishing Bluestine—the departure of his former boss would leave him as the company's top financial officer. Imitating the membership committee of an exclusive men's club, they each

125

cast a ballot on Bluestine's fate. The verdict was unanimous. Bluestine had to go. And so he went, cast out of Wedtech's inner circle for attempting to con the con artists.

One benefit of getting rid of Bluestine was that Moreno, Guariglia, and Shorten would not have to divide the F.H.J. spoils among as many. With Bluestine's departure, they would each get one-sixth of the loot instead of one-eighth.

To build the pontoons, Wedtech needed a very large manufacturing facility. Fortunately, at about the same time as the executives heard about the pontoon contract, they learned of the availability of one of the biggest industrial buildings in the Bronx, at 977–89 East 149th Street, near the Hunts Point section. Further inquiry revealed that the building was owned by the City of New York but was on a long-term lease to PDJ Realty Corp. PDJ Realty was a partnership owned by none other than Pat Simone and his son, Joe.

No introductions being necessary, the Wedtech team met with Simone to discuss leasing the building. Simone didn't want to lose control of the building by selling or assigning the lease outright. He was, however, willing to work out a deal.

The deal was extremely complex. The Wedtech executives formed a partnership called Jofre Associates. The name Jofre was derived from *Jo*hn Mariotta and *Fre*d Neuberger. The executives' ownership interests in Jofre was the same as their cuts from the F.H.J. account. Jofre and PDJ Realty then formed a partnership called PJ Associates; Jofre had to pay $1 million for its interest in PJ Associates, which was assigned the lease on the 149th Street facility. Finally, PJ Associates subleased the facility to Wedtech. The upshot of all this was that Wedtech was paying Simone and its own executives for use of the building at 149th Street.

Mario Biaggi was furious when he heard about the Jofre arrangement. He may not have understood the whole thing, but he understood enough to know he wasn't part of it.

"Why didn't you let us know about this?" he asked Moreno. "Are we partners or aren't we? We should have gotten our five percent of whatever you did there."

Moreno attempted to mollify the congressman by explaining that the Jofre deal was a personal one, not involving corporate funds. Biaggi apparently wasn't satisfied, because he later called Simone to demand a piece of the action. Guariglia walked into Simone's office just as the conversation was ending.

Simone maintained his offices at Hunts Point Auto Wrecking, a sprawling junkyard along Sheridan Boulevard. Security was tight; at least one visitor concluded the offices were designed to minimize the chances of a rubout. Nevertheless, one of Simone's own sons had been gunned down a few years earlier at the junkyard. The tall, burly Simone had taken a fatherly interest in Guariglia. Simone was attracted by Guariglia's style. Unlike many of his neighborhood buddies, Guariglia had left the streets and gotten educated. But he seemed to harbor a hidden desire to be a wiseguy. And wiseguys with Guariglia's accounting background were always valuable.

As Guariglia recalled it, Simone hung up the phone and snarled that he had been talking to Biaggi, and "that S.O.B. just asked for five percent of the building." Simone went on to say there was no way he wanted Biaggi as a partner in the 149th Street deal: "Screw Biaggi, he doesn't deserve it on this one."

Guariglia, still concerned about Biaggi's ability to cause trouble for Wedtech, mentioned he had heard from Ehrlich that the congressman was very upset about being left out.

"Don't worry about it," Simone replied. "I *own* him."

When Wedtech leased the 149th Street building, it was, as the navy team correctly noted, little more than a shell. A great deal of construction work was going to have to be done to put it in shape to function as a pontoon manufacturing plant.

According to the Wedtech executives, Simone offered to do some of the work himself, hinting there was money to be made on the roughly $3 million in improvements that would be required. To work out the details, Mariotta and Guariglia met with Simone at his junkyard office. At first, Simone asked for 50 percent of the construction kickbacks. Considering that Simone was going to establish the "actual" cost of construction in the first place, 50 percent seemed steep. The Wedtech executives said they'd get back to Simone with a counteroffer.

Negotiations over the kickback percentages were difficult, particularly because Simone refused to carry on any discussions over the phone. Guariglia became a messenger boy, driving between Wedtech headquarters and Simone's offices, carrying offers and counteroffers. At the end of the shuttle diplomacy, a deal was struck: the Wedtech crowd would get 74 percent; Simone would get 20 percent, plus 5 percent to pay off the contractors that were going to generate the padded invoices and 1

127

percent to pay the bank that was going to launder the funds and provide the cash.

Simone began construction even before the pontoon contract was officially signed, and cash from kickbacks started to flow into management's pockets in early 1984. Some of it went for the union payoffs and the Ramirez bribe; much of the rest went to pay for the executives' increasingly extravagant lifestyles.

A great deal of the cash was generated through an electrician named Hector Vasquez. According to Guariglia, Vasquez had been instructed to pad his payroll with fictitious names, cash the payroll checks, and turn the cash over to Simone. Over the course of two years, Wedtech would pay Vasquez almost $1.5 million for work supposedly done at the pontoon plant. Of that, some $300,000 was kicked back to the Wedtech executives.

Throughout 1984, Guariglia would go to Simone's office and pick up grocery bags full of cash. On one occasion, his secretary drove him and waited outside while her boss went in to pick up the loot. On another, Shorten accompanied Guariglia. He later described driving into Simone's used auto parts lot to pick up the cash: "There was a guy with an automatic weapon . . . black guy . . . ugliest thing I had ever seen in my life." When Guariglia got back to 595 Gerard, he'd divide the contents of the grocery bags among Wedtech Corporation's senior executives.

In addition to a manufacturing plant, Wedtech needed a place to test the pontoons—to put them in the water, make sure that they floated and the propulsion systems worked. Naturally, the company had no such place.

Finding a site should not have been that difficult. The Bronx has rivers on three sides. Initially, the company leased a waterfront parcel from the Consolidated Rail Corp., but the navy pointed out that the site was unsuitable. (With typical Wedtech inefficiency, the company never bothered to terminate the lease with Conrail and spent about $60,000 in lease payments for a piece of land it never used.)

Shortly thereafter, the ever-helpful Pat Simone told the Wedtech group about One Loop Drive—a city-owned site in Hunts Point that included a building and a large parking lot. The parking lot, he said, might be a suitable site for the final assembly of the pontoons and their launching for sea trials. The Wedtech executives asked Ehrlich to look into the site; he contacted the Bronx borough president, Stanley Simon. As leaders of one of the up-and-coming firms in the South Bronx, the Wedtech officers had met Simon before. At first, the meetings were purely social. In 1981, Simon had helped his brother-in-law, Henry Bittman, get a job at Wedtech. By late 1983, Simon felt comfortable enough with his newly wealthy constituents to ask for another favor.

Though a lawyer, Simon was neither particularly brilliant nor smooth. For a while his idea of graft was to have someone pick up his breakfast tab at the local diner. Apparently deciding to be more aggressive, he approached Fred Neuberger and asked that Wedtech pay for some of his meal expenses during an upcoming trip he and his wife were taking to the Mullet Bay resort in St. Maarten.

Neuberger was somewhat taken aback by the request. How, he asked, did Simon propose to handle this? Was Simon going to have the headwaiter send Wedtech a bill every time the borough president finished a meal?

Simon said he's give the matter some thought. After Christmas, the two spoke on the phone. Neuberger asked Simon what plan the borough president had worked out. Forget it, Simon replied, it had been taken care of.

After hearing from Ehrlich about Wedtech's interest in One Loop Drive, Simon assigned one of his aides to escort Ehrlich, Mariotta, and Moreno through the facility.

At the time, the building was occupied by another minority-owned firm, a food processor called Freedom Industries. Freedom's president, Henry Thomas, was a street-smart black man who liked to say he graduated from "UCLA"—"the University of the Corner of Lenox Avenue." (Lenox Avenue is one of the main thoroughfares in Harlem.) Freedom's legal counsel was the firm of Biaggi & Ehrlich, though relations between counsel and client had been strained even since Ehrlich had asked that the law firm be given stock in Freedom.

Ehrlich, feeling a little uncomfortable about his role in helping one client take over a facility from which the other had yet to be evicted, suggested the group go through the side door so that Thomas wouldn't know they were there. The Wedtech representatives liked what they saw. They told Ehrlich they were interested in the site.

The next step was to get the approval of the City of New York, which owned the site and had restricted its use to activities involving agriculture and foodstuffs. Wedtech didn't bother approaching

129

the city through normal channels using routine procedures. Within an hour of the tour, Stanley Simon called City Hall and set up a meeting.

Simon introduced the Wedtech group to Susan Frank, the commissioner of ports and terminals. This was the agency responsible for approving use of the waterfront properties. After a short while, the outline of a deal was struck. The city would evict Freedom on the grounds that it was behind on its rent. (Thomas was maintaining that Freedom deserved rent *credits* because vandalism and a city-hired plumber had rendered the facility unusable.) Hebrew National, a Queens-based meat processor looking for a new location, would get the building. Wedtech would get the parking lot. Henry Thomas would get the boot.

On June 5, 1984, Frank sent Mariotta a letter formally offering the property; Wedtech could lease 100,000 square feet at One Loop Drive for $50,000 a year for three years, with an option for four more years. That the city agreed to help a company promising to employ a lot of people in the Bronx was not surprising; the speed with which the bureaucracy moved was. Ehrlich bragged to Moreno that the haste was not accidental. Congressman Biaggi, Ehrlich said, had called Susan Frank on Wedtech's behalf.

The final step in securing the site was approval from the city's powerful Board of Estimate. Chaired by the mayor, the Board of Estimate was composed of the presidents of the five boroughs, the president of the city council, and the city comptroller. Simon, a member of the board, worked to get the matter on the June agenda.

On the day of the meeting, Moreno, Ehrlich, and Carlos Cuevas, Jr., a young associate from the firm of Biaggi & Ehrlich, showed up on Wedtech's behalf. Carlos Cuevas, Jr. was the son of Carlos Cuevas, Sr., the deputy Bronx borough president who often sat in for Simon when he couldn't attend the board meetings. Even Ehrlich was perceptive enough tó recognize the potential conflict of interest this caused, so he told Cuevas, Jr. to leave. Simon's help notwithstanding, it became increasingly obvious as the meeting dragged on that the board wasn't going to take up the Wedtech lease. Moreno asked Ehrlich what had gone wrong. Ehrlich was blunt: "Simon didn't move his ass."

Actually, a couple of other factors prevented Wedtech from getting the rubber stamp for which it had hoped. Donald Manes, the Queens borough president, wasn't keen on Hebrew National leaving his borough for the Bronx. Henry Thomas, meanwhile, had gotten Pentagon officials to call certain board members to explain why Freedom needed the building to produce emergency rations for the military.

After the meeting, Biaggi called Simon and chewed him out. The congressman warned that Simon's re-election depended on his support and, if he wanted it, he'd better get the matter taken care of. Thus motivated, Simon managed to get the matter on the agenda—and approved—at the next Board of Estimate meeting. Mayor Koch hailed the good news for Wedtech and Hebrew National at a City Hall press conference.

The Wedtech crew was ecstatic. Wedtech's allies were also pleased. But again they were looking for tangible expressions of gratitude. The feeding frenzy was spreading.

Ehrlich told Moreno the law firm's retainer didn't cover the special work it had done on One Loop Drive. At a meeting in the congressman's Bronx office, Ehrlich informed Biaggi that Wedtech had agreed to pay an extra $50,000 above the annual retainer of $150,000 for the special services. Biaggi grumbled that $50,000 didn't seem like much in return for all he and Bernie had done. For once, Moreno held his ground and $50,000 was the amount they settled on.

Simon also wanted to be recognized. During a function at Yonkers Raceway, the borough president approached Neuberger and said he wanted to form a betting "partnership." This partnership consisted of Neuberger giving Simon $50 or $100 to bet on each race.

Apparently having established that Neuberger was a source of funds, Simon pulled Neuberger aside for some serious talk about money. Simon faced a tough re-election challenge in 1985. He needed help badly. Neuberger never enjoyed being shaken down by politicians, so he didn't make it easy.

What kind of help do you expect? he asked, assuming Simon would ask for the "normal" few hundred or few thousand dollars.

Say, $75,000 or $100,000, Simon replied.

That's ridiculous, Neuberger responded. Apparently feeling as though he needed to back up his position, Neuberger added that the request was illegal. Simon and Neuberger either missed the slapstick quality of their exchange or were masters of self-control. In any event, Simon had a ready response. Give the money to me in the form of donations to synagogues and churches and pick up

131

some of my expenses. Neuberger, realizing that appeals to lawful conduct weren't going to carry the day, agreed to $50,000.

Having made the deal, Neuberger left the mechanics to others. He instructed Ceil Lewis to given Simon a credit of $50,000 in the F.H.J. account and draw against it whenever Simon received funds.

For Stanley Simon, the son of a Tremont Avenue candy store owner, having Wedtech in the Bronx was like having his own candy store. It was an irresistible source of treats. Once, when Simon needed money, he called Moreno and demanded a $5,000 check *that day*. When Moreno protested that he was too busy, Simon told him, "Let's see how we can organize for you to take some time off." Moreno complied.

As Neuberger had discovered, the Bronx borough president liked to gamble, especially with other people's money. When he learned that the Wedtech executives were becoming high rollers in Atlantic City, he insisted on tagging along for the ride.

One time, Simon told Moreno he wanted to go to Atlantic City and use one of the Wedtech executive's apartments there. He also told Moreno he wanted some money to gamble with.

Moreno directed Ceil Lewis to make a withdrawal from the F.H.J. account; she took out about $7,000. When Simon's messenger—a New York City employee named Ralph Lawrence who served as Simon's driver, advance man, and overall "super schlep"—arrived at Wedtech, Lewis had the cash but not the keys to the apartment. Moreno, who'd left the keys at home, ordered a Wedtech employee to go to his house and get them for Simon.

One weekend in late 1985, Simon and his wife, Ehrlich and his wife, and Moreno and his companion all went to Atlantic City in the Wedtech station wagon. They arrived around noon on a Friday. The Simons checked into one of Moreno's apartments; Moreno and Vazquez shared a two-bedroom suite with the Ehrlichs. That night, Moreno took them to dinner at the Tropicana, and later they gambled. Simon, having been safely re-elected, used some of his own money, but he much preferred using Moreno's. That first night, Moreno gave him $500 or $600 in chips.

The next day, Peter Neglia and his wife arrived and checked into a room Moreno had arranged using his "comp" account at the Tropicana. The SBA regional administrator was somewhat upset to see the highly visible Simon in the group, but he didn't let it ruin his weekend.

132

The group went to dinner Saturday night and spent a few hours in the casino. This time, according to Moreno, he gave Simon and his wife about $3,000 in chips to play with and about $1,000 to Peter Neglia's wife. Afterward, the happy band took in a Diana Ross concert at the Tropicana's lounge.

Aside from his assistance on the One Loop Drive site, Simon's deeds in return for the Wedtech largess were rather modest. One time, he invited Moreno to join him at George Steinbrenner's box at Yankee Stadium. He also tried to help Moreno get a retroactive variance for some improvements the Wedtech executive and his companion had made to their Bronx home.

Stanley Simon was not the only Bronx politician who saw Wedtech as a source of goodies. Robert Garcia, the United States congressman in whose district most of the Wedtech facilities were located, also found the company irresistible.

Garcia, the son of a Pentecostal minister, was a native of the South Bronx. After high school, he joined the army, winning two Bronze Stars in Korea before returning home to continue his education as a computer programmer. In 1966, he became the first Puerto Rican elected to the New York State Assembly, and in 1980 he was elected to Congress. Although he looked tough, Garcia developed a reputation as one of the friendliest, least devious members of Congress.

Befitting the district he represented, Garcia had seemed to be a man of rather modest tastes, known for his rumpled suits and scuffed shoes. That seemed to change after his 1980 marriage to Jane Lee Matos, who had grown up in comfort as a member of the prominent Lee family in Puerto Rico. It was the second marriage for him, the third for her.

As one friend characterized the change, "Before Jane, Bobby was never concerned about his appearance. He looked like an unmade bed. Jane provided the spin for a better life. She got him jogging. He took off weight. Started dressing better."

He also started living better. For Jane Lee Garcia, one disadvantage of being married to the congressman who represented the South Bronx was that she had to live there. One of the first nights she spent at the congressman's Bronx apartment, a rat ran across the bed. Soon they moved to a fancier apartment in the Bronx and started spending more time in Washington, Puerto Rico, and their newly acquired, sixty-five-acre horse farm in upstate New York.

The problem with the Garcias' new lifestyle was it cost money, more money than a congressman without independent means could afford. According to the government's indictment of the congressman and his wife, they turned to Wedtech to supplement their income. The payments allegedly began after the Garcias dined with Mario Moreno at a Manhattan restaurant in the spring of 1984.

As usual, there was dissention within the executive suites at 595 Gerard Avenue. Neuberger, who seemed to understand that the less they gave other people the more they would be able to keep for themselves, was opposed to paying Garcia. He pointed out that, as a liberal Democrat, Garcia consistently voted against defense bills. Neuberger saw no reason to help a congressman whose votes could hurt Wedtech's defense business.

Mariotta's argument in favor of paying Garcia was somewhat less lucid. Mariotta seemed to think it was unfair that Wedtech was giving money to politicians right and left but not to its very own congressman, and one who was Hispanic, at that. Garcia was on the banking and post office committees—maybe he could be of some assistance there. As usual, Mariotta prevailed.

The mechanics of bribing a public official were always tricky. Wedtech allegedly disguised the bribes as payments of a $4,000 monthly retainer to Puerto Rican lawyer Ralph Vallone, Jr. Vallone, in turn, paid Jane Lee Garcia for "public relations" work. Between mid–1984 and early 1986, Wedtech paid Vallone a total of $86,100; Vallone allegedly returned $76,000 to Jane Lee Garcia.

In addition to the cash, John and Jennie Mariotta allegedly gave Mrs. Garcia a diamond-and-emerald necklace worth more than $25,000 during a September 1985 trip to the Virgin Islands. The Garcias were also alleged to have received a $20,000 interest-free loan from Mario Moreno, funnelled through the Bronx Pentecostal church where the congressman's sister, the Reverend Aimee Garcia Cortese, was the minister.

The most bizarre story to emerge from the Wedtech-Garcia connection was the possibility that Wedtech may have supplied some of the hush money paid to Jessica Hahn, the church secretary whose sexual encounter with Jim Bakker triggered the downfall of Bakker's PTL television ministry.

Aimee Garcia Cortese was on the PTL board, and she was the board member located closest to Hahn, who lived on Long Island. In late 1984, Cortese served as the conduit for a $10,000 payment to Hahn. In February 1985, PTL agreed to a $265,000 out-of-court settlement with Hahn, and the following month Mariotta told Ceil Lewis to prepare an F.H.J. check made out to Aimee Cortese's church. Mariotta said the $65,000 was to help the church pay its mortgage. Mariotta and Lewis delivered the check to Cortese, who blessed them but did did not seem overwhelmed by their generosity. In July, 1985, PTL gave $50,000 to the church.

Although none of the Wedtech money was traced to Hahn, it was apparently commingled in the same account with at least some of the PTL money. And there was one night during which Hahn and Congressman Garcia were said to be at the church at the same time, taking care of their respective businesses.

Thus, two of the biggest scandals of the 1980s—Wedtech and PTL—intersected at a church in the Bronx, its name the Cross Roads Tabernacle.

135

# 13

# A License to Steal

**N**ow that it had located a manufacturing plant and a testing site, all Wedtech had to do was actually manufacture the pontoons. The company's political allies could help it get the contracts and find the facilities, but at some point it was going to have to produce and deliver a product that met the navy's stringent standards. Unfortunately, Wedtech didn't have a clue how to accomplish that.

In terms of capabilities, Wedtech was still a small-time machine shop, even though it had acquired some sophisticated machinery and larger facilities. Mariotta and Neuberger knew something about the technical end of the metal bending business but were incapable of managing a complex manufacturing operation. Guariglia, Shorten, and Moreno were numbers men, not production experts.

Besides, they were all crooks. Each devoted more time and energy to developing schemes to defraud the shareholders and the government than to managing the business. With every passing day, Wedtech was becoming less of a corporation and more of a racketeering enterprise. It had become difficult, if not impossible, to bring honest and competent leaders into the ranks of top management; sooner or later, they would undoubtedly detect the massive fraud and theft.

When the company was awarded the pontoon contract by the navy, it still hadn't delivered any of the six-horsepower engines to the army. By the time the first fifty engines were delivered in November 1984, nine months behind schedule, Wedtech had received $1.8 million in progress payments. In other words, Wedtech was producing at a rate of $36,000 per engine. Under the terms of the contract, Wedtech would have to produce at $2,116 per engine just to break even. Productivity was going to have to improve remarkably for the remaining 13,050 engines.

Not surprisingly, the company immediately fell behind on the pontoon contract as well. The contract called for delivery of the first pontoon in six months—October 1984. Wedtech would be lucky to have the manufacturing facility ready by then! Everybody knew it—the Wedtech executives, the government contract administrators in New York, the naval officers overseeing the pontoon program. Everybody, in fact, except the political appointees in a position to direct contracts to Wedtech. They either didn't know or, more likely, didn't want to know.

When Wedtech received the pontoon contract, it realized the facility at 149th Street in the Bronx wasn't going to be sufficient to handle the job, even when it was fixed up. Therefore, the company moved to acquire a bankrupt shipyard in the Upper Peninsula of Michigan.

Wedtech heard about the shipyard from Richard Ramirez, who had visited the Upper Peninsula the previous year as part of a navy team. Ramirez left the navy in February 1984, apparently convinced he could make even more money in the private sector. He hooked up with the Washington consulting firm of Gnau, Carter, Jacobsen & Associates. (One of the partners, John R. Gnau, a Detroit-area businessman who was President Reagan's 1980 Michigan campaign chairman, would later plead guilty to conspiracy in connection with a massive postal service kickback scheme.) Shortly after joining the firm, Ramirez told Wedtech officials that the assets of a shipyard in some place called Ontonagon were being auctioned off, and the facility would be ideal for making pontoons. His consulting firm would be glad to broker the deal.

To the people of the economically depressed town of Ontonagon, Michigan, the possibility of their shipyard being purchased by Wedtech seemed like a second coming. Wedtech, they heard, was a rapidly growing company with seemingly unlimited potential. It already had a contract to build ships worth tens of millions of dollars.

The excitement built when Mariotta and other Wedtech officials visited Ontonagon to inspect the facility. They arrived in a chartered jet—said by some to be the biggest plane ever to land at the town's airport—and were greeted by a crowd of enthusiastic locals.

Perhaps the first indication that the Bronx company was not a typical corporation came at a bankruptcy court hearing at which Wedtech asked for more time to put together its bid, despite the presence of another bidder for the assets. John Mariotta was so overcome by emotion he started to cry. Whether because of, or in spite of, Mariotta's histrionics, Wedtech ended up getting the shipyard for a little more than $5 million.

Shortly after the shipyard acquisition, in September 1984, Bob Wallach asked Wedtech for $500,000 as prepayment for his 1985 and 1986 fees. The Wedtech executives agreed to $300,000. The request and payments came at a time when Wallach was representing Meese in the hearings on his confirmation as attorney general of the United States.

According to the Wedtech officers, Wallach indicated he needed the money since he was not being paid to represent Meese. The officers also said Wallach indicated he wanted the money paid then because he expected to be serving in a high-level position in the Justice Department after Meese was confirmed. It would present an "ethics" problem for him to receive compensation from Wedtech while he was a government employee. The executives believed that by making the prepayment of Wallach's fees, they were assuring themselves of greater access to Meese and the administration.

Guariglia delivered the check for $300,000 to Wallach in October 1984 in the restaurant of the hotel in which Wallach was staying. Two weeks later, Wallach sent a letter to Guariglia in which he acknowledged receipt of the money: "I am, of course, delighted to have played a role in assisting the company's acquisition of this very desirable new venture." The venture to which he was referring was the shipyard in Ontonagon, Michigan. Both Guariglia and a key executive directly involved in the transaction deny that Wallach had any role in the purchase. Wallach, however, says he was "heavily involved" in the Ontonagon acquisition. If, as Guariglia contends, Wallach had minimal involvement in the shipyard purchase, his agreeing to misrepresent his payment allowed Guariglia to falsify the company's financial statements, improving the picture of Wedtech's profitability in 1984.

Wallach wasn't the only one to use the consultant-for-the-Ontonagon-transaction story. Deciding they needed to increase their personal cash flow, the Wedtech officers had Pat Simone set up a phony company, Consultants Supreme, to which Wedtech paid $150,000, supposedly for assistance with the Ontonagon deal. Of that amount, Simone got $75,000; the Wedtech executives split $75,000. Later, rumors began to surface that Simone's front man for the deal was a drug-gang enforcer who had served twenty years in prison for murder.

Had Wedtech been able to use the trained work force and the shipyard established in Michigan to build all its pontoons, the company would have been better off. But that would have compromised its position in the 8(a) program. The rationale for giving Wedtech the contract was to bring employment to the South Bronx. To preserve their cover stories for helping Wedtech, the politicians had to be able to point to the jobs being created in the Bronx. And to put people to work building pontoons in the South Bronx, the company had first to prepare its manufacturing facility.

Efforts to renovate the 149th Street building were troubled from the start. There was, for example, the question of what to do about the double railroad tracks running through the center of the building. First it was decided to fill them in with concrete. After that was accomplished, someone decided the tracks might be useful for shipping materials to and from Michigan. The cement—about 4 feet deep and 150 feet long—was chipped away. Ultimately, it became apparent there was no need for the tracks; they were recovered with cement.

About $1 million was spent to put a roof over the 200,000-square-foot building. But the roof leaked constantly, mainly because workmen kept drilling holes in it without authorization to install various cables and wires. In the early days, there was no water in the building. So Wedtech hooked up hoses to the fire hydrants on the street. This was illegal at any time, but the offense was particularly egregious because at the time it was committed, New York City was in the midst of a drought.

To paint the pontoons, Wedtech paid nearly $1 million for a German-made, state-of-the-art spray painting machine, then spent another $1 million or so installing it. The machine was so big the company had to break down walls to get it in the building, then build a separate, twelve-foot foundation to support it. The fume-spewing monster turned out to be in violation of U.S. government

139

standards, and Wedtech was fined $28,000 by the U.S. Environmental Protection Agency. The machine never painted a single pontoon that was delivered to the navy.

To heat the plant, eighty-six gas space heaters were hung thirty-five feet in the air. Naturally, the hot air was promptly sucked out by the ventilation fans in the roof. Wedtech was heating the South Bronx, but not its own factory floor.

In addition to the problems with the facility at 149th Street, Wedtech didn't have a work force with the skills required to build the pontoons. Qualified welders were in particularly short supply. Despite Mariotta's rhetoric about reducing joblessness and employing the unemployable, finding trained workers in the South Bronx wasn't easy. The company resorted to hiring just about anyone who applied, virtually none of whom had the necessary skills. These new employees also changed the character of the work force.

Before the pontoon contract, most of the blue-collar workers were Puerto Ricans, many of them members of the Pentecostal churches that had sprung up throughout the South Bronx. Mariotta used to recruit them after the Sunday services at John 3 : 16 Christian Church. To these workers Mariotta was a hero, and Wedtech was more than just the place they worked. They shared with most of their fellow workers the same heritage, language, neighborhood, and church. Wedtech was their community.

At the pontoon plant, the melting pot was a muddle. With Russian engineers, quality-control personnel from India, and Hispanic and Jamaican craftsmen, the building was a Tower of Babel. Information posted about quality control and welding techniques was unintelligible to a large portion of the work force.

Further, the new workers didn't have the same feeling for Mariotta or sense of community as did the older workers. There were more hardcore cases—drug users and criminals. Wedtech had to hire undercover security men to curb rampant pilferage and theft of tools.

Morale was bad, and for good reason. The safety devices on some machines were disabled so the workers wouldn't be slowed by automatic shut-off switches. Pollution in the building was terrible. Toxic fumes from the portable generators mixed with dust from a cement-crushing plant across the street to form a stifling cloud that hung below the building's ceiling. Things got so bad that in August 1984 the Defense Contract Administration Service recommended that DCAS employees be removed from the plant for their own safety.

Just as the blue-collar work force was unqualified, so was management. No one at Wedtech had ever manufactured a ship of any type; no naval architects were on the payroll. If management had tried to apply itself to the task, it might have coped with the difficulties presented by expansion into a new product line. But it didn't. Moreno and Mariotta, in fact, were spending much of the summer in Europe, arranging kickbacks from suppliers in Italy and Great Britain.

Recognizing a disaster in the making, the government, having made the decision to award the contract to Wedtech, attempted to rally around the company to help it produce. The navy dispatched engineers; DCAS brought in extra personnel to try to help the company establish quality control and production reporting systems.

There was only so much they could do, however, and four months into a multiyear, multimillion-dollar project, the situation was looking grim.

In Washington, in early August, Everett Pyatt had been confirmed as the assistant secretary of the navy for procurement. (The Wedtech officers believed, though it was never proved, that Pyatt's nomination was held up by Wedtech's allies until the company got the pontoon contract.) While assisting Wedtech to get the contract may have helped Pyatt get his job, the company's performance, or lack thereof, could now do his career great harm.

So four days after his confirmation, Pyatt appointed a new deputy, Wayne Arny, to monitor matters related to 8(a) contracts, including Wedtech's execution of the pontoon contract. By late August, it was clear the company was losing ground fast. Arny, a former aide to Sen. John Tower, met with Wedtech and the navy program managers, only to witness a great deal of finger pointing and name calling. Wedtech's executives had perfected the art of blaming others for their own incompetence. Wedtech claimed the disappointing results were the navy's fault for failing to deliver promised equipment. The navy hotly denied it and accused Wedtech of mismanaging the whole project.

In October 1984, the month in which the pontoons were due, Wedtech delivered—not the first pontoon, but a letter to the navy blaming delays on the government and requesting an extension of the delivery dates. In a rather unusual procedure, Wedtech consultant Mark Bragg had Arny review the letter before it was formally submitted.

In response to the letter, the program manager, Capt. Dave de Vicq, pointed out that the government had already expended extraordinary efforts to help Wedtech, and the company wasn't meeting its own revised delivery schedules. The delays meant no powered pontoons would be available for loading on the first three rapid deployment force supply ships before they sailed.

Despite the chaos on the production floor, by the fall of 1984 the Wedtech team was focusing on winning an option—an add-on contract—to build even more pontoons during the next fiscal year.

Wedtech's initial $24.2 million contract award had included the potential for two options, one for fiscal year 1985 and one for fiscal year 1986. For Wedtech, it was essential that those options be awarded.

It was the options that had made the pontoon contract so attractive in the first place. Wedtech was unquestionably going to lose money on the initial contract. The price was too low, the start-up costs were too high, and the learning curve was too steep. The Wedtech executives justified their pursuit of the contract by saying the entire pontoon program could be worth $500 million. Wedtech hoped to make enough money on the options to make up for the initial losses.

From an accounting perspective, getting the options was essential so the massive start-up costs could be spread out over three years, making the basic contract look profitable in the company's financial statements. At least this was the rationale for public consumption. In reality, the Wedtech executives in the Bronx were so inept at running an efficient manufacturing operation that it really didn't matter how many option years they received. They probably wouldn't have made a profit if the government had tripled the price it was paying for each pontoon.

Still, the options were essential if the company was to survive. Money was pouring out far faster than it was coming in. No company could pay the bribes, consulting fees, and kickbacks Wedtech was paying and survive for long. A new infusion of cash had to be found quickly or the pyramid would soon collapse.

From the the personal perspective of Wedtech's top executives, the options were essential if they were to continue to be able to live in the style to which they had become accustomed. They were all making and stealing hundreds of thousands of dollars a year, driving company-provided luxury cars, and using their expense accounts to travel and dine lavishly—all while maintaining "disadvantaged" business status.

This way of life would come to an abrupt end if Wedtech went under. As Tony Guariglia was fond of saying, "We may never have another opportunity like the one we have now."

The navy had committed itself to negotiate with Wedtech for ninety days on the price of the 1985 option. If no agreement was reached by October 15, 1984, the navy threatened to terminate the negotiations and take steps to award the contract to another company, which, it was hoped, could produce pontoons in time to be loaded before the next support ships sailed. The negotiations did not get off to a good start. Wedtech demanded $68 million for the 1985 option; the navy believed the fair market price was $42 million.

Even without the controversy over the price, the naval officers overseeing the pontoon program had grave doubts about giving Wedtech the option. Vice Adm. Thomas J. Hughes, the deputy chief of naval operations for Logistics; Captain de Vicq, the pontoon program manager; and Col. Don Hein, the commander of the Defense Contract Administration Service in the New York region, all opposed awarding the 1985 option to Wedtech. Citing the company's problems establishing a production line and meeting a schedule, they made their position clear to Arny.

Given their propensity for personalizing all disputes, it was not surprising that by now the Wedtech team had elevated Captain de Vicq to the top of its enemies list, displacing Dr. Keenan and Carlos Campbell. Despite the sizable difference over the contract price, Mariotta and Moreno believed it was de Vicq who was standing in the way of their receiving the 1985 option. Therefore, they began focusing their attention on getting rid of de Vicq, rather than on delivering pontoons on time or within budget. For this, the Wedtech executives turned again to their favorite politicians and consultants.

Bob Wallach, as always, was ready with advice. In a November 12 memo to the Wedtech officers and directors, Wallach wrote:

> As we discussed, a private meeting with Captain D. should be arranged at the company as soon as possible . . . Generally speaking [you should make an] implicit suggestion that if he wants his record to look good, obtain a promotion, etc., that by working with you and your working with him, that is the most efficient way to achieve everyone's common goal.

He should be aware of Wedtech's general ally structure.
He doesn't have to know it in detail. The fact that we have
it, and his awareness of it, ought to be gently indicated so
that he understands that we will view favorably with all
we know, his efforts to legitimately conclude this agreement and fulfill the Navy's responsibilities to the public.

Soon after receiving the memo, Moreno decided to go over de
Vicq's head to try to get him fired. To this end, Moreno took the
usual route of trying to enlist Biaggi, D'Amato, and Addabbo in
the campaign.

The company also asked Mark Bragg for his help in securing the
1985 option. Nofziger's partner agreed to try, but he knew it was
going to be an uphill battle, and he wanted a substantial fee. At a
meeting in the Washington office of Nofziger and Bragg, Mariotta
and Moreno agreed to give Bragg $200,000 if the company was
awarded the 1985 option and an extra $200,000 if the company
got the options without price negotiations (meaning the company
could almost name its price). When Wallach, waiting outside,
heard of the commitment to Bragg, he demanded comparable pay
and settled for a promise of $150,000 if Wedtech succeeded in ob-
taining the options.

So the battle lines were drawn. De Vicq and the uniformed navy
were opposed to giving Wedtech the 1985 option at any price;
Wedtech and its allies were urging the company be awarded the
option and a blank check.

On November 18, Arny received a memo from the Office of Naval
Operations documenting Wedtech's problems and stating that the
company would not meet the launch schedule for the supply ships.
The very next day, an extraordinary thing happened: Arny signed
a memorandum directing that Wedtech be awarded the 1985 option by December 3 and that the award be made by "letter contract."

A letter contract was essentially the blank check Wedtech
wanted. Letter contracts were an exceptional way of contracting,
intended to be used for emergencies only—say, for example, a ty-
phoon wiping out the communications facility of an isolated naval
base; in that case, it would be appropriate for the commander to
use a letter contract to have a replacement facility constructed as
quickly as possible, with the price to be determined later.

What a letter contract does is award the contract without a fixed

144

price and authorizes the contractor to begin spending money immediately, with the government committed to reimbursing the contractor for its costs. By awarding the 1985 options to Wedtech under a letter contract, the navy would essentially be giving Wedtech a "cost plus" contract—paying the company its costs plus a fair profit. The company would have no incentive to finish negotiating the total price of the contract, knowing that whatever it spent in the interim the government was going to have to reimburse.

When they received Arny's memo, de Vicq and his colleagues were aghast. In his entire navy career, de Vicq had only known of two letter contracts, one dealing with a water crisis at Guantanamo Bay, Cuba, and the other with a severe storm on the West Coast. De Vicq marched over to headquarters.

"I can't do this," he declared. "It's lunacy. It's a license to steal."

De Vicq's superiors, including Adm. John Paul Jones, Jr., the commander of NAVFAC, agreed. Jones replied to Arny, "respectfully" requesting that he reconsider the letter contract issue. Five days later, Jones's superior, Adm. Richard Miller, called Pyatt to complain about Arny's directive. Faced with the vociferous opposition from the uniformed navy, Arny backed down. Instead, he directed that expedited price negotiations continue.

Arny would later claim he hadn't prepared the memorandum himself and he didn't know what a letter contract was at the time he signed it. He conceded, however, that Bragg had urged him to exercise the options. Senate investigators interviewed more than twenty navy officials in an effort to locate the source of the extraordinary November 19 memo; not one recalled seeing it before it was signed.

As the price negotiations resumed, Wedtech still hadn't delivered its first pontoon to the navy. It finally attempted to do so in late December. De Vicq brought a crowd of officials to the Bronx for the big event, having to keep them there—away from their families—from Christmas through New Year's.

When Wedtech finally presented its pontoon for the important "first article test," the product failed miserably. The navy noted no fewer than eighty-eight deficiencies. Despite the use of sledgehammers by Wedtech's team of manufacturing specialists, the pontoon wasn't even square. (Apparently the first pontoon was made on the floor of the building while the cement was still settling; a one-eighth-inch error at one end became a six- or eight-

145

inch error at the other.) For de Vicq, the man in charge of getting pontoons out to the fleet, the episode was one of the lowest points in a long career.

Unfortunately, the navy was stuck. The deadline for finding a second source to produce pontoons was long past. Bringing in a new contractor would have meant at least another five months of delays, probably more. The best they could hope for was that with a little more time and money, the Wedtech situation could be salvaged. Hope springing eternal, Hughes and de Vicq bit the bullet and recommended that Wedtech be awarded the 1985 options.

After a few more weeks of dickering, the fiscal 1985 pontoon options were awarded to Wedtech on March 15, 1985, at a price of $51.5 million. Wedtech now had navy contracts worth $75.7 million. It had yet to produce a single acceptable pontoon.

# 14

## Dodging a Bullet

**F**or all its Washington clout, Wedtech's by now habitual style of trampling rules, regulations, and competitors was bound to bring it unwanted attention, and sure enough, in the aftermath of the pontoon contract victory, the House Small Business Committee, the panel responsible for monitoring the 8(a) program, began probing into the company.

When the Wedtech executives learned of the committee's interest from Peter Neglia at the SBA, they automatically assumed that the probe had been sparked by an enemy trying to get even. Specifically, they suspected that John Grayson, president of Univox Corp., had contacted committee chairman Parren Mitchell after Univox got shut out of the pontoon contract. It appears, however, that the tip simply came from someone at SBA headquarters in Washington who'd become disgusted with the favoritism Wedtech consistently enjoyed. The would-be whistleblower told Representative Mitchell, a veteran Democrat from Baltimore, that although Wedtech had gone public and its officers had made a killing, Mariotta was still certified as "economically disadvantaged."

Mitchell, a black lawmaker known as the father of minority business programs, called in his senior legislative counsel, Thomas Trimboli, and asked Trimboli to look into the matter.

Trimboli, thirty-seven, was a Brooklyn native and graduate of

Georgetown Law School. He had worked in the New York City corporation counsel's office for a couple of years after law school before going to Washington as a staff aide for Rep. Joe Addabbo, the Queens Democrat who was a senior member of the small business panel. Trimboli knew all the in and outs of the 8(a) law: he had helped write it on Capitol Hill and then implement it as an SBA district administrator in Arizona.

A pale man with slouching posture and soft brown eyes behind wire-rimmed glasses, Trimboli was not an imposing figure physically. But he had a reputation as a tenacious investigator with a strict ethical code. He didn't accept anything—gifts, meals, any favors—from anyone.

Knowing that Wedtech had gone public, Trimboli started his investigation by researching the company's filings at the Securities and Exchange Commission. Flipping through the documents, he began to formulate questions about the economic disadvantage of the owners, their compliance with securities laws, and the involvement of the Biaggi & Ehrlich law firm. He reported back to Mitchell that there was cause for suspicion and suggested as a next step that Wedtech files be obtained from the SBA.

Trimboli was so suspicious, in fact, that he didn't want to follow the standard procedure of sending the SBA a letter to request the files, thereby giving any SBA insider the chance to sanitize them by removing any incriminating documents before the committee could see them. To preserve the integrity of the investigation, he told Mitchell, the files should be confiscated in person and without advance notice. Mitchell agreed.

The confiscation took place on July 27, 1984, with the precision of a police raid. Trimboli and another staff attorney, David Robinson, flew to New York with a letter demanding production of the Wedtech files. Arriving at La Guardia Airport, they called back to their offices, whereupon two other committee staff members were dispatched to the SBA headquarters in Washington carrying the same letter. Almost simultaneously, the committee investigators in New York and Washington served papers on startled SBA officials.

Trimboli accompanied the New York district director to the file room. The Wedtech files were voluminous. Trimboli and Robinson took as much as they could carry; the rest was packed in boxes, sealed, and put in the mail to Washington. The SBA officials were cordial and offered no resistance.

148

As soon as Trimboli and Robinson left to catch a flight back to Washington, however, phone lines up and down the East Coast lit up. Neglia called Ehrlich to tell him what had happened; Ehrlich passed the disconcerting news to Moreno. Within minutes, word of the raid—of Trimboli's "Gestapo-like tactics"—spread throughout Wedtech's network of allies.

No sooner was Trimboli back at his desk in Washington than Joe Addabbo, his old boss, called. Neglia had apparently called Addabbo in an effort to find out what the hell was going on. Addabbo asked Trimboli what was happening. Trimboli explained the investigation. Addabbo said he didn't have any problem with that, but added, "Be careful." Trimboli interpreted the caution as fatherly advice, not a threat.

A few minutes later, Steve Denlinger of LAMA called. Denlinger was not so cordial. He read Trimboli the riot act. "This is the flagship of the Hispanic enterprise movement! What are you doing?" the lobbyist screamed. Trimboli told Denlinger to talk to Representative Mitchell if he had a complaint.

Denlinger wasted no time setting up a meeting with the committee chairman. Deciding to turn the meeting into a show of support for Wedtech, the lobbyist put together a delegation of Hispanic businessmen to accompany him. On August 3, Denlinger and about ten members of LAMA trooped into Mitchell's office. Denlinger and the congressman traded speeches—Denlinger saying that Wedtech was a national model for minority businesses, Mitchell assuring the group he had no intention of treating Wedtech unfairly.

Formalities having been dispensed with, Mitchell reminded Denlinger he had agreed to meet with the lobbyist in person, not with a big crowd. The two men adjourned to the hallway for a franker discussion.

Strolling around the third floor of the Rayburn House Office Building, Denlinger expressed his concern that the investigation was a smear by a disgruntled competitor. News of a congressional probe could hurt Wedtech's ability to secure options on the pontoon contract. Mitchell, who'd begun to get reports from Trimboli about the content of the SBA files, responded that the issues were too substantive to dismiss out of hand. The investigation would continue.

Denlinger was bitterly disappointed, as was the gang in the Bronx when he relayed the decision. But one of the people who'd attended the Washington meeting, Fernando De Baca, was more sanguine.

"... Wedtech has made some very powerful and loyal friends.... This became evident immediately when the call for help was sounded to Wedtech's defense," the consultant wrote to Mariotta and Moreno. "You have earned the respect and admiration of many, many people on 'the Hill' and in the White House because of your honesty, straightforwardness and good work."

As Trimboli continued to comb through the boxes of files, he found some interesting items: correspondence from Nofziger and Bragg ... a memo from Neglia indicating White House involvement ... the approval of financial aid to Wedtech, apparently before the company even formally applied for it. . .

They got goddamn lots of money in goddamn short periods of time, Trimboli thought. He'd seen other people go through hell trying to get far lesser amounts out of the SBA.

Trimboli went back to Mitchell, this time accompanied by Major Clark, the staff director. There are questions, he told the congressman, about Wedtech's 8(a) eligibility, administration of its contracts, and possible favored treatment. It would be an enormous job to get to the bottom of everything. For starters he'd have to stop everything else he was doing and begin pulling people in for interviews.

Mitchell said he didn't want to shut down the committee. The best approach, the congressman decided, would be to write SBA administrator Sanders demanding an internal investigation.

Back at Wedtech, the gang began an effort to nip the investigation in the bud. Almost reflexively, the first stop was Mario Biaggi's office. Not wishing to overlook anyone who might help them quash the probe, the Wedtech executives also contacted Representative Garcia, two Hispanic congressman from the West, Senator D'Amato, Bob Wallach, and Mark Bragg.

Biaggi said he'd talk to Joe Addabbo and see what the two of them could do. At the same time, Mariotta sent a letter to Addabbo. The letter contained little more than a repetition of the Wedtech theme song: the company was taking people off welfare, putting them to work in the South Bronx, saving the taxpayers millions of dollars, etc.

Trimboli soon got another call from Joe Addabbo. This time the congressman wanted to see Trimboli in *his* office. Trimboli went, along with Clark. Trimboli laid out, more specifically this time, what he was on to. Addabbo stood up. "Go do what you got to do," the portly lawmaker said. To Trimboli that meant proceed with the investigation.

By now the Wedtech executives were really worried. The old techniques weren't getting any results. "It appeared we were doomed," Moreno recalled.

Then Richard Strum walked into Moreno's office.

Strum, a short, heavy-set, balding man who resembles the actor William Conrad of "Cannon" fame, was Wedtech's assistant vice-president for marketing. His path to the executive suite had been unusual, to say the least. Immediately before joining Wedtech in October 1983, he had been serving a four-year sentence for wire fraud at the Allenwood Federal Prison in Pennsylvania.

Strum's felony conviction hadn't dissuaded Fred Neuberger from recruiting him for Wedtech's marketing staff. Mariotta was always jabbering about how Wedtech was making productive citizens of ex-cons and junkies, so perhaps Neuberger thought that with Strum he was conducting his own exercise in rehabilitation. In all likelihood, however, Neuberger hired Strum because their concepts of "marketing" were so similar.

Strum didn't know anything about the House committee investigation when he entered Moreno's office in mid-September 1984, but he couldn't help notice Moreno's troubled countenance. When the fifty-six-year-old ex-con asked what was wrong, Moreno filled him in on the Mitchell investigation and explained the implications.

Hearing the name Mitchell, Strum asked if Moreno was referring to Parren Mitchell, the black congressman from Baltimore. Moreno said that was the guy. Something flashed in Strum's memory. His long-time friend and business associate, Tony Loscalzo, had mentioned the Mitchell family many times and had bragged about how close he was to them. Loscalzo was one of the "marketing reps" that Strum had brought with him when he was hired by Wedtech. Another of these reps was Len Lockhart, whose chief qualification seemed to be that he had been Strum's bunkmate at the "Club Fed" prison. After coming aboard, Loscalzo, Lockhart, and two other reps had kicked back to Strum some $150,000 of the "retainers" they received from Wedtech.

Without going into details, Strum mentioned to Moreno that he

151

had a contact who might be able to help the company. Moreno, growing desperate, was willing to try anything. Give him a call, he told Strum.

Strum went back to his office and called Loscalzo. Loscalzo gave him the phone number of Clarence M. Mitchell III and Michael B. Mitchell, the congressman's nephews. Over the next few days, Strum left repeated messages at the Mitchell brothers' office in Baltimore, but to no avail. They never called back.

The Mitchell brothers were scions of Baltimore's most powerful political family, a family sometimes referred to as the "black Kennedys" of Maryland. Their father, Clarence Mitchell, Jr. had been the Washington lobbyist for the NAACP and was so respected that he was known as the "101st senator" on Capitol Hill. He had led the law firm of Mitchell, Mitchell & Mitchell until his death in March 1984. Their mother, Juanita, was the first black woman to graduate from the University of Maryland Law School.

Clarence III and Michael, however, had never achieved the prominence of their parents or their uncle, Rep. Parren Mitchell. Clarence III was a member of the Maryland state senate. His political career had been stunted, however, by press reports that he'd failed to file income tax returns, by his arrest for carrying a loaded revolver in his luggage, and by his having been charged with housing code violations on rental properties he owned. Michael, six years younger than Clarence, was a lawyer and member of the Baltimore city council.

Unable to reach the Mitchells directly, Strum called Lenny Lockhart, his marketing consultant in the Baltimore-Washington area, and explained the problem. Yes, Lockhart knew the Mitchell brothers, too. After establishing that there might be some money in it for him, Lockhart agreed to help. Strum flew to Baltimore, where he met with Lockhart, Lockhart's father, and Maryland state senator Harry McGuirk at the Hyatt Regency. They assured him they were very friendly with the Mitchell brothers. To prove it, they took Strum to a phone, called Clarence Mitchell, and made a phone introduction of Strum and Mitchell. Strum chatted with Clarence Mitchell briefly, then rejoined the Lockharts and McGuirk in the cocktail lounge.

According to Strum, the Lockharts and McGuirk made it clear that they weren't willing to help Wedtech purely because of their commitment to minority business development. They told Strum they wanted $20,000 to help Wedtech with its problem, of which they would kick back $5,000 to Strum personally.

Loscalzo, however, advised Strum to deal directly with the Mitchells. So Strum arranged a meeting with Michael Mitchell at Tug's, a restaurant on the first floor of the downtown Baltimore office building in which the Mitchells had their office.

At Tug's, Strum explained to Mitchell the problem Wedtech was having with his uncle's congressional committee. Mitchell said he could help, but it would cost. The fee would take the form of a retainer to his law firm. Strum told Mitchell he would discuss it with the senior executives of Wedtech and get back to him.

That night, Strum called Loscalzo at his friend's favorite place of business, the Sundance Social Club at the Blackhawk Hotel in Davenport, Iowa. Strum filled Loscalzo in on his discussion with Michael Mitchell. Loscalzo told Strum that the Mitchells normally gave him one-third of the fees they received from his referrals. In this case, since Strum had helped set the whole deal up, Loscalzo offered to split his third with his old buddy.

Strum flew back to New York the next day to report on his activities to the Wedtech bosses. Mariotta was skeptical. What are they going to do for us? he wanted to know. Moreno, as always, was prepared to pay. Let's go to the meeting, he urged, and if it seems likely they can help us, we'll pay them.

The same day Strum and Michael Mitchell had met at Tug's, Tom Trimboli had finished composing his letter to Sanders. The letter was signed by Mitchell, stamped *Confidential*, and sent to the SBA. It asked twelve tough, pointed questions. They included: Had Wedtech received preferential treatment from SBA employees? Did the White House influence decisions? Had the SBA given prior approval to various changes in Wedtech's structure? Had the company disclosed all payments to consultants? Truthful answers to any of the questions could have brought about the downfall of Wedtech.

The letter to Sanders was quickly passed to Neglia, which at the time would have been rather like telling Oliver North to investigate the Iran-Contra affair. The SBA regional administrator promptly convened a strategy session with Ehrlich and Moreno at their favorite Italian restaurant, Villa Pensa, in lower Manhattan. Neglia pulled the letter from his jacket pocket and passed it over. Because the letter was marked *Confidential*, the SBA regional ad-

153

ministrator said he couldn't give Ehrlich and Moreno a copy. They would have to read the letter and return it to him.

Moreno and his cohorts were alarmed. Clearly, Mitchell's committee was getting too close for comfort.

Strum was at home when he received a call from Larry Shorten. Shorten was in a panic. The investigation was heating up. When are we meeting with the Mitchells? he wanted to know. Strum hung up and called Michael Mitchell; a meeting was arranged for the following Monday, October 1.

Strum flew to Baltimore and met Loscalzo at the airport. Mariotta and Moreno flew to Washington, met with Denlinger, and took a limousine to Baltimore. Everyone was to gather at Tug's. While they waited for the Mitchells to arrive, Moreno cautioned the unpredictable Mariotta about being too explicit in the discussions. The Mitchells might be wired to record their conversation, Moreno suggested.

When the Mitchells arrived, Moreno opened the meeting by explaining the seriousness of the situation for Wedtech. Michael Mitchell assured them the problem could be dealt with; Mariotta and Moreno beamed. Michael Mitchell reminded the Wedtech executives that his fee would be $50,000, disguised as the payment of a retainer to the law firm of Mitchell, Mitchell & Mitchell.

The disguise was fairly transparent. Mitchell, Mitchell & Mitchell was a small general practice firm that handled such things as personal injuries, bad checks, and drunk-driving cases. It did not have large corporate clients. The Wedtech payment would be by far the biggest the law firm had received, and all too likely to stand out like a sore thumb. Nevertheless, papers were drawn up designating the firm as Wedtech's new "corporate counsel for the mid-Atlantic area."

The Wedtech group returned to New York that night. The next day, the accounts payable department was directed to issue a check for $50,000 made out to the Mitchells' law firm. The check was then given to Mario Rosado, Jr., the eighteen-year-old son of the former "pastor" of the evangelical chapel at Welbilt. Rosado, Jr. was told to deliver the check by hand to the law firm in Baltimore, which he did. No one had mentioned to Mariotta and Moreno, of course, that a portion of the fee would be kicked back to Loscalzo and Strum. A few days later, Loscalzo got his one-third "referral fee" from the Mitchells and gave half, $8,333.33, to Strum.

Shortly after the $50,000 payment, the investigation went into a lull. Just why remains something of a mystery. The SBA clearly had reasons of its own for trying to duck the issue. At SBA headquarters in Washington, the letter from Mitchell was regarded as a political gambit designed to embarrass the Reagan administration just before the 1984 elections. Sanders believed that Parren Mitchell wanted to focus attention on what Mitchell regarded as Republican favoritism of Hispanics at the expense of blacks. The SBA administrator didn't want his staff spending hours and hours to provide Mitchell with election-year ammunition.

"If they want answers to all these questions, they can come in here and go through all the records, but we don't have time to search out all their questions and get back to them in two weeks," Sanders told his staff.

At the regional office in New York, Peter Neglia was also all too willing to let the matter rest.

Given the SBA's reluctance to investigate, the question then becomes why the congressional committee did not exert more pressure. There is no direct evidence that the Mitchell brothers ever contacted their uncle about the matter, or that Parren Mitchell ever ordered the committee staff to back off. It may just be that the investigation fell through the cracks as the 1984 congressional session came to an end and members went home to campaign for re-election.

In the eyes of the Wedtech executives, however, the $50,000 payment had done the trick. So pleased were they, in fact, that a few months later they decided again to avail themselves of the services of the Mitchell brothers. This time they wanted help not in fending off an investigation of themselves, but in initiating the investigation of a rival.

The rival's name was Ernie Green. Green had played professional football for the Cleveland Browns before he became a businessman. Because Green was black, his firm, Ernie Green Industries of Dayton, Ohio, was certified to participate in the 8(a) program. Green was also a very capable businessman; he had been named Subcontractor of the Year by General Motors Corp. Ernie Green didn't know it, but he had a problem. His problem was that his company and Wedtech wanted the same contract.

The army's Ammunition and Munitions Command at the Rock Island Arsenal in Illinois was about to award a potentially lucrative contract to manufacture chemical decontamination canisters.

Unfortunately for Wedtech, Ernie Green had heard about the contract first and had already initiated a "search letter." If approved by the command, the letter would have the effect of setting the contract aside for the 8(a) program and awarding it to Green. As a capable manufacturer and first in line, Green clearly had the inside track.

How was the Wedtech gang to deal with Green? Strum and Loscalzo had a brainstorm. Remember how worried they'd been about the Mitchell committee investigation? What if the committee were to launch an investigation of Ernie Green? Think of what it would do to his chances of winning the contract . . .

Strum's superiors at Wedtech thought the idea brilliant. So what that they'd be smearing the reputation of a talented minority businessman? As Larry Shorten put it, "All we cared about was the contract. Ernie Green could have been the man in the moon."

Without a shred of evidence, it was decided that the investigation should be based on an allegation that Green was a front for white owners. Strum and Loscalzo flew to Baltimore and met again with Clarence and Michael Mitchell. The Mitchells assured them that what they were requesting could be arranged—for a fee, of course. As before, the fee was $50,000. Strum told the Mitchells he'd discuss it with the senior executives back in the Bronx.

Back at 595 Gerard, it was agreed that another $50,000 would be a small price to pay if it led to a multimillion-dollar contract award. Another check was issued. This time, however, the results were not as positive. There is no indication that the promised investigation was ever initiated and, in fact, Wedtech did not get the contract. But neither did Ernie Green. The contract was eventually awarded to a third party.

Back in Washington, meanwhile, Tom Trimboli was getting impatient. The new Congress had convened, and he still hadn't received any response to the twelve questions in the letter of September 25. Tired of getting put off, he met on March 6, 1985, with Robert Turnbull, the SBA's associate deputy administrator. Turnbull revealed that the SBA's central office hadn't yet gotten around to investigating the issues raised in the earlier letter.

Trimboli was furious. He drafted a new letter, demanding answers to the twelve questions. The letter, dated March 7, was stamped *Confidential*, signed by Parren Mitchell, and sent to Sanders.

"I wish to stress that I consider the matters raised by the Wed-

156

tech case to be exceedingly grave," the letter concluded. "I can only draw negative inferences from the failure of your staff to initiate this review. Accordingly, please be advised that this committee expects to receive your full, written report within the next thirty (30) days."

As word of the new letter reached the Bronx, the Wedtech executives panicked. What the hell's going on? they demanded of Strum. We've paid all this money and the investigation is back.

Strum called Michael Mitchell. Mitchell told him to relax. The problem was the "unguided missile" on the committee, Trimboli. Quashing the investigations was just a formality, crossing the *t*'s and dotting the *i*'s. Seeing an opportunity to shake more loot from the Wedtech money tree, Mitchell added that it would take another $10,000 to make sure things stayed under control.

The Wedtech executives were understandably annoyed. Guariglia muttered something about extortion. Still, not making the payment would be too risky. Another check was issued.

On April 4, 1985, Sanders responded to the letter of March 7 with a five-page letter of his own; answers to the original twelve questions had been drafted by SBA staffers and were forwarded to Peter Neglia. The answers were a masterful combination of lies, obfuscation, and doublespeak. The bottom line: everything was fine. Every action and activity of the SBA relative to Wedtech had been proper and appropriate.

With that, the investigation went into remission. Neglia assured the Wedtech crowd that the matter would be buried in the files and never see the light of day. Wedtech had dodged another bullet.

157

# 15

## "The Sprouting Whale"

**A**s 1985 began, the Wedtech gang had good reason to feel smugly pleased. The $51.5 million option for the pontoon contract would soon be in hand. The Mitchell investigation appeared quiet. The company's backlog of contracts was significant enough to prompt glowing reviews by Wall Street analysts. To paraphrase President Reagan's re-election theme, it was morning in the South Bronx (at least at 595 Gerard Avenue). In fact, the whole Wedtech crew would soon be going to Washington to attend Reagan's second inaugural.

The company officers first heard about the invitations from Bernard Ehrlich. In late 1984, Ehrlich bustled into the executive suites, announcing that everyone had been invited to attend the inaugural festivities. The Wedtech executives—visions of waltzing with Nancy Reagan and conducting intimate tête-à-têtes with cabinet officers dancing in their heads—were perfect foils for Ehrlich. Trying to mask their delight with an air of world-weary sophistication, they asked Ehrlich how he had managed to get the invitations. Pressed, Ehrlich acknowledged that the invitations had come through the New York State Republican Committee and were a reward for the money the Wedtech officers had raised for Reagan's re-election campaign.

Ehrlich also let drop that Wedtech was going to be expected to pay for a few people to attend the inaugural in addition to its officers. He gave Larry Shorten a list. It included Mr. and Mrs. Richard Biaggi, Mr. and Mrs. Peter Neglia, Mr. and Mrs. Joseph Neglia (Peter's father), Mr. Zack Gertler (one of Ehrlich's close friends) and guest, and, of course, General and Mrs. Bernard Ehrlich.

Guariglia and Shorten were left with the task of making the reservations and taking care of the payments. Guariglia handled the hotel rooms. He had his secretary, Margie Colon, make reservations for everybody at the Sheraton-Washington Hotel on Woodley Road in northwest Washington. Ehrlich had pointed out that the reservation for Peter Neglia could not be made in his own name; Neglia was, after all, still a government employee who was not supposed to accept favors from private interests. Guariglia's secretary, unused to concocting phony names, made the reservations for the Neglias in the name of Mr. and Mrs. Marguerita Colon.

The hotel rooms were not the only expense Wedtech would have to bear. Not wanting to miss any of the fun, the gang bought tickets, costing at least $4,800, for the Inaugural Ceremony, the Inaugural Ball, the Vice-Presidential Gala, and the Presidential Gala. Wedtech also paid $5,000 for a table at the Hispanic Inaugural Ball and another $1,725 for limousines. It had turned into a very expensive event for the company—and it would become more expensive before it was over.

Wedtech's senior management cut a striking presence at the inaugural: John Mariotta, the hero for the eighties, and his wife, Jennie; Fred Neuberger, fifty-seven, and his third wife, Eileen, thirty-eight, with their nine-month-old adopted daughter, Lisa, and her Hispanic nanny; Mario Moreno and his long-time companion, Caridad Vazquez; Tony Guariglia and his wife, Cynthia; Larry Shorten and girlfriend (Shorten was separated from his wife at the time).

The group tried its best to maintain a façade of elegance and sophistication but wasn't always successful. On the way to one of the balls, for instance, Fred Neuberger suddenly ordered the limousine driver to stop at a convenience store. Neuberger jumped from the limo and, in tuxedo and black patent shoes, dashed into the store. He emerged with a box of Pampers for his baby daughter back at the Sheraton.

Frigid weather gripped the nation's capital that inaugural weekend; the temperature plunged to four below zero and the wind chill was close to thirty below. It was so cold, in fact, that the inau-

159

gural parade had to be cancelled. But the weather didn't put a damper on the Wedtech group's celebrations. On Sunday, the company threw a Super Bowl bash in one of the hotel suites, complete with big screen TV, open bar, and plentiful snacks and sandwiches.

Only John Mariotta, it seemed, was worried that Wedtech was getting too big for its britches. "Be careful," he recalled someone warning him at the inauguration. "The sprouting whale gets harpooned." (Mariotta often spouted malapropisms.)

The inaugural weekend wasn't all fun and festivities for Wedtech. There was also business to be discussed. Naturally enough, it was illicit business.

The time had come for Peter Neglia to present his bill for services rendered. For two years, the slender bureaucrat had been essential to the company's efforts to win government contracts. Without his help, Wedtech probably could not have stayed in the 8(a) program or been awarded the two major contracts it had received. In return, the company had bought him some meals and taken him to the inauguration—pretty small recompense for the risks Neglia had taken. Now Wedtech was going to be asked to do more.

Early in the weekend, Ehrlich, Neglia, and Moreno were having drinks at the Sheraton. Carrying water for Wedtech hadn't harmed Neglia's career; in fact, he had recently been promoted to chief of staff at the SBA's national headquarters in Washington. Ehrlich announced that the time had come to discuss compensation for Neglia, particularly the possibility of giving him some stock.

Moreno pointed out that it is difficult for a public company to give away its stock. He suggested stock options instead. One advantage of options, Moreno continued, was that you didn't have to put any money down right now. You paid only when you exercised the options. With the future looking so bright, the price of Wedtech stock could go to $50, maybe as high as $100, a share. If Neglia got 20,000 options to buy Wedtech stock at $20 per share, and the price went to $50, he would make $600,000.

That all sounded nice enough, but Ehrlich wasn't through. Sometime in the not-too-distant future, he said, Neglia was planning to leave government service and go to work in the private sector. In fact, Neglia already had an offer: from the law firm of Biaggi & Ehrlich. The law firm was to pay Neglia $100,000; it would be nice if Wedtech were to provide half of that. Moreno indicated he didn't think that would be a problem.

At about this point, the threesome was joined by Peter Neglia's father, Joseph, the Brooklyn Republican boss. Ehrlich and Moreno, wanting to share the good news, told Joe Neglia they were making plans to take care of Peter once he left government.

"We never forget," said Moreno, nobly.

Joe Neglia played the role of proud father perfectly. He indicated his gratitude and his pleasure that Peter was going to continue to associate with such a fine group of people.

By the time of the Super Bowl party on Sunday, Mariotta, Neuberger, Shorten, and Guariglia had all been briefed on the preliminary commitment to give Neglia 20,000 stock options and to pay 50 percent of his salary when he left government. Shorten alone had his doubts. He might not know anything more about ethics than that they were usually inconvenient, but might it not be considered unethical to grant stock options to a public official whose actions could affect the stock price? No problem, said Ehrlich. We'll put them in the name of one of Neglia's friends.

On the night of the inauguration, the whole gang dined at an Italian restaurant, Il Giardino, on 21st Street. The Wedtech officers were all there with their spouses or "companions," as were the company's ever-expanding group of hangers-on. There must have been two dozen people in all. When the check came, it went on the Wedtech tab: another $1,926.

By now the thrill of the inaugural weekend had begun to pale. The hotel . . . the tickets . . . the cars . . . the Neglia payoff . . . the restaurant check. The members of the Wedtech party were beginning to feel that they had been invited only to handle the logistics and pay the bills. For all the money the company was spending on limousines, John Mariotta—the chairman of the board, for chrissakes—couldn't get the use of one when he wanted it. After his wife questioned him about this, Mariotta complained to Moreno and Shorten: "Everybody's always got their hands in our pocket and they should at least treat us like human beings."

Moreno, always quick to jump to the defense of those he was bribing, disagreed. These are "very important people," he contended. "We can't afford to have them upset with Wedtech."

At the time of the inaugural in early 1985, cash was flowing through the F.H.J. account in record amounts. In 1984, almost $1.2 million of money stolen from the company was deposited in the account; the Wedtech executives took out almost $1.1 million. The

161

major contracts were producing a steady stream of cash. From the pontoon contract, Wedtech had received $9.2 million in progress payments, the engine contract had produced $1.3 million in progress payments, and the contracts for parts for the M–113 armored personnel carrier had yielded $23.6 million in progress payments.

Of course, the company was terribly behind the required delivery schedules for all of the contracts; the difference between the progress payments received and the value of the products delivered—the amount Wedtech owed the government—was $5.2 million. But the financial statements showed that the company was making a profit, so it had been able to sell $40 million in bonds in the summer of 1984 in a second public offering. The proceeds from the bond sale plus the progress payments equalled a lot of funds from which to steal.

Wedtech's executives began leading lifestyles befitting their newfound wealth. But the more they spent, the more they needed. Their greed had become insatiable.

The side of the Wedtech parking area reserved for the executives began to resemble a luxury car dealer's lot. For management and its cronies, Wedtech was leasing seven Mercedes, four Lincolns and four Cadillacs.

Perhaps believing that the group that steals together ought to vacation together, Mariotta, Neuberger, Moreno, Guariglia, and Ceil Lewis all purchased homes near the water in Apollo Beach, Florida, about twenty-five miles from Tampa. They also gambled together: Mariotta, Moreno, and Guariglia bought seven apartments at the Ritz-Carlton in Atlantic City for about $2 million.

The executives had varying approaches to the gaming tables. Neuberger stuck to blackjack, usually at the $50 minimum tables and limiting his bets to $200 a hand. This was enough to prompt the casinos to give him free rooms, food, and occasionally a limousine.

Guariglia and Moreno were the real high rollers. Guariglia played blackjack, occasionally roulette. He enjoyed the thrill of high stakes, often playing at the $100 tables. As one of Wedtech's senior executives, he could take frequent "business" trips to the Bahamas, Las Vegas, Puerto Rico, and London—places in which he could indulge his passion for casinos.

Moreno got the red carpet treatment at the Atlantic City casinos, and a $60,000 credit line. No wonder. He would later claim that his gambling losses in the mid–1980s amounted to $1.1 million.

162

Caridad Vazquez generally stuck to the slot machines, but Moreno enjoyed the more sophisticated games. It wasn't unusual for him to gamble from dusk to dawn. The weekend of November 23 and 24, 1985, he gambled at the Tropicana from 8:10 P.M. to 5:40 A.M., taking a break from 9:55 P.M. to 1:35 A.M. His average bets were between $75 and $150. The most Moreno ever won in a single session was about $50,000; he once dropped $100,000.

For the money that didn't end up with the casinos, each member of the Wedtech team pursued a different investment strategy.

Mariotta was perhaps the most conservative. Jennie Mariotta controlled the family finances, and since she was a cautious investor, much of their wealth was invested in real estate—in addition to their homes in Scarsdale and Florida, they bought a condo in Puerto Rico decorated with Oriental furnishings—and certificates of deposit. Still, they led a life of expensive meals and frequent travel. "If you travel like you are well off, people will accept you," Mariotta would explain. He strove mightily for acceptance, dining at company expense at such restaurants as the Caribe Hilton in Puerto Rico, and the Rainbow Room, the Waldorf-Astoria, and the Palm in New York. His average restaurant tab, invariably charged to Wedtech, was about $180. With dining habits like these, Mariotta's weight reached some 210 pounds on his five-nine frame, and his double chin became even more pronounced.

Fred Neuberger was far less cautious. He did not invest for the long-term. As one of his lawyers later put it, "Fred Neuberger is a survivor. He lives for the next 24 hours. For him, the future is tomorrow." For a man who had reported adjusted gross income of $13,115 in 1975, being at Wedtech a decade later must have been like winning the lottery. Neuberger had Gold and Platinum American Express cards, a gold Mastercard, and three Visa cards. He played the stock market (oil company stocks were a favorite), invested in other businesses (including a shipyard in Great Britain and a safe company in Israel), and acquired a multinational real estate portfolio. Neuberger had so many houses, in fact, that he couldn't keep track of the keys to all of them.

Neuberger's real estate holdings included, at one time or another, a townhouse on fashionable Sutton Place; a home in Weehawken, New Jersey; four houses in Apollo Beach, Florida; ski houses in the East (Windham, New York) and the West (Jackson Hole, Wyoming); a condo in Atlantic City; a co-op in Forest Hills; an apartment at 111 East 85th Street in Manhattan; twenty acres

163

in Titusville, Florida; interests in four properties in the city of Long Beach, New York; and a house on Priory Lane in London. One of Neuberger's prize possessions was a forty-foot Hatteras yacht, worth about $200,000, which he docked at the Norwalk Cove Marina in Connecticut during the summer and at Pier 66 in Ft. Lauderdale during the winter. Neuberger kept a small motorcycle on board, a 350 Honda. In a romantic gesture, the boat was christened the *Ee Vee*, after the initials of his wife's maiden name, Eileen Vanora (which was about as far as his fidelity at sea extended).

The newly rich Neuberger was not much of a yachtsman. He'd show up for an expedition carrying a straw basket and wearing knee socks—looking for all the world like a tourist visiting the Bahamas. The first time he tried to operate the boat himself, he smashed the top against a drawbridge. Neuberger apparently thought the bridge would open automatically as he approached, like a door at the supermarket.

Neuberger's lust for money was matched only by his lust for women. Or, as one friend summarized Neuberger's philosophy, "Money buys pussy." This friend viewed Neuberger as an insecure man who needed constant sexual conquests to feed his ego and provide self assurance. Moreno once described Neuberger's lunch hour visits to the hookers of Hunt's Point this way: "He would leave, he was like a panther in heat. When he came back, he would be peaceful and tranquil."

Aware that his sex appeal went about as far as his bank account, Neuberger sought to enhance his attractiveness to women by becoming a superb dancer and skier. He also tried to do something about his physical appearance. His costly hair transplants were notably unsuccessful, however, leaving only scattered plugs of frizzled hair adorning his scalp. Nor did all the expensive clothes and jewelry he was buying help. He continued to look dumpy. Still, he managed to find plenty of women attracted to dumpy rich men.

The yacht proved to be a particularly useful in satisfying Neuberger's sexual appetites. In New York, he entertained a series of girlfriends aboard the *Ee Vee*, sometimes in full view of the Neubergers' apartment overlooking the East River. In Florida, Neuberger would hang out at Shooter's, a nightclub near the dock, pick up women, and bring them back to the boat. One former Wedtech employee recalls a girl knocking on the door of the boat and asking where Neuberger was. "He owes me a Camaro," the young lady explained plaintively. "Freddie told me if I spend the day and night with him, he'd buy me a car."

Neuberger's style of seduction wasn't terribly subtle. John Mariotta recalled his partner in action:

> One time I saw him. He goes to the woman at the coat check in this hotel. Immediately he says, "Oh, I own two companies. I own two boats. I have so many cars. I have so many houses. By the way, my name is Fred Neuberger. What are you doing tonight?" I said, "Why can't you say you're a simple dishwasher and find out what love is really all about?" He says, "Hey, I just want to rent the thing. I'm not interested in inheriting the thing." They were not in love with Freddie. They were in love with his money. I guess Freddie never knew what love really is. And he does not care to have love. That would conflict, psychologically, [with his view] that this world is not right.

Jennie Mariotta had a blunter and less complex explanation of Fred Neuberger's success with women: "He's a good bullshitter." He must have been, because his office files contained missives from various women bullshitting him right back. One example, scrawled on a brown paper bag:

> Hi Love . . . You are incredibly good to women. Only a man who truly loves and appreciates the female in the world could be so charming and wise, not to mention gracious and entertaining . . . Men electrify me, put me on a tight rope, take me into the jungle. You do all those things, but gently, so that it is enjoyable instead of tedious and mind-wrenching. You give love so beautifully, having come to know yourself so well . . . Don't you ever travel to Seattle anymore? Or LA or Frisco?

Even Neuberger would joke about his popularity with the opposite sex. "I must be a good-looking guy," he told one Wedtech employee. "Look at all the girls I have."

As for Mario Moreno, much of the loot he didn't gamble away went into the house he occupied at 3337 Sedgwick Avenue in the Bronx. He claimed that his companion, Caridad Vazquez, had

165

bought the house in 1981 for $85,000, and indeed from the outside it was nothing special: a squat former boardinghouse with a red brick front obscured by three spruce trees. Inside, it became a textbook example of overbuilding the neighborhood.

Moreno spent approximately $1 million on renovations to the $85,000 house. At the rear, he built a $200,000 greenhouse, furnished it like a lanai and, to complete the effect, added a miniature tropical rain forest along the edges. One level down, Moreno had a team of workers (most of whom would have probably scattered to the winds at the mention of the words *green card*) chisel an indoor swimming pool out of the bedrock. This cost another $500,000. When it was done, Moreno possessed what was undoubtedly the only indoor grotto in the Bronx. The grotto was heated by the sun-warmed air circulated from the rain forest above. Lights shining through the turquoise water shimmered off the chiseled walls and ceiling. (Although Vazquez was technically the owner of the house, there was little doubt for whose pleasure the pool was built: Caridad couldn't swim.)

Adjacent to the grotto were the walk-in wine cellar, the media room equipped with a big screen TV, stereo and video games, a playroom, and an office. On the first floor, Oriental furnishings competed for attention with Art Nouveau. Decorated according to the concept that if one is good, two are better, the rooms were crammed with lacquered and inlaid Chinese furniture, Lalique vases, and hyperdetailed scrolls. The dining room was dominated by a huge table whose glass top was supported by the arched necks of four painted swans.

The exterior featured a garden with seminude statuettes and stone lions atop brick columns. The whole compound was wired with an elaborate intercom system and surrounded with a black wrought-iron fence. Puzzled neighbors assumed Moreno must have been some sort of Colombian drug kingpin; Moreno would explain he was just a successful businessman showing his commitment to the rejuvenation of the Bronx.

Even with all this, Moreno still had money left over to spend on a $250,000 home for his son in Puerto Rico, an apartment in Greenwich Village, an interest in a 4,000-square-foot farmhouse on 80 acres in the upstate New York community of Chatham, a four-bedroom apartment in Bal Harbour, Florida, and an interest in a Long Island City apartment building. He also owned a majority interest in the Trocadero, a catering company and dance hall in

Manhattan, and a condominium in Nanuet, New York, occupied by his estranged wife.

Tony Guariglia also went into real estate in a big way, though unlike Moreno he chose new construction over remodeling. A couple of weeks after the inaugural, on February 8, 1985, he paid $325,000 for a wooded parcel of land in the fashionable village of Matinecock on Long Island's North Shore near Oyster Bay. There he began building a home reflecting his new economic position in life.

An estate at the end of High Ridge Lane, set back a suitable distance from the road, its style was contemporary, with a flagstone front, wood siding, and a cedar roof with numerous skylights. The blueprints included a three-car garage (to shelter a Mercedes, Jaguar, and another auto) and a large wood deck out back. The interior of the 12,093-square-foot house featured a bowling alley, a $26,600 swimming pool enclosed with redwood, a cabana, an entertainment room, a spiral staircase, and bleached wood cabinets. The utilities were enough to service a small hotel—eight heating zones, two furnaces, and two 70-gallon water heaters.

Guariglia's estate would ultimately be worth $2.4 million. Even with his 1985 salary of $189,423 plus all he could steal, Guariglia needed help financing the construction. For that, he turned to Pat Simone, who always seemed to have plenty of cash at his disposal. Simone gave him a loan for more than $1 million. While the estate was being constructed, Guariglia and his wife continued to live in their half-million dollar home on High Pound Road in Jericho, New York. The Guariglias also bought a condo along the boardwalk in Atlantic City worth about $265,000.

Though not in the same womanizing league as Neuberger, Guariglia was also cheating on his wife. He made about twenty trips to London during his tenure at Wedtech, about a half-dozen of those on the Concorde at $6,000 per round trip. Most of the extramarital affairs took place in London, "one or two" in the United States.

The fifth and final member of Wedtech's senior executive team, Larry Shorten, was also quick to spend his ill-gotten gains. Shorten bought a luxury apartment at 630 First Avenue for $591,000 and later a weekend home in Connecticut for about $160,000. At one point, he had more than $125,000 hidden in a cardboard box in a closet at his condo. He drove a Mercedes 380SEL leased by the company, bought suits costing close to $1,000 at Barneys, and dined at fine restaurants. Unfortunately for

167

the Shorten family budget, his wife, Susan, also had expensive tastes—perhaps in retaliation for his philandering. In one year alone, she is said to have spent more than $150,000 on clothing.

Shorten's career did not keep pace with his income, however. More of a follower than a leader, Shorten was relegated to minor roles within the company. Mariotta berated him regularly, once calling him "a plant, good for nothing but standing still and being watered." Neuberger sneeringly referred to him as the "vice-president of the hallways" because he seemed to spend most of his time strolling up and down the corridors. Guariglia once remarked that "If Larry would spend less time trying to fuck everything in a skirt, he might be able to get his job done." Still, Shorten's four years with the company would bring him $3.1 million. He could afford to live without the others' esteem.

# 16

## Labor Pains

**W**ith such conspicuous executive lifestyles widening the gap between the managers and workers, it is not surprising that the first half of 1985 at Wedtech was dominated by labor problems.

The first major incident occurred shortly after the inauguration. It would go down in Wedtech lore as the day of the wildcat strike.

The episode began in the morning when an altercation broke out between a foreman and a worker at 1049 Washington Avenue, the old corporate headquarters. The worker claimed that the foremen had hit him. The worker went to see the plant manager, Vijayan Pazhangaitu, at 595 Gerard Avenue to argue his case. Pazhangaitu, born in southern India, had been with the company for several years. His name, too complicated even for the heterogenous group working at Wedtech, had been anglicized to V. J. Nair. A diminutive Indian known as a tough disciplinarian, Nair was not the ideal judge before whom a worker would choose to appear with an appeal. After consulting with the in-house attorney, Nora McCarthy, and talking to the union representative by phone, Nair suspended the worker for three days, pending an arbitration hearing.

The worker, having gotten no satisfaction from Nair, marched downstairs and told his story to the shop steward. The story of the dispute spread like wildfire through the shop floor. Soon workers had quit their machines and were gathered in little groups throughout the plant, excitedly exchanging rumors. They began threatening a wildcat strike. Nair recognized that the situation was getting out of control, so he went upstairs to the executive offices looking for help. Mariotta was at the dentist for root canal work. That left Fred Neuberger in charge.

By now it was lunch hour. A union official, Frank Casalino, had arrived on the scene, as had the New York city police. Casalino went immediately to Neuberger's office and asked what the plan was. Neuberger said he was going to fire anyone who walked out. Casalino, rather than argue the union member's case, told Neuberger a wildcat strike could actually be a golden opportunity for management. If those guys walked out, he explained, they would in essence be nullifying the union contract. In that case, management would be able to fire anyone it wanted—deadwood, troublemakers, anti-union agitators, senior guys with high wages. Neuberger decided that Casalino's reasoning was splendid. He headed downstairs to the factory floor.

Neuberger began to address the workers. Curt to the point of rudeness in the best of times, Neuberger was not the one to defuse a potential riot. His speech was short and abrasive. Anyone who didn't come back to work after lunch, he said, would be dismissed for cause. The workers were furious. Their machismo was being tested. An angry undertone of muttering turned into defiant shouts. They'd shut the place down and starve before they'd let Neuberger and Nair treat them this way. Neuberger and Casalino retreated upstairs.

Just as the situation was tipping toward violence, Mariotta returned from the dentist. Seeing the squad cars in front of the building, he dashed in the main entrance, up the stairs, and past the Defense Department plaque proclaiming Wedtech to be a quality contractor. Ceil Lewis, in a state of near panic, filled Mariotta in on the morning's events. "John, you've got to stop it!" she implored.

Mariotta headed down the hallway, where he encountered the raving Neuberger.

"Come back here, you moron!" Neuberger screamed as Mariotta went right by him. "You don't know what you're doing!"

"Fred, if I'm a moron, what are you doing with me?" Mariotta shot back. "For heaven's sake, I'm going to stop this thing."

Mariotta proceeded to the factory floor. As the workers saw him, they began murmuring, "Here's the boss, here's the boss." Elbowing his way through the mob of excited workers, Mariotta felt "like Moses splitting the water," as he later put it. Mariotta climbed onto a box. In his high-pitched voice, he began to address the workers in Spanish.

"Please, fellows," he urged, "calm yourselves. I know there has been abuse. I know because I have been abused myself. I, too, am a Puerto Rican. When they spit in your eyes, they are spitting in my eyes. You are my people!"

The workers roared their approval.

"No one is going to fire one of my people!"

More cheers.

"If anyone is getting fired, it is the foreman and the managers!"

Pandemonium. By now the workers were chanting Mariotta's name, beside themselves with the euphoria of a victory over management. The strike was over.

Back upstairs, Mariotta was thrilled with his performance. The rest of management, and the Teamsters local leaders, were appalled. Mariotta had trampled the arbitration procedure, undercut lines of authority, and squandered a golden opportunity to streamline the company.

Mariotta and Neuberger were soon nose-to-nose over the morning's events. Neuberger called Mariotta an idiot.

"Freddie, you used to be able to play cards with the fellows," Mariotta said. "Now you've got a little bit of money and you cannot communicate with the people that have made you rich."

Then, hearing that reporters from the New York papers were on their way to cover the story, Mariotta closed the plant and sent the workers home for the afternoon.

Nora McCarthy, the in-house counsel who'd helped fashion management's response to the work stoppage, quit in disgust after Mariotta berated her for her role. After tempers had cooled, Mariotta came to her office and handed her a $5,000 check, telling her to forget about what had happened. McCarthy looked at the check, shook her head, and tore it up. "No," she said. "I'm leaving." She walked out and never came back.

V. J. Nair didn't have the same choice offered to him. Within a week of the wildcat strike, he was forced to resign. A year later, with his manufacturing management skills in demand and changes made in upper management, Nair was rehired.

In the aftermath of the wildcat strike, the union leaders decided

171

Mariotta was an uncontrollable screwball. To strengthen the union, the other managers agreed to let the union win some arbitrations for a change. They also embarked on a strategy of promoting troublemakers out of the union into management positions, just to be able to fire them after they'd lost their union protection.

The next labor crisis arose just a short time later at 350 Gerard Avenue, a large three-story structure that overlooked the Major Deegan Expressway where it rounded the southern tip of the Bronx. Formerly the site of a commercial laundry, it had been vacant for several years and, as happens to empty buildings in the Bronx, it had been vandalized and heavily damaged. In an effort to halt the deterioration, Wedtech decided to turn a couple of guard dogs loose in the vast empty space. Within a few days, the head of security went to check on the two German shepherds. He entered the building, prepared to cope with a pair of snarling dogs. He heard nothing. After a few moments of eerie silence, he discovered why the dogs hadn't reacted to his presence. The resident rats had not taken kindly to sharing the building with the dogs, and there had been a struggle for control. The dogs had killed a good many rats, some of them the size of cats, but there had been too many rats for the dogs to handle and eventually the rats had prevailed. Both dogs were found dead, their bloated, half-eaten corpses testimony to who ruled the animal kingdom in the South Bronx.

When Wedtech bought the building, it needed more than a thorough extermination of the resident vermin. Extensive repairs and renovations were required before it could be used as a manufacturing facility. Mario Moreno suggested using an electrical contractor called Adequate Power and Lighting. Moreno contended that Wedtech needed a company that understood its way of doing business—in other words, one willing to make kickbacks to the Wedtech officers. Moreno knew Adequate was that kind of business because it was owned by his brother-in-law, Reynaldo Berney.

Moreno and Berney had great plans. In the flush of the inaugural celebrations, Moreno had discussed some of these plans with the Neglias and Ehrlich. Berney, he said, was Hispanic and could get Adequate Power qualified as an 8(a) company. Ehrlich chipped in the thought that with all the repair work that was going to be done on the New York City subway system in the next ten years, Berney's status as a minority contractor could enable him to generate a lot of business. Why, it might turn out to be even bigger than Wedtech! Ehrlich gushed.

When the Wedtech officers met to discuss ways to handle the nonelectrical renovations, Mariotta asked Guariglia how much they could pad the construction costs. Guariglia's estimate was $1 million. Guariglia also mentioned that because Wedtech was a public company with an obligation to its shareholders, the officers would have to make it appear they had awarded the work to the lowest bidder. He had a ready answer to this problem. *He* had a relative in the construction business who, for a price, could be persuaded to provide "proper" bids.

Reynaldo Berney had another suggestion as to whom Wedtech should hire as a general contractor. Berney knew a man who owned construction companies and could be counted on to do business "the Wedtech way." The man was Mahmoud Yaghoubi. Berney neglected to mention that Yaghoubi, like himself, was Moreno's brother-in-law.

"Moe" Yaghoubi was an Iranian immigrant with a dark complexion, thick glasses, and a receding hairline. Like Mariotta, he was living in the affluent Westchester County suburb of Scarsdale. On Moreno's recommendation, he was chosen as the chief contractor for all the work to be done at 350 Gerard.

To make it appear that more than one firm was benefitting from the millions of dollars that Wedtech would spend, Yaghoubi created four companies—Only Mechanical, Builtmore, Today's Construction, and Dimo. Unbeknownst to his partners, Mario Moreno owned 20 percent of these companies. Reynaldo Berney also owned 20 percent, and Yaghoubi owned the other 60 percent.

With this setup, the senior executives could begin to bleed Wedtech in earnest. From 1984 through 1986, Yaghoubi's four companies received about $8 million from Wedtech. Some $2.6 million of that was kicked back to the Wedtech officers. Moreno, of course, was benefitting at both ends.

There was, in fact, a strange lack of honor among the Wedtech thieves. Guariglia and Shorten, not to be outdone by Moreno, arranged a scam of their own. Guariglia would intercept the padded invoices coming in from Dimo Construction and would then substitute a phony invoice for a higher amount. Through various manipulations, Guariglia and Shorten would pay the original Dimo invoice and keep the difference for themselves. The arrangement netted them some $200,000 each in eighteen months.

173

Although they could never catch him at it, the others suspected that Neuberger was siphoning off money that was being sent to Wedtech's subsidiary in Israel, Carmo. Because Neuberger's cronies controlled Carmo, however, it was hard for Moreno, Guariglia, and Shorten to get a handle on what was going on. Later, when Neuberger learned of his three partners' own schemes, he just laughed: "They ought to get a medal. They're better thieves than I am."

Of course Wedtech had to account for all the money it was pouring into renovation work. The company reported that some $11.25 million of improvements had been made to 350 Gerard. That led to an appraiser issuing a written report that the building's "market value" was $14.6 million. The appraisal led, in turn, to Wedtech being able to issue inflated reports of the value of its assets and borrow more money against those assets than they were worth. It later turned out that the building's actual market value was $5.7 million.

Understandably, with so much money at stake and going into so many pockets, not everything went smoothly at 350 Gerard. In early spring of 1985, Moreno received an urgent call from Yaghoubi. Representatives from Local 17 of the carpenters' union had appeared at the job site and were protesting the use of nonunion labor. Moreno told Yaghoubi to have them come to 595 Gerard to talk to him.

Two representatives soon showed up at corporate headquarters. They were ushered into Moreno's office where Guariglia, Shorten, and Neuberger joined them. Moreno offered to hire four union workers at 350 Gerard. This was not what the union reps had in mind. They threatened to close down not only 350 Gerard but also 595 Gerard. To emphasize that he was serious, one of the Local 17 reps, who was shouting by now, warned that "some people could get hurt."

The Wedtech executives couldn't help but feel this was a little unfair. They were paying Teamsters officials a lot of money for labor peace, and now they had a major labor problem on their hands.

Neuberger's initial reaction was that it was Yaghoubi's problem. Yaghoubi was, after all, general contractor at the site. What Neuberger didn't realize was that as far as Moreno was concerned, Yaghoubi's problems were *his* problems. Passing the ball back to Yaghoubi was not a satisfactory solution.

174

In a search for a way out of the dilemma, the Wedtech officers decided to talk to their respective contacts. Guariglia would approach Pat Simone, and Neuberger would get in touch with the officials at Teamsters Local 875.

Simone was unhelpful. He had wanted the construction work at 350 Gerard, and the greedy Wedtech officers had kept the contracts for themselves. Simone decided to use the opportunity to show he couldn't be cut out with impunity. He told the Wedtech gang the carpenters' union was their problem; they should solve it themselves.

When Neuberger explained the problem to Richard Stolfi at union headquarters in Queens, Stolfi appeared reluctant to get involved. These are very tough people, he explained to Neuberger. Stolfi and Neuberger then got in a car, drove up a hill on Queens Boulevard, and parked along the curb. Stolfi said that as a "favor" he would take care of the problem. But the favor was going to cost $150,000. Neuberger said that he would have to consult with his associates before he made a commitment that big.

Neuberger reported Stolfi's demand to his cronies, suggesting again they simply tell Yaghoubi to pay the money. Moreno was getting concerned about all this talk of passing the problem on to Yaghoubi. If his brother-in-law had to make the payment, it would reduce Moreno's cut significantly. "Moe can't afford to make a payment that size," Moreno snapped.

When in trouble, go to Biaggi. For several years, that seemed to have been the credo by which Moreno lived. So he explained the situation to Ehrlich and asked him to have Biaggi intervene on Wedtech's behalf. Ehrlich reported back that Biaggi had been in touch with "certain people" but had been unable to get the Teamsters to reduce their "fee." Wedtech should either hire the carpenters' union workers or pay the $150,000 to the Teamsters bosses.

Neuberger bargained Stolfi down to $100,000. Guariglia, the money man, suggested that they make the payment in two installments of $50,000 each. Guariglia also arranged for Yaghoubi to submit two additional phony invoices to generate the cash to make the payments. Yaghoubi submitted the invoices to Wedtech; Wedtech (at the direction of Moreno and Guariglia) paid them; and Yaghoubi kicked the money back into the F.H.J. account.

Neuberger made the first payment. He put $50,000 in cash into a manila envelope which he delivered to Stolfi. A few weeks later, Guariglia put $25,000 in $100 bills into a brown paper bag and,

175

early one morning, met Casalino at a diner at the corner of Glen Cove Road and Jericho Turnpike on Long Island. Over breakfast, Casalino told Guariglia that Wedtech was lucky the Teamsters were able to take care of the problem. He also swore to Guariglia that he and Stolfi were not getting a piece of the action. Guariglia passed the paper bag to Casalino under the table.

About two weeks later, Guariglia met Casalino at the same diner. This time, he didn't have the cash with him. Casalino followed Guariglia to his house in Jericho. Casalino waited at the doorstep while Guariglia went to his bedroom, put another $25,000 in an envelope, and returned to the front door. Casalino took the envelope and left.

The $100,000 did the trick. The carpenters' union wasn't heard from again.

Even with these payoffs, however, Wedtech was unable to keep labor peace for long.

In March 1985, with the cash situation again tight, all nonunion employees were hit with a 10 percent pay cut. The clerks, secretaries, and draftsmen at company headquarters had to suffer for the incompetence and corruption of management, but short of quitting, there was nothing they could do. That same month, Mariotta, Neuberger, Moreno, Guariglia, and Shorten helped themselves to $434,790 in stolen funds from the F.H.J. account.

The griping by the white-collar workers at 595 Gerard Avenue was minor, however, compared to the dissatisfaction among the blue-collar workers at the pontoon plant. The new government contract had required a rapid expansion in the size of the work force. The 350 workers who were hired in the Bronx to build the pontoons were not recruited from the Puerto Rican Pentecostal community, as were many of the workers hired up to then. In fact, most of the new workers were black, and they did not identify with John Mariotta the way the Puerto Ricans did. They particularly took exception to the part of the Spiel in which Mariotta referred to "spearchuckers." These workers had to be motivated with money, not Mariotta's exhortations.

Accordingly, when management promised, but did not deliver, $500 bonuses for Christmas of 1984, labor relations quickly soured. By the spring, sabotage was not uncommon. Management brought in a group of hardworking rednecks from Arkansas as supervisors, and predictably the mixture didn't work. The workers grew in-

176

creasingly restless about wages and conditions (while the working environment at 595 Gerard was relatively clean, the pontoon plant was a much dirtier environment). They felt like second-class citizens and responded by working like third-class labor. Early in the summer it was decided that the situation was critical. The first acceptable pontoon had finally been delivered on May 25, 1985—seven months behind schedule—and someone needed to talk to the workers and motivate them to start producing pontoons at a faster clip.

Given Mariotta's unpopularity with this new group, the executives decided Tony Guariglia was the man for the job. Late one morning, the workers were assembled on the shop floor of the cavernous facility at 149th Street. After some opening remarks by Mario Moreno and Ceil Lewis, Guariglia drove up in his company car, a sleek dark blue Mercedes 300SD costing more than $25,000. He parked just outside the loading bay doors, in full view of the assembled workers. As Guariglia mounted the platform that had been built for him to speak from, the workers also got a clear view of his exquisitely tailored Italian silk suit, his custom-made, monogrammed shirt, his diamond ring, and his heavy gold watch. Guariglia began discussing the need for the workers to make sacrifices now for the sake of a brighter future.

As Guariglia was expounding on the desperate financial straits in which the company found itself, one of the Jamaican workers could stand it no longer.

"Fuck you, mon," he burst out. "Fuck you. You full of shit. How you say company don' have no money when you up dere in you fancy clothes, drivin' you big car? I don' believe you, mon."

With that, the workers began to vent their frustrations on the hapless Guariglia. Recognizing that his forte was bedazzling accountants and investment analysts, not malcontent blue-collar workers, Guariglia soon returned to his big car. A few days later, the leadership of the Teamsters local met with the workers without management present. Only then was any semblance of labor peace restored.

The incident at the pontoon plant didn't seem to chasten Wedtech's high-living executives. By September, they were back where they started the year: in Washington, D.C., hobnobbing with the power elite. This time the occasion was the annual Ambassadors Ball to benefit the National Multiple Sclerosis Society.

177

Ursula Meese, the wife of the attorney general, was the co-chairman of the ball. It would be wise, Bob Wallach had suggested, for Wedtech to participate. Wallach assured the Wedtech gang that its tables would be grouped together in a prominent place, and there would be "a minimum of five ambassadors, and probably more, available for Wedtech's selection." Four representatives of Wedtech were also invited to a cocktail party reception at the home of Barbara Bush. Best of all, Wallach added, the event would be a good opportunity for the Wedtech officers to meet "my friend." Wedtech purchased three tables at $5,000 apiece, indicating that the corporate officers would like to be seated with the ambassadors from West Germany, Egypt, Pakistan, Israel, and Italy.

The Wedtech executives got to dine with three of the ambassadors on their wish list, and they also got the chance to meet Wallach's friend. Wallach proudly escorted the group into the presence of Ed and Ursula Meese.

"This must be the Wedtech clan!" Ursula Meese exclaimed.

For the next three to five minutes, the chief law enforcement officer of the United States chatted casually with the Wedtech crooks. Meese inquired as to the company's progress on the pontoon contract. Tony Guariglia, who knew first hand what a disaster the situation was becoming, listened as Meese was assured that everything was coming along just fine. Guariglia left the ball with the impression that Ed Meese was still a member of the Wedtech fan club.

# 17

# Feeding the Beast

In mid–1985, Wedtech had thirteen government contracts. For two, the products were not yet due to be delivered. For two others, the government was late in providing the company with necessary materials. On the remaining nine, Wedtech was behind schedule. For almost any other company, such a woeful performance would soon be reflected in its income statement. Delays in production would show up as cash flow problems. The company would begin to report losses.

But Wedtech was not a typical public company. Despite its horrendous manufacturing problems, it continued to report rapidly rising revenues and consistent profits. So far as the public could tell, Wedtech was a fast-growing, solidly profitable venture when, in fact, it was insolvent.

How could this have been?

Simply put, Wedtech was cooking the books. It perverted both the military procurement system and the public accounting system to defraud the government and the public. The company was collecting millions of dollars from the government for products never delivered, while issuing public financial statements that not only hid its losses but painted a highly profitable picture.

The person almost solely responsible for Wedtech's ability to pull the wool over the eyes of its auditors and, hence, the financial

179

community was Tony Guariglia. Fast-talking and supremely self-confident, Guariglia simply outwitted those who were too trusting, too lazy, or too insecure to challenge him. As one Wedtech employee put it, "I never saw Tony bested in any discussion when it came to finances. It was two minutes before [the people he was talking to] were lost. They didn't know what the hell he said, but it sounded awfully good."

Guariglia's financial sleights of hand found an appreciative audience in his colleagues. Each quarter, Guariglia would explain to them how he had persuaded the auditors to accept his latest phony figures.

Mariotta didn't quite follow all the mechanics, but he got the drift. After listening to Guariglia's explanations, Mariotta would shake his head and exclaim that Tony had a tremendous ability "to stretch the rubber band." To make sure no one was missing the point, he would take an actual rubber band and stretch it. Mariotta explained his analogy to mean that, just as the company had stretched its cash to the breaking point, Guariglia would use the phony financial statements to pull off another public offering or bank financing. The next time, Mariotta would add, Guariglia would need a bigger rubber band.

Guariglia's colleagues were not the only ones impressed with his ability to lie and deceive. After he had succeeded in persuading the auditors to accept some particularly blatant falsification of the accounts, Guariglia would often swagger down the hall and announce to his cronies, "Either they are awfully stupid or I'm awfully smart."

The explanation of how Wedtech cooked the books begins with the government's system of "progress payments" to contractors. In theory, the progress payments system is fair for both the government and the contractor. The system allows the contractor to receive government payments for expenses incurred. The payments are not necessarily related to actual products delivered. By the end of August 1985, for example, the amount of progress payments Wedtech had received on the engine contract exceeded the value of the 191 engines actually delivered by $13.5 million.

Contractors like the progress payment system because their upfront costs are reimbursed relatively quickly. In this way, the contractors are not forced to bear the full burden of starting a production line, purchasing material, and training a work force for the entire life of the contract.

The government benefits because the progress payments allow a company to perform a contract more cheaply, since it doesn't have to borrow funds to pay the up-front expenses. Without the progress payment system, many small, undercapitalized companies simply could not afford to become government contractors.

Typically, a small government contractor is entitled each month to request and receive up to 95 percent of its costs. If the company were losing money and collecting progress payments at the 95 percent rate, it could conceivably be in a position to pass on costs to the government that exceeded the total value of the contract. In such a case, the government's contract administrator would supposedly adjust the rate at which the contractor received progress payments.

Wedtech subsisted on progress payments once its officers discovered that the payments could be manipulated to mask the penalties of inefficiency. As the Main Hurdman accountants detected in the 1983 audit for the initial public offering, the company had even devised a fairly elaborate scheme for falsifying progress payment requests to speed up the payments.

Understanding how Wedtech was able to disguise its huge losses as profits also requires an explanation of the "percentage-of-completion" method of contract accounting—an explanation clearer, that is, than that contained in the Wedtech prospectus:

> . . . fixed price contract revenues are recognized in proportion to the percentage that costs incurred to date bear to total estimated contract costs less revenues recognized in previous periods. As a result, as the rate of production increases and additional manufacturing commences, greater costs are incurred and greater revenues are recognized. Losses, if any, on U.S. Government contracts are recognized in full at the time the estimate of total cost indicates a loss will occur.

Put more simply, this accounting method, much like the concept of progress payments, ties earnings to expenses, not to products delivered. The method allows companies to book earnings based on their current costs and the estimated costs to complete a project. For example, if Wedtech was supposed to make a 10 percent profit on a $100 million pontoon contract, and it spent $50 million in the first year on the contract, it would be able to record a $5 million profit. Investors would be in for an unhappy surprise, how-

181

ever, if the company had to spend more than another $50 million to complete the contract, or if the contract were cancelled in midstream.

Wedtech's contracts themselves were fixed price—the government was going to pay Wedtech a specified amount to produce a certain number of engines or pontoons. Each time a financial report was issued, it showed an increase in costs Wedtech had incurred to date. Thus, the only way Wedtech could maintain that the contracts were profitable was to pretend that the cost to complete the contracts was decreasing.

The deception required Wedtech to increase, on paper, the total value of each contract. This could only be done by "pooling"—getting additional contracts or options for the same item. For example, if the fixed price for a contract was $30 million and the company had reported that costs to date were $20 million, the company was likely to lose money if it had only delivered one-quarter of the required items. However, if the company had also been awarded an option worth another $30 million, it could then claim that it had spent only $20 million of a total of $60 million (the original $30 million "pooled" with the $30 million option). The company could contend that costs were much higher manufacturing the first one-eighth of the items (when it was working the kinks out of the production line) than they would be for the remaining seven-eighths. Thus, the company would argue, it could deliver the remaining items *and* make a profit for the $40 million left in the "pool."

This was how Wedtech had "pooled" the 1985 option on the pontoon contract with the initial contract to credit itself with revenues from the option even before the initial pontoon contract was completed.

Guariglia, being more financially sophisticated than the rest, understood he was playing a dangerous game. "Feeding the beast," he called it. He would tell his colleagues that every quarter he had to use part of the unfilled backlog of manufacturing orders—the "pool"—to justify the revenues he was booking. The beast was the backlog; as it was used to create revenues, it had to be replaced with new contracts that would replenish the pool. If the flow of new contracts stopped, the "beast"—the backlog— would soon disappear and with it the ability to pretend that expenses were generating profits. All the company would be left with would be the requirement to deliver pontoons, engines, suspension kits, and the like without any money coming in to buy the materials or pay the workers.

182

Fooling unsophisticated investors in a bull market isn't terribly difficult. The more troubling question is how Wedtech was able to fool for so long the "experts" who are supposed to prevent this kind of chicanery.

With respect to the government regulators, the answer seems to be a combination of dishonesty, incompetence, and timidity.

Some bureaucrats unquestionably failed because of a lack of integrity—they were greedy, and Wedtech was willing to pay them enough to make them neglect their duty to the American taxpayers who were paying their salaries.

Other bureaucrats lacked the ability or the dedication to perform their functions properly. Rather than doing the investigation and analysis necessary to sort through the competing claims in the various Wedtech issues, they simply relied upon the assertions and puffery that Wedtech and its politically powerful allies passed off as facts. Still others focused so hard on the political benefits of propping up a Hispanic-owned enterprise in the South Bronx, an enterprise obviously favored by the White House, that they let the facts and regulations fall by the wayside.

In several instances, career civil servants wanted to do the right thing but were trampled by their political bosses. In other cases, civil servants failed because of ineptitude. They were too easily fooled (the best and brightest lawyers and auditors tend to flock to the private sector, not lower paying government jobs). Others were competent and honorable; what they lacked was the stomach to push a point of view unpopular with their political masters.

The mid-level contract administrators, the people who had to approve or disapprove the requests for progress payments, found it less risky to go along with Wedtech than to fight the company and its powerful allies. They knew Wedtech's demands were contrary to both the letter and the spirit of the regulations; in fact, they appear to have so informed their superiors. But for many mid-level employees, that was where their responsibility ended; if the superiors didn't see fit to enforce the regulations, there was nothing more the guys in the middle could be expected to do.

The Small Business Administration's extreme favoritism toward Wedtech occurred in part because a senior official, Peter Neglia, was corrupt. There was more to it than that, however. As the head of the SBA, James Sanders, explained, "It's very much like what happens to large banks that loan too much money to one company. They get in so far, they can't let the company go under. So they loan them more money. I think we [at SBA] were very much in the situation that as this company [Wedtech] got more and more contracts, we felt we had to keep them going." The SBA had committed so much money to Wedtech and had so much prestige riding on its success that there was enormous pressure on the agency to prop the company up. Reality had to be made to correspond to hype.

The government's systemic failure also has to do with the famed "revolving door" of the military-industrial complex. Wedtech used this to great advantage. At one time, Wedtech had no fewer than four former employees of the Defense Contract Administration Service on its payroll. All four were in position to work directly with their former colleagues at DCAS. Hired by Wedtech at salaries far in excess of their government pay, these individuals were able to use their personal relationships with the DCAS auditors and inspectors to smooth over differences.

Even if government officials didn't blow the whistle on Wedtech, the public accounting firms that audited its financial statements should have. They didn't.

When Wedtech went public, its auditor was the Big Eight firm, Main Hurdman. Main Hurdman auditors discovered both the progress payment fraud and the F.H.J. account theft during the audit in 1983. Although both illegal acts were recorded in its work papers, Main Hurdman continued the audit engagement and issued a "clean opinion" that Wedtech was able to use in the prospectus for its public offering. A "clean" or "unqualified" opinion is a statement by the auditing firm that the company's financial statements accurately represent its financial position in conformity with generally accepted accounting principles.

What the prospectus didn't reveal was that the man instrumental in issuing the clean opinion, Richard Bluestine, had already agreed to join Wedtech in return for a multimillion-dollar compensation package. And although the prospectus did disclose that one of the company's officers, Anthony Guariglia, was formerly employed by Main Hurdman, an investor had no way of knowing that Guariglia had been Main Hurdman's audit manager for the Wedtech engagement and had left in the middle of the audit to go to work for the company.

So Main Hurdman was compromised, almost from the outset, in its relations with Wedtech.

After Bluestine and Guariglia left, along with two other Main

184

Hurdman employees also hired by Wedtech, a new audit team was assembled. Some of the team had previously worked together on the account of Grumman Corp., the major aerospace contractor headquartered on Long Island.

Despite the expertise of the new Main Hurdman team, Wedtech was successful in getting the Big Eight firm to continue to certify financial statements which turned out to be false. Main Hurdman performed two additional audits—the year-end audit for 1983 and the year-end audit for 1984. The financial statements that Main Hurdman certified showed that Wedtech was making money and growing rapidly. For 1983, the company reported a $4.9 million profit on revenues of $27.4 million. For 1984, the company reported earnings of $4.7 million on revenues of $72.4 million.

These audited statements were used by Wedtech to issue more securities, acquire a subsidiary, and persuade the city of Mount Vernon in Westchester County to issue Industrial Revenue Bonds to finance a new facility for Wedtech's coating division. They were also used by hundreds of small investors as the basis for their decisions to buy Wedtech's common stock and bonds.

How to explain the auditors' incompetence? One explanation is that they didn't do their homework. Evidently, they were not aware of the enormous problems Wedtech was having getting a production line running and delivering small engines and pontoons on schedule, although the Wedtech files were filled with letters and memos reflecting the difficulties. The auditors never interviewed the pontoon project manager, Captain de Vicq, who certainly would have told them about Wedtech's production problems. The auditors also missed technical discrepancies. For example, Wedtech was charging the expense of acquiring Mazak milling machines to the engine contract when, in fact, the machines were for the suspension kit contract and weren't even located in the engine facility. The auditors certainly never rediscovered the F.H.J. account, nor the hundreds of thousands of dollars that were being siphoned off through padded invoices for kickbacks.

Perhaps the most serious failure had to do with the analysis of what it would cost Wedtech to complete its government contracts. By the end of 1984, even Guariglia's sleights of hand could no longer conceal evidence of enormous cost overruns in the pontoon program. The auditors calculated there would be such overruns even though Guariglia had persuaded them to allow the company to "pool" the 1985 and 1986 pontoon options. (In fact, the options

185

had not yet been awarded to the company and there was no guarantee they would be.)

Main Hurdman insisted that Wedtech establish a "reserve" of $14 million to allow for the anticipated overruns. When a company shows a reserve in its financial statement, it means it believes there is a reasonable chance that a loss is going to have to be recorded in the future; it decreases the size of its assets to reflect that possibility.

Guariglia balked. If Wedtech were to take such a large loss reserve, its stock price would plummet and the government might have to question Wedtech's financial ability to complete existing contracts. Worst of all, Wedtech's credit would likely evaporate. The company's revolving credit agreements with several banks, including Chemical Bank and Bank Leumi, had covenants requiring the company to show at least $5 million of net income. If Wedtech violated the covenants, the banks could call existing loans and cancel the agreement to extend additional credit. The company might then collapse.

So Wedtech had another crisis on its hands. Supported by the company's accountants, Guariglia and Shorten met with the auditors late into the night. For all Guariglia's legerdemain, the auditors refused to budge. The meeting broke up without a resolution.

The dispute was now so serious that it had to be taken to the board of directors. On April 1, 1985, a meeting was convened in the Fifth Avenue offices of Squadron Ellenoff, the corporate counsel. Howard Squadron, although not a member of the board, attended. After the auditors made their presentation, Squadron spoke up. He suggested that Main Hurdman seemed more intent on forcing Wedtech to violate the banks' restrictive covenants than on reserving a specific amount in the financial statements. Squadron was right. If the trouble couldn't be avoided, the auditors didn't want the banks to be able to say that Main Hurdman hadn't warned them. On the other hand, by forcing Wedtech to violate the covenants, Main Hurdman would shift at least part of its financial oversight burden to the banks.

Everyone wrangled for a while over the merits of various technical arguments on the amount to be reserved. Finally, Squadron suggested a compromise. Why not agree to reserve an amount that would have the effect of reducing Wedtech's net income for 1984 to just over $5 million?

The auditors were in a quandary. On the one hand, they should

186

have been insisting that the amount reserved be based on a factual analysis and have nothing to do with the $5 million net earnings covenant. On the other hand, Squadron's suggestion came very close to what Main Hurdman wanted to accomplish. One of the auditors excused himself and went to use the phone. He returned with another suggestion. Why not set the reserve at $6.7 million, which would reduce the net earnings to just *under* $5 million?

Now it was Wedtech's turn to leave the room. Guariglia made a couple of hurried phone calls to the banks. Upon learning that the banks would be willing to waive the $5 million covenant, Guariglia returned. Wedtech could live with the auditor's suggestion, he announced.

The compromise was reflected in the company's earnings announcement. For all of 1984, Wedtech reported net income of $4.7 million on sales of $72.4 million. For the fourth quarter of 1984, however, it reported a pretax loss of $2.2 million. The press release quoted John Mariotta, chairman and chief executive, as giving a detailed explanation of the accounting issues involved in the surprising fourth quarter results (amusing in itself since Mariotta didn't know a debit from a credit). Gross profits, Mariotta "explained," had been eroded by $9.5 million because of additions to the costs of goods sold and by $2.1 million because of a year-end reserve for the cost to complete the pontoon contract.

Although Guariglia could live with the compromise, he knew Wedtech couldn't live much longer with Main Hurdman. They were getting too close to discovering the truth about the contracts and Wedtech's financial situation.

Shortly after the financial statements were published, Guariglia fired Main Hurdman.

When a public company changes auditors, it is required to notify the Securities and Exchange Commission. The rule is designed to alert the public to any disagreements and to discourage companies from "audit shopping" for a favorable opinion. Wedtech's SEC filing disclosing the replacement of Main Hurdman was dated April 26, 1985. It said:

> There have been no disagreements between [Wedtech] and KMG Main Hurdman on any matter of accounting principles or practices, financial statement disclosure, or auditing scope or procedure during the fiscal years ended December 31, 1983 and December 31, 1984.

187

Main Hurdman, required to confirm Wedtech's assurances regarding the change, sent a letter to the SEC which said, in part:

> . . . we concur with the statement made by [Wedtech]
> and confirm that . . . there were no disagreements between
> Wedtech Corp. and us on any matter . . . which would have
> caused us to make reference to the subject matter of such
> disagreement if not resolved to our satisfaction.

Obviously, both versions were misleading, at best. There had
been disagreements, and they were significant.

Main Hurdman had served as Wedtech's independent auditors
for slightly more than two years. In that time, the firm collected
about $1.3 million in fees—$286,000 in 1983, $440,000 in 1984, and
$622,000 for just the first four months of 1985. With those kinds of
fees at stake, it becomes easier to understand why Main Hurdman
was reluctant to make public its differences with Wedtech.

Main Hurdman was replaced as Wedtech's independent auditor
by another Big Eight accounting firm, Touche Ross & Co. One
thing Touche Ross had in common with Main Hurdman was that
both were former employees of Anthony Guariglia. Rather than
use the Touche Ross office in New York City, as would have been
usual for a New York City company, Guariglia shrewdly chose to
use the auditor's Long Island office, a much smaller operation.

One reason for this decision was that Richard Kron, a long-time
friend of Guariglia, was a partner in that office. No doubt another
factor was Guariglia's calculation that it would be far more difficult for the partners at the Long Island office to risk losing one of
their largest accounts than it would be for the New York City office
to risk losing an average one.

Remarkably, what the highly qualified and compensated accountants at Main Hurdman and Touche Ross didn't detect was
discovered by both an inexperienced Wedtech employee and a federal bureaucrat.

The employee, Gil Tenzer, had joined Wedtech in 1984, right out
of college. Initially employed as a systems auditor at about $20,000
per year, he resigned a year later. Before he left, he wrote an internal memo, dated June 19, 1985, which he distributed only to the
senior executives. Although he didn't uncover the criminal activity, he didn't miss much else. His insights and conclusions are

188

striking, especially considering how dramatically they differed from what the supposedly independent auditors were providing to the public. Among his conclusions:

> Today's Wedtech is a very sick company. Arguably, it has reached a terminal stage . . . [There is] virtually no control, planning, and true "management" at either the manufacturing or financial areas . . . Unless costs are brought under control and use of costly debt financing for daily operations is terminated, Wedtech is spiraling toward bankruptcy.

The federal bureaucrat who correctly analyzed Wedtech's dire financial situation was Samuel H. Cohen, an industrial engineer with the Defense Contract Administration Service. In March 1985, the fifty-seven-year-old Cohen was asked to analyze how much it would cost Wedtech to complete both the basic $24.2 million pontoon contract and the $51.5 million option for fiscal 1985.

Cohen was no rookie. He had degrees in industrial engineering and mechanical engineering from New York University, and he had just presented a scholarly paper titled, "A Refutation of T. P. Wright's Cum Average Learning Curve Theory; and Resulting General Learning Curve Law." Balding, with thick glasses, he worked independently, "like Columbo," the television detective.

When Cohen visited the Wedtech pontoon plant in March 1985, he was astounded. The company had already gone through $18 million of the original $24.2 millon and still hadn't produced an acceptable pontoon. Cohen analyzed the records carefully. At the rate the company was going, he calculated, it would cost $380 million to complete the $75 million pontoon package!

Cohen figured his margin of error to be 20 percent at most. Clearly the government had a big problem. In his report issued April 30, 1985, Cohen wrote, "One must conclude that a cost overrun on both the basic and option contracts is highly probable."

Two weeks later, Cohen was told that the navy would not accept his recommendations. Another engineer was assigned to analyze the situation without using the traditional standards. Cohen protested that this was tantamount to giving a math professor a problem and saying, "Don't use numbers or letters." The other engineer's calculations were more to the navy's liking; Cohen's warnings were ignored.

189

# 18

## One That Got Away

**E**ven a captive auditor couldn't help the Wedtech executives if they couldn't keep "feeding the beast." They had to continue getting contracts; unfortunately for them, their only source—the 8(a) program—was not going to be available forever. Soon, even the efforts of Neglia would not be sufficient to prevent the SBA from "graduating" Wedtech from the program. When that occurred, the company was going to have to win contracts the old-fashioned way: in competition with other firms. Looking ahead to that unhappy day, Wedtech started keeping an eye open for non-SBA opportunities.

When the U.S. Army Armament, Munitions and Chemical Command (AMCCOM) in Rock Island, Illinois issued an invitation for bids on a maintenance vehicle, Wedtech was extremely interested. Not that Wedtech had ever built anything similar to the maintenance vehicle or had any expertise in the manufacturing operations involved. But as in the case of the six-horsepower engines and the pontoons, Wedtech was not going to let such minor considerations of capability stand in its way.

What really excited the company executives was that the army planned to award a multiyear contract which included the possibility of additional option years. In other words, this contract represented another "pool" Guariglia could use to feed the beast. It would make a major contribution to propping up Wedtech's increasingly precarious Ponzi scheme.

The maintenance vehicle was intended to be a repair shop on wheels. Rethinking its tactics for a war in Europe, the army had concluded that certain units ought to be virtually self-sustaining. They would need a carrier containing tools, basic repair parts, and diagnostic equipment with which mechanics could go to inoperable vehicles and fix them on the spot, rather than have to get the vehicles to a repair shop in the rear.

The maintenance vehicle contract required the contractor, using a government-furnished truck chassis, to add a new sheet metal body and compartment, upgrade the electrical system to supply the necessary power, and equip it with the appropriate tools.

Wedtech was one of twelve companies that responded to the army's bid solicitation. On March 19, 1985, the army opened the proposals. Wedtech bid $30.2 million for the five-year contract to produce 3,021 maintenance vehicles, or roughly $10,000 a vehicle. The next lowest bidder was Libby Corp., which bid about $39 million, some 30 percent higher than Wedtech.

John F. Hayden, the contracting officer at AMCCOM in charge of the procurement, was amazed. The Wedtech bid was so far below any other bid that Hayden sent a telex to Wedtech suggesting that the company may have made an error. He requested that Wedtech review its estimated costs.

Indeed, even the bid estimators and engineers at Wedtech weren't at all confident about the company's bid. One sent a memo to Shorten in which he expressed concern about the various assumptions used to arrive at the price.

What the engineer didn't realize was that it didn't matter to Shorten and his cronies whether Wedtech could manufacture the maintenance vehicles at the bid price; they just wanted to keep cash flowing into the company, to feed the beast and maintain the illusion of growth. The engineer's concerns were ignored. Wedtech responded promptly to the army that it had reviewed its prices and the bid was correct.

The Wedtech executives were euphoric at having been the low bidder. Not only did it appear that they had pulled another rabbit out of the hat, but apparently they had won their first major competitive contract. The only hurdle left was the pre-award survey.

The survey involved an inspection of the facility at which Wedtech planned to manufacture the maintenance vehicle, a review of

191

production plans, and discussions with key manufacturing managers and engineers. It would be conducted mainly by representatives from the New York office of the Defense Contract Administration Service with technical assistance from AMCCOM.

Unfortunately for Wedtech, one of the DCAS engineers assigned to conduct the survey was Sam Cohen, who had recently completed his devastating analysis of the pontoon contract. More than any other outsider, Cohen knew how desperately the company needed more money to cover its losses on the pontoons.

The government inspectors had been told that Wedtech was going to acquire a company on Long Island, Euclid Equipment Inc., and that Euclid would be used to manufacture the maintenance vehicle. The inspectors had been through this with Wedtech all too recently—indeed, they were still feeling the heat from the delays caused by awarding Wedtech the pontoon contract without an adequate production facility. The acquisition discussions with Euclid were in the very early stages; there was no assurance that Wedtech would ever complete the deal.

Moreover, the Wedtech staff had not developed any detailed production plans; the company had not even plotted what the production layout would look like . . . the same point the Army and Navy procurement staffs had raised regarding Wedtech's ability to manufacture the engines and the pontoons.

Perhaps the most damning indictment was the recitation of Wedtech's performance on government contracts awarded previously. The DCAS survey team reported:

> Records in this office indicate that the bidder has completed three . . . contracts in the past 12 months. All 3 contracts were completed in a delinquent status . . . The bidder is currently performing on 13 contracts administered by this office. Of the 13 contracts all (13) are in a delinquent status. The main causal factors for the delinquencies have been poor production planning and difficulty in obtaining vendor items.

The report could have gone on to explain that the difficulty in obtaining material from vendors was caused primarily by Wedtech's failure to pay its bills on time. By now many vendors had learned to deal with the company only on a cash-on-delivery or cash-in-advance basis, and since Wedtech's cash was usually going into the pockets of its executives and their cronies, making prompt payments to vendors was not a priority.

No facility. No coherent production plan. Delinquent on 100 percent of its government contracts. It seemed an open-and-shut case. On May 3, the DCAS officials made their recommendation to AMC-COM: the government should not award the maintenance vehicle contract to Wedtech.

Wedtech's executives were disappointed but not overly concerned. Initial rebuffs had never before proved insurmountable in the company's pursuit of contracts, whatever the facts of the case, and there was no reason to assume that the DCAS's facts would have anything to do with the award of this one. Wedtech had been down this road before and felt it shouldn't be all that difficult to have the recommendation reversed.

The plot of the maintenance vehicle procurement was all too familiar. The government had solid and substantive reasons for not awarding the contract to Wedtech; Wedtech would stall for time to get its political allies involved in deflecting attention from substantive issues to the theme of "resurrecting the South Bronx." As the procurement actually unfolded, the various players acted out their roles as if they had been scripted.

The first thing Wedtech had to do was delay the award. Moreno fired off a letter to the General Accounting Office formally protesting the award of the contract to any other bidder. In the letter, Moreno contended that the recommendation against awarding the contract to Wedtech should be reversed "based on the lack of full and complete information by the survey team due to such data not being seasonably [sic] requested plus the lack of timely facts on the status of extant contracts and erroneous and arbitrary conclusions by certain members of the team unsupported by any qualified technical and factual data." (The windy prose style was typical for Moreno and his administrative assistant, Deborah Scott, the two regarded as the most accomplished writers in the company.)

The next step was to turn up the political heat. Moreno and Ehrlich flew to Washington to review the situation with Representative Biaggi at his office in the Rayburn Building. Moreno and Ehrlich were joined by Vito Castellano; the three went to see Representative Addabbo.

Vito Castellano, like Ehrlich, was a major general in the New York National Guard. And, like Ehrlich, he was a crook. Although

193

he looked more like a clerk than a general, Castellano had a certain flair about him. He had worked for Bob Guccione at *Penthouse* magazine, supposedly as a consultant on how to get space in magazine racks at PXs around the world. Actually, Castellano later admitted, his real service to Guccione was to help him get a loan from a bank in Buffalo that was run by another National Guard officer. In return, Castellano received the use of a Lincoln Town car and $35,000.

As head of the National Guard, Castellano controlled the state's armories, including the Seventh Regiment Armory, located on Park Avenue between Sixty-fifth and Sixty-sixth streets. The armory was a huge old building, resembling what an aircraft hangar would have looked like if the Victorians had built aircraft hangars. Its vast open floor, used for assembling formations of troops and their equipment, was unlike any other space in midtown Manhattan. The armory's unique size and location made it a magnet for trade shows, and it was Castellano who determined which groups got to use the facility. One of the events he approved was a fur show, which Castellano visited with his wife and daughter. After some not-so-subtle hints, Castellano's support was acknowledged with a gift of fur coats for both Castellano ladies.

Perhaps the most bizarre of Castellano's crimes involved his marital status. He married his first wife, Dorothy, in 1947. They were divorced in 1979, the same year he married his second wife, Linda. His marriage to Linda lasted only two years; they were divorced in 1981. The next year, apparently missing Dorothy, Castellano remarried her. The next year, apparently missing Linda, he remarried her. He neglected, however, to divorce Dorothy a second time before marrying Linda the second time. Somehow he maintained two wives and two homes (one in Westchester County and one in Albany, about 125 miles to the north), until Dorothy died in 1986.

Understandably, these five years were a confusing period for Castellano. To lessen the confusion, Castellano had the same front door lock installed at both houses. That way he only had to carry one house key and didn't have to explain to either wife why he had the front door key to another house in his pocket.

Castellano was close to Addabbo, so the Wedtech team thought he would be helpful on the maintenance vehicle contract. At Addabbo's office, the group met with one of the congressman's aides. After explaining the situation, they received a promise that Addabbo would intervene with the army. A short time later, Ehrlich was told that Addabbo and his assistant had each made calls to top army officials.

On leaving Addabbo's office, the trio beat the well-worn path to the fifth floor of the Hart Senate Office Building, where they met with Senator D'Amato and one of his assistants. D'Amato later sent a letter to the secretary of the army, asking why the maintenance vehicle contract had not yet been awarded to Wedtech. "The hallmark of the company's success has been its ability to produce a quality product at a competitive price," the senator wrote. (D'Amato's efforts on behalf of Wedtech over the years didn't go unrewarded. Between 1981 and 1985, Wedtech executives contributed $11,000 to the senator's re-election campaign. According to Moreno, Wedtech also funneled $30,000 in illegal donations to the D'Amato campaign. D'Amato denied any knowledge of having received illegal contributions. Moreno also stated that Wedtech gave illegal campaign assistance to Addabbo in the form of subsidized advertising and taxi services.)

Meanwhile, Wedtech had succeeded in getting the award delayed and had written to Hayden, the procuring contracting officer, to request a second pre-award survey. The company claimed it now had a firm agreement to acquire Euclid Equipment, thus satisfying one of the government's objections in the first pre-award survey.

Hayden wrote back that AMCCOM did not intend to conduct a "re-survey" because there was no reason to believe the production and technical recommendations would be any different. After a lengthy and detailed analysis of the facts in the case, he had made his recommendation. Despite its bureaucratic style, the recommendation was direct and to the point: "There is no evidence that the lack of perseverance of this bidder, indicated by its poor performance history regarding government contracts, would improve in the performance of this award." Hayden went on to say that he would override any recommendation to reverse the first survey—rather like the president threatening to veto a bill passed by Congress.

To Hayden's dismay, Wedtech was successful in forcing a second survey. (By now, Hayden must have been feeling like Keenan had several years earlier.) Hayden was directed by "higher headquarters" to request a follow-up pre-award survey of Wedtech's capabilities "due to the substantial passage of time" since the first survey. On September 4 and 5, 1985, the second survey was conducted.

Since the initial survey, Sam Cohen had been a target of Wedtech's wrath. In correspondence with high-ranking federal officials, the executives had ridiculed his analysis and challenged his credibility. Cohen was instructed to go back to Wedtech as part of the survey team. This was the first time in his long experience that he had participated in a "re-pre-award survey."

As he walked into 595 Gerard Avenue, Cohen felt intense pressure; he had been told that the request for a second survey had come "from the highest positions in the army." If he wavered, the system was going to suffer; if he didn't, he was way out in front where all of the Wedtech's weapons would be trained on him. He knew he had to be on solid ground with his findings.

The night after he visited Wedtech, Cohen woke up at 4 A.M. thinking about what he had seen and been told. Unable to get back to sleep, he got up and began to reanalyze the Wedtech figures. It was clear to him that they were wrong, that Wedtech had made major miscalculations.

In the office that morning, Cohen did his own calculations. They showed that it was going to cost Wedtech $25 million to $30 million *more* than it had bid to build the maintenance vehicles. In fact, according to Cohen's calculations, experienced truck manufacturers such as Fruehauf and Mack Truck could not have built the maintenance vehicles for anything close to the price Wedtech had bid.

On September 11, Cohen issued his report. After a detailed and very technical analysis of Wedtech's capabilities, the engineer made his recommendation. He said he would "be remiss in (my) professional and government obligations" if he found Wedtech's bid to be suitable.

"Therefore," he concluded, "it is strongly emphasized that Wedtech Corporation's submission be rejected, because it not only fails in providing adequate manpower needs, but also fails to provide a sufficient plant layout, and its management lacks the necessary experience needed to achieve the solicitation's requirements."

It was, Cohen said later, "the strongest language I could possibly use."

The results of the second survey must have been a bitter surprise to Wedtech's managers, so accustomed by how to getting their way. The situation was especially worrisome because for the first time the SBA was not involved; since the contract was not being set aside for an 8(a) company, Neglia couldn't intervene on Wedtech's behalf.

The company was a long way from giving up, however. Its contracts attorney in Washington asked the United States Court of Claims for an order preventing the army from awarding the contract to the next lowest bidder, an action withdrawn when Wedtech learned that the army was going to delay the contract award. By late fall, Wedtech had completed the acquisition of Euclid and convinced the army to conduct its own survey. Two army colonels, one from the Pentagon and one from the DCAS office, visited for a couple of days in mid-December.

In early January, Wedtech learned that the army concurred in the decision not to award it the maintenance vehicle contract. Cited were Wedtech's uncertain manpower estimates, its inadequate profit margin, a technical error in its bid submission, and a general lack of faith in the company by army contract managers. One DCAS official was quoted as telling Wedtech that he lacked a "warm feeling" about the company and its bid.

With this new setback, it was time to bring out the heavy artillery in Washington. Jim Jenkins was no longer Meese's deputy; he had left the White House staff in May 1984 and had become a Wedtech consultant in October 1985. Jenkins had helped pull the army engine contract out of the fire when the situation looked bleak. Maybe he could deliver again.

In late January 1986, Jenkins met with both Jack Marsh, the secretary of the army, and James Ambrose, the undersecretary of the army, to discuss the maintenance vehicle contract. In the space of six days, Jenkins followed up with three "Dear Jim" letters to Ambrose.

In the first, Jenkins said he had "asked the Company to *commence* (emphasis added) the industrial engineering work necessary to produce a Production Plan ..." Jenkins's next two letters focused on whether anyone in the army had acted against Wedtech out of "prejudice." Evidently Wedtech, desperate to divert attention from its capabilities and its record, was suggesting that the army's decision might be based on bigotry against minority companies.

On Capitol Hill, meanwhile, Representative Addabbo was weighing in with telegrams and letters to Army Secretary Marsh. Addabbo, however, was dying of cancer. The once rotund Queens congressman was now startlingly thinner and older-looking. His clout was deteriorating along with his physical condition.

With Addabbo near death, Wedtech began cultivating a new ally, one of even more powerful position and reputation. On January 28, 1986, Moreno wrote to Rep. Les Aspin, a Wisconsin Democrat and the chairman of the House Armed Services Committee, urging a reevaluation of the army's position.

Wedtech's entrée to Les Aspin was through his brother, James, who ran an aviation services business in New York's Lower Hudson Valley. Jim Aspin, who had an MBA from the Wharton School of Business, would be hired in June 1986 as Wedtech's senior vice-president of marketing. In early 1986, he apparently alerted a staffer at the Armed Services' panel to expect a letter from Wedtech. Les Aspin answered Moreno's letter just two days after he'd received it, saying he had asked the army to provide him with a response to the issues Wedtech had raised. (There is nothing to suggest that Les Aspin received any improper payments or compensation from Wedtech.)

The Army's next and final response arrived six weeks later in the form of letters from J. R. Sculley, the assistant army secretary in charge of acquisition, to Les Aspin and D'Amato. The army, intentionally or not, took the one avenue that Wedtech could not dispute—it cancelled the entire procurement. The letters cited "a number of inquiries and complaints concerning this matter" and stated that the need for the vehicles "may be seriously overstated."

Aspin forwarded Sculley's letter to Wedtech, commenting that in view of all the confusion regarding the proposed contract, cancellation of the solicitation seemed to be the best solution. D'Amato evidently demanded a reevaluation, because on May 12 Ambrose sent another letter to the senator stating that the government's assessment of Wedtech's capability was "inadequate and incorrect." Nevertheless, the undersecretary of the army added, "the procurement was flawed and should be cancelled."

Wedtech had lost. Realistically, there was no way it could overturn the army's decision to cancel the purchase. Even Wedtech could not get away with insisting that the army should procure vehicles it now said it probably didn't need.

Wedtech's failure to obtain a contract through competitive bidding did not bode well. This had seemed to be the best shot at winning a competitive contract, but the Wedtech crew had been unable to pull it off. And without new contracts to feed the backlog, the beast might soon starve.

Even more troubling, the failure was a crack in the company's facade of invincibility. Always, until now, the civil servants who manned the middle ranks of the procurement bureaucracies had proved no match for Wedtech's powerful allies. Wedtech had been able to bluff, bully, and buy its way into almost any contract and out of any of the consequences of its incompetence and fraud. The maintenance vehicle contract failure suggested for the first time that the company's future might not be nearly as bright as its past.

# 19

# Wedtech High Tech

**D**espite the publicity and praise Wedtech received, the company's business was neither glamorous nor diversified. For all practical purposes, Wedtech had one customer—the United States Department of Defense. (In its only apparent quest for diversity, the company had obtained a small U.S. Postal Service contract by bribing a post office employee.) The company's overall growth was tied to the growth of the defense budget, perhaps not a bad link in the early Reagan years, but one that was becoming increasingly risky with pressures to curb Pentagon spending.

The business itself, reduced to its essence, was metal-bending. The company took large pieces of steel or aluminum and cut, bent, and welded them into the desire shapes. There was nothing wrong with the business; it was just that metal-bending is what financial types call a "mature industry."

The term "mature industry" connotes slow growth in sales and profits. It also insinuates that the industry, either because of its products or its technology, is on the verge of obsolescence. For those reasons, companies in "mature industries" seldom generate much excitement on Wall Street or in the hearts of investment bankers. Without exciting the financial community, a company usually finds its stock price depressed and its ability to raise capital limited.

200

Nevertheless, Wedtech had generated excitement. Part of this was because of its astounding sales growth: the company reported its revenues had soared from $9.8 million in 1981 to $117.5 million in 1985, an increase of nearly 1,200 percent in just four years. Part of the excitement was the result of the publicity Wedtech received from Reagan administration officials and others who saw the company as proof that private enterprise was the last, best hope for the urban wastelands.

But there was another element that contributed to the enthusiasm that always seemed to surround Wedtech. That element was the company's patented coating process, known as low-temperature, arc vapor deposition (LTAVD, for short).

It was this process that led analysts to tout Wedtech as a potentially exciting growth stock, not a company mired in a mature industry. The Wedtech executives themselves appeared to believe the coating process would be their salvation, even if the company got kicked out of the 8(a) program and failed on competitive procurements like the army maintenance vehicle.

LTAVD held out the prospect of an almost revolutionary breakthrough in coating technology. Basically, it was designed to allow certain materials to be vaporized, without high heat, and deposited on various surfaces, called substrates. The process took place in vacuum chambers. According to Wedtech, LTAVD resulted in the deposit of extremely thin, uniform coatings that had excellent adhesion and durability. The company further asserted that coatings deposited by this process were exceptionally pure, and there were no unwanted changes in the material being coated. Because of the relatively low temperatures, combustible materials such as plastics, paper, and wood could be coated using LTAVD. These attributes gave the coating process a number of exciting possibilities, assuming it could be adapted to the commercial marketplace. Ceramics, solar cells, fiber optics, printed circuit boards, turbine blades, the insides of pipes and tubes—all were said to be potential markets for Wedtech's patented process. The company's hype in its annual report would have made a snake oil salesman blush: "The applications of this new coating technology are nearly endless, and more and more uses are being found as testing continues."

The guru of Wedtech's entry into the world of high technology was a Soviet-born scientist named Eduard Pinkhasov. Pinkhasov had come to the United State in 1978 at the age of forty. When Wedtech hired him as a tool- and die-maker in 1980, Pinkhasov, like so many newly arrived immigrants, was driving a cab in New York City.

Pinkhasov had been born in Tashkent, the son of a teacher. According to his resumé, he attended the Electrotechnical Institute of Communications from 1956 through 1961, receiving a degree in electrical engineering. After leaving school, he was assigned to work in Moscow at the Academy of Sciences' electronics institute. During his ten years at the institute, he was introduced to coating technology, particularly in its applications for solar energy and mirrors. He said he received his Ph.D. during this period (and therefore was known to all at Wedtech as *Dr.* Pinkhasov).

In 1972, Pinkhasov returned to Tashkent as the head of the laboratory at the National Gas Industry, where he worked until he emigrated. By then the KGB evidently did not believe that he possessed current scientific or technical information of any importance. Pinkhasov apparently left the Soviet Union at the behest of his wife, who already had family in the United States and was anxious to join them.

During his first year at Wedtech, Pinkhasov was not held in any particular esteem. In fact his supervisors regarded him as rather a mediocre tool- and die-maker. After about eight months, Pinkhasov began pestering his superiors, telling them he'd been working on a great invention. No one took the Russian very seriously.

All that changed, however, the day federal agents came to Wedtech's offices and asked to interview Pinkhasov. They had heard Pinkhasov had been involved in some research regarding the Soviet space program and wanted to find out what he knew. Mariotta served the agents coffee; the agents told Mariotta that, in the Soviet Union, Pinkhasov was a famous scientist.

"I wish he was a famous tool- and die-maker," Mariotta replied.

Exactly which government agency interviewed Pinkhasov isn't entirely clear; the consensus is that it was the CIA. In any event, the debriefing was something U.S. intelligence agencies do routinely. It is known as interviewing "white travellers," people who have had legal access to areas off-limits to U.S. officials. But to John Mariotta, this was James Bond stuff. If the CIA thought Pinkhasov had secret information important to the country, then it must be so. It was as if the United States government had certified that Wedtech was sitting on a gold mine!

Not long afterward, Pinkhasov was in Mariotta's office trying to explain about "coatings." A burly middle-aged man with the

Russian emigrée's seemingly obligatory gold crowns, Pinkhasov was no fool. In his heavily accented English, he made the process sound as exotic and unique as he could. At first, Mariotta thought Pinkhasov was talking about overcoats, some new type of outer garment. No, no, no, said Pinkhasov. To bridge the communications gap, Pinkhasov brought in an elderly associate named Henry Hochfeld with whom he had worked in the Soviet Union.

With Hochfeld translating, Pinkhasov began explaining his process for transferring molecules from one surface to another. Mariotta, who had been fascinated by chemistry since his childhood, became absorbed. He was taken with the sincerity with which Hochfeld described the process. Mariotta also saw in Pinkhasov something of himself—the inarticulate outsider pleading for a chance to prove himself. Based on what Pinkhasov and Hochfeld told him, Mariotta, the high school dropout, decided Pinkhasov was on the verge of a great technological breakthrough.

The next step was to work out an agreement with Pinkhasov regarding what he would do for the company and what the company would do for him. Pinkhasov may have been new to the United States, but he had quickly learned the basic principles of a free market economy. By mid–1981, he was negotiating terms with the company that called for him to receive royalties and maintain control of the process.

A contract between Wedtech and Pinkhasov was signed that fall requiring the company to furnish the Soviet scientist with a laboratory and all the supplies and equipment needed to develop the vapor deposition process. Wedtech also promised that Pinkhasov would get 5 percent of any royalties and 30 percent of any licensing fees earned from his coating process. In addition, his salary was raised from $6 an hour to $600 a week. Pinkhasov estimated he would be able to turn his process into something with commercial applications in six months to a year. The first year's budget for the research effort was $100,000, including Pinkhasov's salary.

In January 1982, Pinkhasov declared success. In a letter to Moreno, he announced that ". . . the program originally contemplated to be accomplished within one year has been actually completed in less than four months at a cost about half of the figure as originally estimated . . . The plant is ready to accept work on a commercial basis."

To perform the work, Pinkhasov submitted a $7.7 million request in March for vacuum equipment, test apparatus, and the upgrading of utilities. At this point, Pinkhasov was working in a large room in the rear of the company's headquarters in the Bronx. He had filed a U.S. patent application entitled "Noncrucible Method of and Apparatus for the Vapor Deposition of Material Upon a Substrate Using Voltaic Arc in Vacuum." The patent for the technique was issued in September 1982.

Eighteen months after Pinkhasov declared he was ready for commercial contracts, the company had yet to realize any revenues from this new coating process. Nonetheless, Mariotta had come to believe in Pinkhasov and his miracle process with the fervor of a disciple. Perhaps it was because the U.S. Patent Office had actually granted Pinkhasov a patent. Perhaps it was Mariotta's willingness to accept on blind faith matters that he didn't fully understand. Perhaps it was because Pinkhasov, with his longish graying hair, heavy jowls, and mysterious foreign accent, so perfectly fit Mariotta's conception of a scientific genius. Whatever the reason, in Mariotta's eyes Pinkhasov held the key to Wedtech's future.

For Mariotta it became imperative to get Pinkhasov to sign a long-term employment contract. Why he imagined Pinkhasov would be able to find anyone else to give him a better deal is hard to fathom. The Soviet scientist had an unproven technology that no one other than Mariotta had ever shown much interest in. Yet Mariotta was paranoid about Pinkhasov leaving the employ of Wedtech and someone else gaining access to Pinkhasov's secrets.

Whether Pinkhasov had deluded himself that the American business community was hungering for his services is unclear. He was, however, smart enough to grab the very good deal that Wedtech offered him. The contract he signed in June 1983 was for five years. It called for a salary of $80,000 the first year, growing to $117,128 in the fifth year. He was also guaranteed four weeks paid vacation per year.

A month after Mariotta gave Dr. Pinkhasov his absurdly generous contract, a technical assessment of the coating technology was completed. The assessment, done by Technology Assessment Group Inc. of Schenectady, New York, contained a number of conjectural findings.

For one thing, the assessment concluded, ". . . the Welbilt coating process has unique features which may permit it to produce good quality coatings in a cost effective manner . . . We have seen no evidence, however, that the coatings produced have any unique characteristics which make them superior in quality to other similar coatings available in the market place."

204

The assessment went on to indicate that "there may be insufficient understanding of the physics and chemistry of the process to permit easy scale up to larger equipment and large size products . . . Despite claims of extreme interest by numerous potential customers, of the four we were permitted to contact . . . only [one] is still sufficiently interested to be considered a real potential customer."

The report also explained at some length that, because the report's authors were restricted in what they were allowed to see and what information they were given, they could not verify most of the claims made for the process.

Wedtech's use of the findings was highly selective. The company was about to go public. The coatings technology would enable investors to think they were buying equity in a sexy, high-tech growth company. Thus, in the prospectus for the initial public offering, the company painted this picture of its coating process:

> The Company believes that the process developed by Dr. Pinkhasov represents a significant improvement over other coating methods . . . A number of prototype applications have been developed and tested . . . and prospective customers have indicated satisfaction with such prototypes.

Based on such optimism, an analyst with Moseley Hallgarten (the underwriter for the initial public offering) listed Wedtech as a "new purchase recommendation." In late 1983 the analyst issued a report stating that "the unique coating process developed by Wedtech Corp. represents an advancement of the state of the art in the coating of metals, nonmetals . . ."

Once again, bombast had supplanted fact.

Pinkhasov, recognizing Mariotta as a true believer, poured it on. He forwarded to Mariotta an article from *USA Today* entitled "Coming Soon on Moon" with a cover memo which announced:

> You will note that a study has been conducted by NASA scientists involving the production of water and oxygen-bearing substances by thermal processing lunar rocks . . . I, personally, was also involved in a similar study while in the Soviet Union. Several devices, designed under my guidance, proved the feasibility of such a project . . . I propose WEDTECH send [a letter] to NASA in the hope of exploring and establishing working relationship with NASA

205

. . . I feel that to participate in such an undertaking would offer great prestige and publicity to WEDTECH.

Despite Wedtech's expression of interest, NASA, luckier or more nimble than the Pentagon, managed to escape the company's embrace. Pinkhasov nevertheless was later granted patents for processes to obtain water from lunar rocks. At considerable expense, Wedtech paid for the filing and protection of these patents, although how the company expected to make money from moon rocks was never clear.

Mariotta, unable to promise Pinkhasov the moon, remained panicked at the idea that he would defect from Wedtech, despite a contract that was good through 1988 and a "do not compete" clause effective through 1990. In an effort to keep his resident scientific genius happy, Mariotta had the board of directors provide him a house. Not just any house. It was to be in Westchester Country, worth up to $500,000, and chosen by Pinkhasov. Pinkhasov would lease the house from Wedtech for approximately $1,000 a month. Naturally, Pinkhasov chose a house in Scarsdale.

When Pinkhasov had marital problems, he apparently convinced Mariotta and Moreno that his estranged wife was liable to gain some control over his patents as part of their divorce settlement. They arranged for Squadron Ellenoff to handle the divorce—at a cost of $30,437 to Wedtech.

In early 1984, Pinkhasov moved his research lab from the Bronx to a pseudo-Georgian building situated just off the Hutchinson River Parkway in a secluded wooded park in Mount Vernon, N.Y. Wedtech had acquired the 51,000-square-foot building in conjunction with a $5 million Industrial Revenue Bond offering through the City of Mount Vernon. About $2 million of the money was used for renovations and decorating.

And what decorating it was! The Wedtech crowd apparently decided that a parklike setting in upscale Westchester County demanded an English country look. So with a heavy hand they set about trying to achieve what they believed an English country house cum corporate offices cum laboratory should look like. Rooms were stuffed with reproduction Chippendale chairs and tables. Bookshelves were filled with untouched leatherbound editions of great works and endless brass figurines. Walls were covered with mirrors, clocks, and prints. To many visitors, the lobby—with its spiral staircase, high-back chairs and chandeliers—resembled nothing so much as the entrance to a bordello.

In the labs, security was the order of the day. In addition to TV camera surveillance and a guard inside the front entrance, all of the interior doors had locks that could be released only by inserting a personalized entry card into the mechanism. Pinkhasov was the only employee whose card allowed him entry to all the rooms; the others were restricted to entering and leaving the lab in which they actually worked.

Virtually all the "scientists" who worked in the labs were from the Soviet Union. Many could barely speak or read English. Instructions, written in Russian, were taped to the sides of the vacuum chambers and other equipment. Pinkhasov was the only one who knew what was going on and he wasn't talking, at least not to anyone competent to evaluate the technical aspects of what he claimed he was doing.

"Pinkhasov ran it like he was developing the A-bomb," recalls one former Wedtech employee.

Pinkhasov, perhaps because of his training in the Soviet Union, perhaps to preserve the aura of mystery that surrounded his coating process, refused to allow even "official visitors" access to the labs. One confrontation occurred when inspectors from the U.S. Department of Labor demanded entrance to perform safety inspections. Pinkhasov refused them. They blustered and threatened to get court orders, but Pinkhasov held firm. In the end, the Labor Department apparently decided it wasn't worth the trouble.

The Teamsters representatives wanted to survey the jobs being performed by the machine operators to determine if some of them should be classified as union positions. Pinkhasov refused to allow them in. They blustered and threatened to call a wildcat strike. Pinkhasov held firm and the union backed down.

The risk appraisers from the company providing the property insurance wanted access in order to determine the insurance rates. Pinkhasov refused. They appraisers shrugged and said if they didn't get access, they had no choice but to charge the company the highest possible rates. Pinkhasov held firm and Wedtech ended up paying exorbitant property insurance premiums.

With the new building came a new list of equipment demands. The price tag was $4 million.

Pinkhasov and his technical sales force never had any problem getting people interested in the process. With the extravagant claims being made for it, it should have been no surprise that many companies wanted to visit Mount Vernon and to send samples to be coated. The difficulty came when Pinkhasov was unable to deliver what he had promised. Often, customers would receive coated samples and, after testing them, discover that they were unsatisfactory in terms of adhesion, purity, uniformity of thickness, or smoothness. After a couple of such failures, the prospective customer would lose interest.

AMP Inc. had connector housings coated with aluminum in October 1984; it reported that "the adhesion was marginal." Morgan Semiconducter Inc. had a silicon nitride coating applied to a crucible; it reported that "the very rough surface prevented the process from producing any usable crystal." Hughes Aircraft had sample quartz tubes coated with silver; according to an internal Wedtech memo, "their tests revealed that our deposit of silver was too porous . . . This was our third attempt at this application. Hughes stated that they are discontinuing this approach and are therefore not interested in any more samples." Motorola showed initial enthusiasm in early 1985, but further testing revealed that the "initial samples consisting of copper deposited on aluminum oxide exhibited very poor adhesion . . . Deposition uniformity is a problem . . . In view of the above, the coating appears to be unsuitable for our application, and any further investigations on our part cannot be justified."

Despite these failures, hope sprang eternal. The Wedtech crowd had been repeating the same overblown claims about Pinkhasov and his coating process so often they seem to have convinced themselves that it was all true. Pinkhasov's star never dimmed, and the enthusiasm remained high.

In July 1985, Touche Ross was brought in to do a market development analysis. (Throwing lucrative consulting contracts to Touche Ross was part of Wedtech's strategy for attempting to compromise the independence of its new auditors.) The financial projections it prepared, based on management's estimates, showed revenues for 1986 of $21 million and net income of $2.1 million. The projections for 1987 were even rosier, showing revenues of $33.2 million and net income of $5.4 million. Actual revenues in 1986 turned out to be less than $250,000 (derived from fees Wedtech charged to coat samples); the coating division had a net loss of about $4 million.

Partly as a result of these fantastic projections, Wedtech had established a wholly owned subsidiary, incorporated as Vapor Technologies Inc. The plan was to put all of the assets of Wedtech's coating division into Vapor Technologies and take it public just as soon as the first big order was received. Taking Wedtech public had made them all very rich; repeating the trick with Vapor Technologies would have been like hitting the daily double. The Wedtech executives even met with lawyers from major firms for preliminary discussions about using Vapor Technology to raise venture capital.

Wedtech also hired a Washington representative for Vapor Technologies—John R. Zagame, a former top aide to Senator D'Amato. Zagame's fee was to be $5,000 a month. He promised to pursue direct federal funding for Vapor Technologies' processes, emphasizing that "Senator D'Amato's office will be a key point of contact in this effort."

Zagame wasn't the only Wedtech consultant trying to hawk Dr. Pinkhasov's miracle process. Jim Jenkins was enamored with the notion of using the coating process in mass production. In one of his more famous experiments, Pinkhasov had succeeded in coating gold onto toilet paper. While the commercial market for gold-coated toilet paper seemed limited, Jenkins had another idea, one with almost unlimited potential. What about applying a transparent coating to United States paper currency? The coating would prolong the life of the bills, reduce the costs of constantly replacing them, and make the currency harder to counterfeit.

After an initial meeting with Treasury Department officials, Jenkins transmitted a euphoric report: "Had excellent luncheon meeting. Enthusiastic response . . . Nothing like this process has ever been suggested. Entire U.S. currency system being revamped in 1987 . . . Potential is huge, I suspect we must form subsidiary company to deal with this special coating aspect effectively."

Wedtech went so far as to spend $206 to buy four sheets of uncut bills with which to experiment. As usual, however, Pinkhasov couldn't deliver.

Jenkins didn't give up. He next decided Wedtech should use its process to put a protective coating on the inside of gun barrels to protect them from wear. After all, Wedtech had been claiming for several years that one of the advantages of Pinkhasov's process was that it could be used to coat tubes and pipes. In his note to Moreno on the subject, Jenkins again waxed euphoric: "Next to paper currency, gun barrells [sic] may be the most numerous items in the world . . . if there's a chance we can coat these, it should be in the presentation Wed. to Dr. Keyworth at the White House." (George

209

A. Keyworth II was the White House science adviser.) After a good deal of thrashing about, it became clear that Pinkhasov could not put the required coating on the insides of gun barrels.

Bob Wallach also was active in trying to market the coating technology. As usual, his contributions were nebulous. He once referred to his "intangible" contributions as his "product of productivity." For the most part, his "product of productivity" seemed to be memos filled with self-important rhetoric and California spinach talk.

As part of the LTAVD sales effort, Wallach had attended a presentation to the Raytheon Corporation in Boston. He memorialized the meeting in a six-page memo. Wallach's "description" of the presentation (the memo went to several people who'd been at the meeting) was essentially a piece of self-puffery explaining how the whole thing would have been a disaster for Wedtech had it not been for his last-minute heroics. ("Right up until the time I arrived . . . no one seemed to know precisely . . . what we were to accomplish . . . My role of introducing the group . . . seemed to be effective.")

As with most communications from Wallach, this one quickly sank under the weight of platitudes ("We simply cannot be going helter-skelter into major presentations"), patronizing pats on the head ("Mario was very impressive . . . John did a very fine job . . ."), and exhortations to win one for Wedtech ("We are a strong company with an excellent product, even a revolutionary one, and we are interested in people who treat us on an equal footing and in good faith.")

Despite all this high-level and very expensive assistance, Pinkhasov and his coating process had yet to land a contract. The lack of revenues, however, did not act as a brake on the rising costs of the coating division.

Pinkhasov entered into yet another employment contract in early 1986, this one even more generous than the previous ones. The new contract ran through 1996, providing a base salary of $125,000. It also guaranteed him raises of 10 percent each year, which meant that by the last year of the contract, Pinkhasov's salary was to be almost $325,000. He was still to receive percentages of any royalties and licensing fees Wedtech received.

Later in 1986, the scientist decided to exercise his purchase option on the house he was "renting" from Wedtech. The house, then conservatively valued at more than $800,000, was sold to Pinkhasov for $500,000. He didn't even pay that much. He received credit for the rent he had paid; and he received another $33,000 credit after complaining that he had spent $53,000 furnishing the house and had been reimbursed "only" $20,000.

By mid–1986, the coating division had thirty-nine employees (including one with the job title of "hostess") and a monthly payroll of $85,000. It was then that Wedtech finally verged on obtaining what looked like a real contract. It was selected to participate in a two-year program with Martin Marietta Energy Systems for developing ceramic coatings resistant to stress damage.

Wedtech estimated that it would cost $955,978 to perform its portion of the contract. To get the contract, Wedtech offered a "cost sharing arrangement" in which Wedtech would bear half of the direct costs and would absorb all capital equipment costs. Pinkhasov submitted a list to Moreno detailing the $456,000 in equipment and materials that he needed for the contract. Despite the ballyhoo, the Martin Marietta contract would be, like all of the other Wedtech contracts, a money loser.

The whole coating division, in fact, ended up just one big money sump. Between 1981 and 1986, Wedtech poured roughly $15 million into Pinkhasov's hobby shop and had almost nothing to show in return. LTAVD did provide one very valuable function, however. It kept investors salivating for the big bonanza just around the corner, which in turn kept the price of Wedtech stock at a premium.

211

# 20

# The Problem of John

**E**ver since the first public offering, the "financial guys" had moved to higher prominence in the Wedtech hierarchy while the "manufacturing guys" had been relegated to supporting roles. The corporate officers and the various consultants increasingly focused on a single variable: the price of a share of Wedtech's common stock. Which was understandable, given the extent to which their personal fortunes were tied up in restricted stock and stock options.

Propping up Wedtech's stock price meant cooking the books to show impressive quarterly increases in sales and earnings. It meant cultivating, and misleading, stock analysts and institutional investors. It meant erecting a veneer of respectability around the company: glossy annual reports; a listing on the American Stock Exchange, then the New York Stock Exchange; a respected corporate law firm, Squadron Ellenoff; Big Eight auditors, first Main Hurdman, then Touche Ross; venerable investment bankers, Moseley Hallgarten and Bear Stearns & Company Inc; a well-regarded investor relations firm, Kehoe, White, Savage & Company Inc.

During 1985, however, it became increasing obvious there was a chink in this veneer of respectability. The chink had a name—John Mariotta. As long as Wedtech's chairman and chief executive remained a machinist who publicly described himself as Chauncey the gardener and said he was living in the Twilight Zone, it would be hard for the company to gain real respectability on Wall Street.

Although Mariotta had founded the company and, in many respects, personalized what Wedtech purported to represent, there was no longer any doubt that the business had outgrown him. "This company is bigger than you and me," he would tell Ed McCarthy, currently vice-president for contract administration. As the focus of management shifted from the shop floor to the board room, Mariotta's ability to exercise direct control weakened. His unique management style became less of an asset and, in many cases, an outright embarrassment.

The disastrous "road show" in connection with the initial public offering convinced Mariotta's colleagues to leave home without him when meeting with buttoned-down representatives of financial institutions and investment houses. Still, they couldn't hide him entirely.

At the first meeting of the Wedtech board of directors in the fall of 1983, Mariotta had sat at the end of the table and spent much of the time filling out Lotto tickets. Asked what he was doing, Mariotta replied, "Don't laugh at me. If I hit the lottery, then we will have the money that we need ...." Mariotta added that his luck might not be sufficient and suggested that everyone else on the board play Lotto as well.

By early 1985, Wallach was meeting with Guariglia, Moreno, Neuberger, and Shorten to discuss how the company could upgrade its image. Wedtech should get a new president to oversee the defense business, it was decided, preferably "a blond-haired, blue-eyed, white Anglo-Saxon Protestant who could be a member of the country club." A country-club WASP was needed because Wedtech's biggest customer was now the U.S. Navy, the most class-conscious of the services.

Wedtech's executive search for a suitable WASP was notably unsuccessful. The company did offer the presidency of the defense division to a retired army lieutenant general, but he wasn't interested in relocating to New York. By this point, of course, it was nearly impossible to bring a newcomer into the ranks of upper management. If they hired someone honest and competent, they risked being exposed as thieves. If they hired a crook, they'd have to share the booty.

Not surprisingly, therefore, the executive WASP search ended in

June 1985 with the appointment of Tony Guariglia as Wedtech's new president. The swarthy Brooklyn native wasn't exactly what the company had started out looking for, but at least he was a CPA who understood public accounting and sophisticated financial transactions. Best of all, he had an uncanny ability to look people straight in the eye and lie.

Bob Wallach remained unflagging in his efforts to enhance the company's image—and his own—especially by way of his friend Ed Meese.

In the spring of 1983, Wallach had convened a San Francisco farewell luncheon for himself at Jack's Restaurant to which he invited some of the most important judges and attorneys of the Bay Area. At that meeting, he announced to the group that he met Ed Meese almost daily, and "through me, you can send messages to this man." Wallach then solicited suggestions of things good for the country. Wallach apparently didn't realize that his constant hints as to how important he was were not very subtle and were, in fact, making him seem somewhat ludicrous. As one of the judges in attendance later put it, "Given a choice between sinister and absurd, it was absurd."

Wallach's relationship with Meese and the proximity to power it gave him seemed to make him almost giddy with a sense of his own self-importance. On a Wedtech trip to Israel to visit the company's subsidiary, Wallach told the Wedtech executives he would have to slip away for a while to take care of some (presumably secret) business with the Israeli government. At one point in 1985, Meese, Wallach, and Neuberger were all in Israel at the same time. Wallach invited Neuberger to get together with him and Meese. What the hell, figured Neuberger. So the crooked Bronx businessman and the attorney general exchanged pleasantries over drinks at the King David Hotel in Jerusalem.

Throughout Meese's years in Washington, Wallach deluged him with memoranda on a variety of subjects, in few of which he had any real expertise. For example, Wallach sent Meese memos advising him on Soviet-Polish relations, on the Pacific Basin, on Afghanistan, on how to settle the war in the Falklands, and one *tour d'horizon* regarding the general world situation. In his memos, Wallach would suggest to Meese at various times that he (Wallach) be appointed the ambassador to the United Nations, a Middle East negotiator, or solicitor general of the United States.

214

Wallach also inundated the Wedtech executives with memos. Even a quick reading suggests Wallach deluded himself into ignoring, overlooking, or rationalizing any indications that Wedtech's managers were other than model corporate citizens. It was as though he bent reality to conform with the idealized vision of Wedtech he had created in his head. As long as he told himself that Wedtech was a social exemplar and its officers a group of lovable bootstrap entrepreneurs, he could continue making a lot of money with very little effort.

In the spring of 1985, not long after Meese was confirmed as attorney general, Wallach introduced to Wedtech two individuals—both epitomizing the kind of sophistication he thought the company needed. Their names were Wayne Franklyn Chinn and Rusty Kent London.

Wallach had met London around September 1983, when London rented him a $2,600-a-month apartment in San Francisco directly below his own. Landlord and tenant quickly struck up a social relationship: they began jogging together, and Wallach represented London in a civil case. In late 1984, London introduced Wallach to a friend and business associate, Frank Chinn. Perhaps the most remarkable thing about Chinn and London was they made the eccentric Wallach look almost dull by comparison.

Wayne Franklyn Chinn was born in Shanghai in 1942 and came to the United States in 1945, a refugee from the war. His first job was as an encyclopedia salesman. Apparently he was extraordinarily successful, ending up managing a sales force in Africa, the Middle East, and Southeast Asia. He claimed that by the time he quit, he was making as much as $50,000 per month.

He then turned his attention to the stock market. During the 1960s, he worked in the San Francisco office of McDonnell & Co., gaining a reputation as an aggressive salesman. After McDonnell collapsed in 1969, Chinn moved on to E. F. Hutton, working as a broker in the firm's San Francisco office. By the mid–1970s, he was self-employed, trading for his own account and doing some financial consulting. He later told the Wedtech executives that he managed about $1 billion in assets for various investors in the Middle East; implausibly, he claimed to have doubled the size of the investment, earning fees of some $200 million.

During this period, Chinn acquired a somewhat unsavory reputation as a trader who played it very close to the edge. A short, slender man with almost aquiline features, Chinn did not radiate the good, gray sobriety often associated with those who make their living persuading others to entrust them with their money. His straight black hair was worn long and parted in the middle. His clothes were Western casual—boots, jeans, and fringed leather jackets. He drove around in a Rolls Royce, a Cadillac, and a Jeep. And, it was reported, he carried a pistol.

Adding to Chinn's mystique was his marriage from 1961 to 1967 to Shadan Shazly, the dark and beautiful daughter of the former chief of staff of the Egyptian army. An organization run by her father was widely reported to have claimed credit for the 1981 assassination of President Anwar Sadat.

About the same time Wallach introduced Chinn to Wedtech, he also introduced Chinn to his friend in Washington, Ed Meese. At the time, Meese, recently confirmed as attorney general, was in the process of liquidating his stock holdings and designating someone to manage his money in a blind trust. Wallach recommended Chinn, who had obtained returns on Wallach's money in excess of 20 percent.

Meese never bothered to check on Chinn's background or reputation. Apparently, his idea of blind trust was to follow Wallach's advice without question. And so the attorney general of the United States invested his $54,581 nest egg not with a major financial institution such as Merrill Lynch or Shearson but with Frankie Chinn, a wheeler-dealer who operated out of a studio apartment on the sixth floor of a residential complex on Jones Street in San Francisco. At the time, Chinn was managing a grand total of four investment accounts: his own, his mother's, Wallach's, and Marymount College's.

Chinn's specialty was trading new stock issues. Through extensive personal contacts, he had become known as a "regular calendar player"—someone whose speciality was buying stock on the first day it was issued. As a regular calendar player, Chinn was often allocated blocks of "hot issues" by their underwriters. The demand for shares of these hot issues was such that their value was almost certain to increase during the first day they were traded. Even if a new issue of stock was not particularly "hot" or desirable, the underwriter was frequently committed to supporting a specific price for a new issue.

Chinn would arrange to buy the stock at the issue price and sell it the same day, a practice known as "flipping." This enabled him to take advantage of any price increase that occurred on that day, either because it was a hot issue or because the underwriter was buying to support the price.

While flipping is disparaged by many money managers (because one is competing with regular customers like Chinn who have better access to new issues), it is not illegal. A couple of Chinn's other practices may have crossed the line, however.

One is called "free riding." A "free ride" means that stock is bought without the money being available to pay for it. In most cases, it is a violation of the credit rules established by the Federal Reserve Board. In Chinn's case, he was able to use different brokerages and clearinghouses to avoid having to put up the purchase price of the new issues he was buying. Chinn's transactions were arranged so that he bought and sold the same shares virtually simultaneously. Thus, the money received from the sale of the shares was used to pay the purchase price for those same shares. On the rare occasions when the price of the stock decreased and the amount realized from the sale was not sufficient to pay the full purchase price, Chinn had to pay only the amount of the decrease, usually quite small.

Chinn's other dubious activity involved rebates of sales commissions. Because of its frequent trading activity, Chinn's small investment firm was often entitled to commission rebates. Rather than pass these rebates on to his clients, Chinn had them deposited in accounts in Hong Kong. From 1985 through 1987 these rebates may have totalled as much as $1 million. Obtaining rebates that aren't shared is the same as receiving undisclosed compensation and is considered to be a fraudulent securities transaction. Further, by moving the money to accounts in Hong Kong, where it was invested in gold contracts, Chinn may have violated Hong Kong's laws.

Chinn's colleague, Dr. Rusty Kent London, had an even more exotic background. London was born in Jersey City, New Jersey, in 1943 as Irving Louis Lobsenz. A brilliant student with wide-ranging interests, Lobsenz graduated with honors in zoology from the University of California at Berkeley in 1963 and received a medical degree from Washington University in St. Louis. While in medical school, he changed his name to Irving Louis London. He then attended a postgraduate research program in pediatrics at the San Francisco Medical Center; in 1969 he was licensed to practice medicine in California.

London was a full head taller than Chinn, slender and athletic

217

looking, with thick glasses and reddish hair. Quiet, courteous and intense, he seemed a man who would have a good bedside manner. But in the early 1970s, London gave up the practice of medicine to devote his intellectual energies to investing and gambling. By 1971, he was an executive with a water bed company known as Innerspace Environments Inc.

Shortly thereafter, London underwent another transformation, this time becoming an author named Ian Andersen. During this period, London became what he described as "a master game player" who "is considered by many to be the best blackjack player in the world . . ."

London/Andersen wrote a book, *Turning the Tables on Las Vegas*, in which he described his system for winning at blackjack. Evidently believing that he had more advice he should share with the world, he wrote *Making Money*, in 1978. This book provided insights into investing in real estate, finding tax loopholes, and setting up foreign bank accounts. In the introduction, London/Andersen stated: "I have been enormously successful at making money. What turns me on is playing games where others make the rules. I like to study all the parameters and systematically approach the problem of how to win—and keep winning."

In 1979, London/Andersen turned his hand to fiction, publishing *The Big Night*, a novel about a scheme that tricked the Las Vegas casinos out of $1 million. The author's blurb on the jacket of the book stated: "Mr. Andersen has parlayed his Las Vegas plunder into seven figures by playing the investment game—negotiations, real estate, the stock market, foreign currencies, etc."

London/Andersen had an unusual relationship with his publishers, first Vanguard Books and then Simon & Schuster. Neither publisher ever met their author and both remained unaware of Andersen's real name. They did not even have a phone number at which to call him. All his royalties were sent to a bank account in Liechtenstein.

By 1983, London underwent still another transformation. He again changed his name, this time to Rusty Kent London.

With their backgrounds and approaches to doing business, Chinn and London were naturals for the Wedtech team. They were introduced at an April 30, 1985 meeting at the offices of Squadron Ellenoff.

Wallach had described Chinn as a shrewd financial consultant who knew the major players in the investment community. Chinn explained that he was an expert in promoting stocks. By that, he meant he was able to raise a stock's price by increasing investor demand. The others at the meeting—Mariotta, Neuberger, Moreno, Guariglia, and Shorten—listened attentively. They held large blocks of Wedtech stock (although, at this time, Mariotta supposedly owned almost all of it), and they had a strong interest in keeping the price as high as possible. They quickly decided to provide Chinn and London with similar incentives. Arthur Siskind, the partner in charge of the Wedtech account, was called into the room and instructed to draw up an agreement for Chinn and London to receive 50,000 stock options apiece in return for their "public relations" services.

In June, a secret deal was struck with Chinn and London, as later revealed by company officers. The two would tout Wedtech stock, which, they assured the Wedtech executives, would cause a run-up in its price. In return, the executives promised to pay Chinn and London 10 percent of any increase of the value of their shares from the then-current price of $13. Guariglia cautioned his cronies that this type of deal involving company insiders was supposed to be disclosed to their lawyers and the SEC. As they had no intention of disclosing it, they agreed to keep it secret.

Chinn's Asian ancestry also proved valuable to Wedtech. The SBA had been raising a number of questions about Wedtech's eligibility to continue in the 8(a) program. One was that the board of directors had more non-minority members than minority members. To defuse that criticism, Wedtech added two individuals to the board who could qualify as "economically and socially disadvantaged." One was retired Gen. Richard Cavazos, the first Hispanic to reach the four-star rank in the army. The other was Frank Chinn. Chinn qualified as "socially disadvantaged" because of his Chinese descent. According to Moreno, Chinn said he could qualify as "economically disadvantaged" because most of his assets were in foreign trusts. (Moreno himself had similarly qualified as "disadvantaged" the previous fall. "Dear Mario: It is a privilege for me to know so many poor and economically disadvantaged people," Ehrlich had written in his congratulatory letter.)

One person not thrilled to see Chinn elected to the board was Jack Kehoe, who handled Wedtech's shareholder relations. Kehoe had known the new director from his days at McDonnell & Co., when he went by "Frankie Chinn" instead of W. Franklyn Chinn.

Kehoe checked with his old acquaintances and was told Chinn had a reputation as a wheeler-dealer who ran with a fast crowd. Kehoe brought his apprehensions to Guariglia and Shorten. "Chinn is in," he was told, and he would just have to figure out a way to work with him.

On the same day as Chinn was elected to the board, Guariglia and Moreno approached him with another deal. Chinn was going to be sitting on the compensation committee, which recommended how much the executives should be paid. Guariglia and Moreno were eager for the board to award them 200,000 stock options apiece. If you help to get those options approved, they told Chinn, we will each give you 20 percent of the number we are awarded. Chinn did, and they did.

It didn't take Chinn long to adapt to the Wedtech style. The company provided him his own Diners Club card, and Chinn began living royally. He jetted between coasts (leaving Manhattan by helicopter) and to Florida, Australia, Europe, and Asia, supposedly on company business. He ran up enormous bills at hotels and restaurants. By the end of the year, Chinn had charged more than $17,000 to Wedtech on the Diners Club alone. The expenses he charged on other cards or directly to the company brought the figure to in excess of $20,000.

Dr. London, meanwhile, was focusing his efforts on the Far East. Being something of a Japan buff, having visited the country twenty or thirty times, he had reportedly become a connoisseur of Japanese antiques and had built a spectacular home in Honolulu by moving it piece by piece from Japan.

London was enamored with Japanese management techniques. In an October 1985 memo to Wedtech's senior managers, London urged that the South Bronx company follow the example of the Matsushita Electric Company and foster the seven values: national service through industry, fairness, harmony and cooperation, struggle for betterment, courtesy and humility, flexibility and adjustment, and gratitude. How the Wedtech team, whose idea of enlightened management was to grease palms, reacted to these suggestions can only be imagined.

Tony Guariglia no doubt tossed them in the circular file, but he did find London useful in another area. On a trip to England, he and London visited one of the casinos. At the high-stakes blackjack table, London stood behind Guariglia, watching him play. At one point, seeing Guariglia hesitate about whether to draw another card, London leaned over and whispered, "Take it, it's a five." Guariglia did, and it was.

The episode made for a good story, and Guariglia was greatly impressed. But London's main mission was to interest the Japanese in Wedtech's patented miracle coating process. If Wedtech could show interest in the process from a reputable company, the stock price would surely get a boost. After extended negotiations, an agency agreement was signed with Sumitomo Corporation, a large Japanese trading company. The agreement did little more than designate Sumitomo as the exclusive agent in the Far East for products using the coating process. In other words, it did not result in any revenues for Wedtech.

London also tried to negotiate a licensing agreement between the two companies in which Sumitomo would pay Wedtech if it used the process in commercial production runs. London's difficulty in negotiating this licensing agreement was not Sumitomo; it was Dr. Pinkhasov and John Mariotta. From the outset, Pinkhasov resisted any arrangement that would enable the Japanese technical experts (or any other technically qualified people) to get more than a superficial look at the process. Pinkhasov argued that if the Japanese had access to his secrets, they would steal the process. Mariotta meanwhile was insisting that Sumitomo make an absurdly high $50 million down payment. Although London appealed to Moreno, Pinkhasov, backed by Mariotta, prevailed. The Japanese, unwilling to enter into a licensing agreement without some assurance they would be provided the necessary technical information, walked away

It didn't take Chinn and London long to agree that something had to be done about Mariotta. Trying to inflate Wedtech's stock price with a loudmouthed "tinsmith" at the helm was like trying to raise the *Titanic*. And it wasn't just a matter of Mariotta's crudeness, now that his paranoia was paralyzing development of the coating process. The newcomers began conspiring with Guariglia to force Mariotta out.

Mariotta may have been irrational at times, but he was no dummy. He quickly picked up rumblings that the others were plotting to get rid of him. Wedtech's explosive growth had scared him; he was losing his grip. Still, no one was going to take away John Mariotta's child without a fight.

By mid–1985, the struggle for control of Wedtech was focused on a particular date: January 1, 1986. That was when Mariotta was supposed to default on the sham stock transfer and the others would get their shares back. Everyone knew, however, there was nothing in writing to prevent Mariotta from buying back the shares.

A few months before the big day, Mariotta told a presumably loyal Mario Moreno that he was exploring ways to buy the stock being held in escrow, especially that of Neuberger, who Mariotta thought was spending more time chasing women than he was working. Moreno was invited to lunch with Mariotta and Ralph Vallone, the Puerto Rican lawyer who would later be indicted for acting as the conduit for bribes to Rep. Robert Garcia.

Vallone, Mariotta, and Moreno met for four or five hours in a Chinese restaurant in midtown Manhattan. They discussed how Mariotta might raise enough money to buy Neuberger's stock and possibly that of some of the others. Vallone and Mariotta kicked around the possibility of a leveraged buyout of Wedtech; that is, they would use the assets of Wedtech to finance the acquisition of its stock.

Moreno reported the conversation to the other Wedtech executives. Although Mariotta had threatened to buy them out in the past, such threats had always been made during one of his tantrums and were not taken seriously. Now the gang was worried. Their concerns increased when, a few days later, Shorten reported on a recent conversation with Mariotta.

Shorten told the others that Mariotta had called him into his office and, in front of Jennie Mariotta, asked for advice about how he could obtain a bank loan of some $3 million using his Wedtech stock as security for the loan. Although Mariotta said he wanted the money for a new business venture, Shorten knew that making the first payment on the stock purchase would cost Mariotta about the same amount. He did not think that the similarity was coincidental.

After his briefing of the other members of the gang, Shorten called Jeffrey Rubin, an attorney with Squadron Ellenoff. He asked Rubin to monitor filings with the Securities and Exchange Commission to see if a hostile group, probably allied with Mariotta, was trying to take control of the company.

The uncertainty about Mariotta's intentions regarding their stock, his increasingly erratic behavior, and the pressure from Wallach, Chinn, and London were all having an effect on Mariotta's cronies. Still, ousting Mariotta carried enormous risks. Without Mariotta, the company would no doubt lose its 8(a) certification. More importantly, Mariotta knew enough about their criminal activities to put them all in jail. Irrational as he often was, they could easily imagine him turning them in, despite the risks to himself, in order to get even.

No one was deluded enough to think that Mariotta would agree to leave voluntarily. In his mind, Wedtech was still his company. Forcing him out was going to be traumatic. They needed an incident that could serve as a catalyst to precipitate action by the board of directors.

At Wedtech, one never had to wait long for the next bizarre incident, especially now with Mariotta becoming increasingly moody and temperamental. Mariotta's fights with Neuberger were already legendary. Neuberger would call his partner "banana head." They'd throw cups of coffee at each other. One story had it that during a lunch with managers from the army's Red River Depot in Texas, an important customer for Wedtech's cooling kits, Mariotta and Neuberger got into a heated argument. When hurling insults at each other no longer sufficed, the two executives stood up and continued the assault with bread rolls.

Shorten had also felt Mariotta's wrath. One tantrum had occurred while Shorten was negotiating a loan with a young banker. Mariotta charge into Shorten's office, his face mottled, eyes bulging, and spittle flying. "I pick you out of the street! I loan you money! And this is the way you treat me!" Mariotta screeched. The banker grew wide-eyed, Shorten grew pale.

"You'll be lucky to get any money out of that banker," a Wedtech consultant who witnessed the incident drily told Shorten afterward. And he was right.

John Mariotta's favorite whipping boy, however, was Mario Moreno, and it was an explosion with Moreno that would become the pretext for trying to force Mariotta out of the company.

One day in November, Mariotta stormed into Moreno's office, furious because he had just seen a list that referred to Deborah Scott, Moreno's secretary, as an "administrative assistant."

Scottie, as she was known, was a skinny widow in her mid-fifties with curly, unnaturally blond hair. Despite having a master's degree from New York University, she seemed to have an attention span measured in nanoseconds and to exhibit rather odd behavior. She talked to herself, muttering in the morning, baying by the evening. She was intensely loyal to Moreno, who reciprocated the attachment. Despite her flakiness, he steadfastly refused to fire her even when urged to do so by his cronies.

"She's no fucking administrator!" roared Mariotta. "She is just a simple secretary. You make her change her title or otherwise she goes out of this company."

Moreno often ignored, as best he could, Mariotta's tirades. This one, however, had the makings of an incident that could be used against Mariotta with the directors. So Moreno pressed the issue.

It wasn't fair, he responded. That woman was doing a lot for the company. She had been very good to everyone. She was very capable. She knew how to write English very well. Then he added, "John, if she goes out of the company, then I am going to go myself, too."

Moreno had no plans to go anyplace. He might delude himself about a lot of things, but he was smart enough to know that no one else would come close to providing him the $254,000 in compensation that he was receiving from Wedtech, much less the opportunity to steal hundreds of thousands more. But he had apparently decided to force a showdown with Mariotta.

Mariotta knew that Moreno was bluffing, but he didn't know that he was playing into his opponents' hands by pressing the point. "So leave the company, resign!" Mariotta screamed. "If you really have a pair of balls between your legs, you will resign immediately!"

Moreno now had the issue he had been angling for. "John, the problem is that you cannot fire me, and if I am going to resign, I will be willing to resign in front of the board of directors and we will bring all our issues out."

As soon as Mariotta had left his office, Moreno met with Neuberger, Guariglia, and Shorten. After describing the blowup, Moreno suggested that they were now in the position to force Mariotta's resignation. The others agreed. The four executives went to Mariotta's office and told him that they believed he should resign. They suggested he take a meaningless position as "chairman emeritus."

Mariotta's reaction was predictable. He refused.

"That is all bullshit," he said, peering angrily through his wire-framed glasses. "If I am in charge, I will be in charge."

The battle was joined.

As the data on which Mariotta would have to make the first stock payment approached, the issue of the tax consequences of his default became more significant. Neuberger had airily dismissed the problem two years earlier, but it no longer seemed so insignificant. The Internal Revenue Service would probably consider Mariotta's default as tantamount to a transfer of the stock to the other executives. If so, they would have to declare the stock as non-income compensation and pay tax on its value. For Neuberger that meant that the default would create a "taxable event" of about $20 million.

Guariglia, always working the angles, had been discussing the situation with Arthur Siskind and Howard Topaz, attorneys at Squadron Ellenoff, and the group soon came to a decision. If Mariotta were to rescind the agreement entirely, instead of defaulting on January 1, there would probably be no tax consequences at all. Their conclusion was based on the notion that rescinding the agreement had the effect of nullifying it. Therefore, the stock would be seen as never having left the control of its original owners. Therefore, no tax would be owed.

In mid-December, Mariotta came to Siskind's office at Squadron Ellenoff. He sat on the couch while the lawyer explained what was being proposed. From a tax standpoint, Siskind said, it didn't make any difference to Mariotta whether or not he agreed to the rescission. But the others believed it would be very helpful to *their* tax positions. Unless John were really intent on hurting his long-time partners, there was probably no reason he shouldn't sign it.

Listening to Siskind's smooth and clever appeal to his sense of fairness, Mariotta made no protest, encouraging the lawyers to draft the agreement. It was sent up to Mariotta's office at 595 Gerard Avenue on December 17, just before he and his wife were to leave for their annual Christmas trip to Puerto Rico. Incredibly, Mariotta signed the rescission, thus surrendering his only effective weapon with which to oppose the rest of the gang. Once he signed, the only power he had left was the ability to be a nuisance.

Why Mariotta was willing to sign the agreements is hard to fathom. He later alleged that he was tricked, that the lawyers merely told him his colleagues wanted to "rescind some documentation" and didn't explain what it was all about. The lawyers, he maintained, "accosted" him and "thrust" the rescission agreements in front of him. He signed them, believing that his colleagues "were acting honestly and in good faith."

It's true that Mariotta was a trusting soul who would often sign documents with only the faintest idea of what he was signing. Still, it strains credulity to think that he would sign such crucial documents on the assumption that people who a short while earlier had tried to fire him would be "acting honestly and in good faith." A more logical explanation would be that Mariotta, desperate to save his job, thought that if he did this favor for his cronies, if he kept his word, they would abandon their efforts to get rid of him.

If that indeed was his reasoning—that if he signed the rescission agreements his partners would leave him alone—he was badly mistaken. Fred Neuberger knew Mariotta best of any of the Wedtech gang. Even after Mariotta signed the agreement and left for Puerto Rico, Neuberger brooded. Mariotta hadn't yet actually returned the stock. He was irrational. If Mariotta decided that he must have revenge, he wouldn't be deterred by the cost to himself. So when Neuberger, Guariglia, and Moreno got together at Neuberger's winter home near Tampa between Christmas and New Year's, Neuberger had another suggestion for how to handle Mariotta.

As Moreno recalled it, Neuberger drew him to the side of his swimming pool and said he wanted to talk. Neuberger was feeling decidedly unsentimental about his long-time business partner. Mariotta, he said, was "a complete idiot" who could cause them a lot of trouble. But there was a way to prevent such trouble. Neuberger said he had contacts with former Israeli agents and could arrange to have Mariotta eliminated. Murdered. If done properly, this would not only prevent Mariotta from blowing the whistle, but Wedtech would solve its latest cash flow crisis by collecting on the $15 million "key man" life insurance policy the company had on Mariotta.

Moreno quickly spread Neuberger's proposal among the others. Despite its obvious attractions, they considered the plan extreme.

According to Moreno, he, Guariglia, and Neuberger celebrated New Year's Eve with their respective women at a Spanish restaurant in Tampa. Against a backdrop of flamenco dancers and castanets, Neuberger pulled the men aside and again proposed having Mariotta eliminated. Moreno and Guariglia again demurred. Neuberger was displeased.

"That's the problem with you people," he growled. "You are Boy Scouts."

August 5, 1980: Presidential nominee Ronald Reagan, speaking to the press during his visit to the South Bronx, pledges incentives for private enterprise in urban ghetto areas. *Wide World Photos.*

John Mariotta and Fred Neuberger in the Wedtech plant at 595 Gerard Avenue.

Lawrence Shorten (*left below*) and Mario Moreno. *Scott Barrow*

Rep. Mario Biaggi at a press
conference in his office, June
3, 1987.  *UPI/Bettmann
Newsphotos.*

Bernard Ehrlich. *Wide World Photos*

January 21, 1982: John Mariotta addresses President Reagan (*far right*) at a conference on urban enterprise zones in the Cabinet Room of the White House. Facing the President, left to right: Mariotta, Senator John Chaffee, Providence Mayor Vincent Cianci, Vice President George Bush, Kansas City Councilwoman Joanne Collin, and Secretary of the Treasury Donald Regan.

Howard Squadron, senior partner of Squadron, Ellenoff, Pleasant & Lehrer. *UPI/Bettmann Newsphotos.*

Richard Bluestine, Alfred Rivera (Wedtech's treasurer), and Anthony Guariglia. *Scott Barrow*

Lyn Nofziger. *UPI/Bettmann Newsphotos.*

Ceremony celebrating award of the pontoon contract at 595 Gerard Avenue. *From left:* Sen. Alfonse D'Amato, Jennie Mariotta, Rep. Mario Biaggi (*speaking*), Rep. Robert Garcia, Peter Neglia (*standing*), Fred Neuberger, unidentified man, and Vito Castellano.

E. Robert Wallach. *Wide World Photos.*

Rep. Robert Garcia and his wife Jane hold hands as they leave Federal Court in New York. *Wide World Photos.*

Maryland state senator Michael Mitchell (*left*) and his brother, former state senator Clarence Mitchell III, talk to the media outside U.S. District Court in Baltimore. *UPI/Bettmann Newsphotos.*

W. Franklyn Chinn. *Wide World Photos.*

R. Kent London. *Wide World Photos.*

The Wedtech float in the 1984 Puerto Rican Day Parade down New York's 5th Avenue.

Eileen Vanora Neuberger. *The New York Post.*

Steve Cossu, special agent for the Office of Labor Racketeering, U.S. Department of Labor.

U.S. Attorney Rudolf Giuliani announces the Biaggi indictments at a news conference on June 3, 1987. Bronx District Attorney Mario Merola stands at right. *Wide World Photos.*

The gang who caught the Gang. From left, Howard Wilson, Edward J.M. Little, S. Alexander Planzos, and Mary T. Shannon. *Faye Ellman*

The Gand indicted, leaving U.S. Court House January 30, 1987: Fred Neuberger (*2nd from left*), Mario Moreno (*3rd from left*), and Anthony Guariglia (*2nd from right*). *N.Y. Daily News Photo.*

The real victims: Wedtech employees and their families demonstrate outside U.S. Court House during the Biaggi trial in August 1987. *John Sotomajor, The New York Times.*

# 21

# A Meeting at the Airport

**W**hen the Boy Scouts trooped back to the Bronx after New Year's, yet another financial crisis was awaiting. Once again, the company's cash was disappearing at a frightening rate.

Wedtech's work force had swelled to about fourteen hundred. Most of the employees were still in the Bronx, but others were scattered at Wedtech subsidiaries on Long Island and in Westchester County, northern Michigan, and Israel.

At least four hundred of these workers had to be concealed from the SBA because companies with more than one thousand employees were ineligible for small business set-asides. To maintain the fiction that Wedtech was still a small business, dummy companies were set up in Michigan and Israel as "employment agencies." Wedtech "contracted" with these dummy companies for "temporary employees." This way, Wedtech was able to assert that most of the workers in Michigan and Israel were employees of temporary help agencies, not Wedtech.

Payroll, taxes, lease payments, insurance, utilities, interest, raw materials, transportation, and all the other expenses of running a large manufacturing operation were costing about $2.5 million a week. That was far more than was coming into the company, and progress payments on the engine and pontoon contracts were nearly exhausted. The company was trying to get another add-on

239

to the pontoon order, but that was at least several weeks away. In the meantime, money was needed to keep the company afloat. Since they couldn't steal it from the government for a while, the Wedtech executives could conceive of only one other alternative—they'd steal it from the public.

Late in 1985, Guariglia had arranged with the company's investment bankers, Bear Stearns and Moseley Hallgarten, to underwrite a new offering of about two million shares of common stock at $11 a share. Everyone knew this would be a tough sell, even in a bull market. Wedtech was going back to the public well for the third time in as many years. Moreover, the Wedtech executives were disclosing plans to unload more than $1 million of their own shares in connection with the offering. It would be doubly difficult to find buyers for a company whose insiders appeared to be bailing out.

By December 1985, Guariglia was worried that the stock offering wasn't going to fly, and if the offering didn't fly, Wedtech was going to crash. Half in jest, he told Chinn and London that if they could help pull off the sale, he'd give them a million dollars.

Jest or not, the figure caught the attention of Chinn and London, who loved both challenges and money. What had been a semiserious comment by the desperate Guariglia was soon hatched into a full-fledged scheme. For $1 million plus expenses, Chinn and London were willing to devote their energies to placing the Wedtech stock. Chinn would talk to securities brokers around the country. London, meanwhile, would try to conclude a new deal with the coating process, just in time for announcement in connection with the offering. Chinn and London allegedly agreed to give Guariglia a $200,000 kickback if he could get the board of directors to approve the $1 million payment.

The deal was in place. Now all they needed was for John Mariotta, who was still Wedtech's chairman and chief executive officer, to sign the prospectus for the stock offering.

While the rest of the gang was in Florida over Christmas discussing whether to bump him off, Mariotta was brooding in Puerto Rico. The more he thought about the events of the past few weeks—the effort to fire him and the rescission agreements—the angrier he became. He got even more upset when Chinn and London called to ask if he was interested in selling them his stock. When Mariotta returned to the Bronx and was asked to sign the prospectus, he refused. "No ways, no how."

Mariotta had never been entirely comfortable with the concept of raising capital through the sale of stocks and bonds. Now, having foolishly agreed to give back to the others the stock he'd been holding, threatening to block the stock offering was Mariotta's only remaining leverage.

The Gang of Four—Neuberger, Moreno, Guariglia, and Shorten—was furious at Mariotta's refusal to go along with the stock sale. Probably he was bluffing, but who could be sure? He might just be willing to bring the whole company down to get even with them.

Given the standoff, Neuberger must have felt that his colleagues might now be more receptive to his earlier proposal about assassinating Mariotta. Sometime during the first week of January, Neuberger called Frank Casalino, the muscular business agent at Teamsters Local 875. Neuberger knew the union bosses hated Mariotta and were fearful he'd go to the authorities if ousted from the company. He also knew his partners would take a proposal from the Teamsters more seriously than one that came from him. After speaking with Neuberger, Casalino called Guariglia and asked to meet with the Gang on January 8.

Because Guariglia and Shorten were leaving that evening for California to promote the latest Wedtech stock offering, the meeting was held at John F. Kennedy International Airport. The group gathered late in the afternoon at the United Airlines lounge on the second floor.

Neuberger opened the meeting. He advised Casalino that Mariotta was acting irrationally and might well destroy the company. He told the union leader that something had to be done and asked if he had any suggestions.

Casalino, following the script, said he, too, was worried. He was concerned that Mariotta would reveal the payments that the company had made to him and Stolfi. Then he got to the point. They had the means to get rid of Mariotta, he said. Should he take care of him?

It is hard to say exactly how serious this proposal was. If the Teamsters really wanted to kill Mariotta, it seems unlikely they would have announced their intentions in advance to four of Mariotta's long-time associates. More likely, Casalino's comments were the Teamsters' way of impressing on the Gang of Four just how serious they were about keeping Mariotta under control and keeping the monthly payments flowing to the union local.

What happened next is a case of life imitating art. As in the 1951

241

Japanese movie *Rashomon,* there are four somewhat different accounts.

Moreno says he, Guariglia, and Shorten balked at the proposal, Neuberger grumbled again about their being Boy Scouts, and that was the end of it.

Guariglia says he told Casalino not to worry. What was happening with Mariotta was a business situation that would be dealt with in a businesslike manner. According to Guariglia, when Casalino asked point blank if they wanted Mariotta "hit," he responded, "Why are you asking us? If you are worried and you really want John Mariotta hit, you certainly don't need our approval. We are not that type of people."

Shorten says Casalino mentioned a specific price: $50,000 to knock off Mariotta. Shorten adds that he was, of course, appalled by the proposal.

Neuberger says he asked Casalino what the Teamsters could do about the increasingly irrational Mariotta and how much it would cost. In Neuberger's version, Casalino was noncommittal at the airport meeting but called back a few days later to say he wasn't interested, that too many people were involved.

In any event, the Gang's solution to the problem of John stopped short of murder. They did have him followed, however. A private detective was hired to report on his movements.

Guariglia's own businesslike solution to the Mariotta problem was to attempt a preemptive boardroom coup to get rid of him quickly. Two days after the airport meeting, a special meeting of the board of directors was called for the following Monday, January 13, at 5 P.M. The purpose of the meeting was to consider a motion to fire John Mariotta. Mariotta didn't know about the meeting until he happened to call his secretary at 3 P.M. Friday. She told him about the agenda.

During his Christmas trip to Puerto Rico, Mariotta had met with his friend and sometime attorney, Rafael Capo. The always emotional Mariotta had poured his heart out to Capo about the plot to take his company away from him. Capo, a former deputy counsel to George Bush, told Mariotta he needed a lawyer—outside of Squadron Ellenoff—to protect his rights. Mariotta asked Capo to represent him. Capo said more powerful legal representation was needed. Back in New York, they went to the prestigious firm of Skadden, Arps, Slate, Meagher & Flom.

242

Mariotta's lawyers worked all weekend. On Monday, Mariotta came to the board meeting at Squadron Ellenoff prepared to do battle. Accompanying him were his wife, Capo, and Thomas Schwarz, Mariotta's attorney from Skadden Arps. The two lawyers brought with them the draft of a lawsuit seeking an injunction against the proposed public offering. The suit detailed a plot to oust Mariotta.

Guariglia and his fellow conspirators were taken aback. They had the votes to get rid of Mariotta, but there was a good chance Mariotta would be successful in getting the injunction, and they couldn't afford the delay an injunction would cause. The money situation was too critical, and the negative publicity alone could be devastating. Mariotta would have to be appeased. The meeting was adjourned without a vote on his status.

Back in the Bronx, Neuberger hissed that he should have hired an Israeli "consultant" to blow Mariotta's brains out. Then they wouldn't be in this mess. But Guariglia and the others thought they knew how to pacify Mariotta, or at least keep him quiet until after the public offering.

Mariotta desperately wanted to remain with Wedtech; he couldn't imagine life without his baby. Knowing this, the Gang offered him a three-year employment contract. The contract "guaranteed" that Mariotta would continue to serve as chief executive officer for at least one year. He would receive a base salary of $150,000, bonuses equal to the highest received by any other executive, and 1 percent of the net revenues of the coating division. Mariotta said he would consider it if his colleagues agreed that Wedtech would maintain its corporate headquarters in the Bronx. There was also some fine print: if Mariotta were terminated "without cause," he would be entitled to a lump sum payment of all three years' base salary, or $450,000.

Mariotta, pleased to have saved his job, agreed to drop the threatened lawsuit. He also agreed to sign off on the stock offering. All that remained was to find buyers for the stock.

Guariglia was still nervous about generating sufficient demand. The "road shows" at which he would tout the stock to investors and brokers, and whatever Chinn and London were doing, might not be enough. Guariglia decided to call an "in-house" sales meeting.

One week before the offering, he gathered a group of clerical and mid-level Wedtech employees in a conference room at 595 Gerard.

243

Assisted by a representative from Moseley Hallgarten, he bally-hooed the future of the company and the value of the stock prepa-ratory to urging the employees to invest in Wedtech and suggest-ing that those with Individual Retirement Accounts use the funds in them to buy shares.

For the most part, the employees in the room were making less than $25,000 per year. Their savings were their only secur-ity—Wedtech had no pension plan—and their investment pro-grams were unsophisticated. Guariglia had worked for almost three years with these people. He knew most of them, had even gotten to know something about their families and their aspira-tions. He knew that they couldn't afford to lose the savings they had scraped together. Yet Tony Guariglia, who was to receive an illegal payment of $200,000 if the offering succeeded, and who two months later would dump his own Wedtech holdings, apparently had no compunction about telling these people to invest their sav-ings in a company he knew was on the brink of bankruptcy.

The offering was completed on January 23. The company sold 1.75 million shares at $10.125 per share. It wasn't as much as Wed-tech had originally hoped, and plans by the insiders to sell some of their own shares had to be shelved. Still, the company walked away with $16.6 million, certainly better than nothing. The under-writers kept $1.1 million in fees.

Six days later, the triumphant Mr. Chinn and Dr. London trav-elled from New York City to Washington. There they had lunch with Bob Wallach and his friend, the attorney general of the United States.

That night, Chinn and London returned to New York, where Gu-ariglia presented them with a Wedtech check for $1 million, made out to a company controlled by London. Later, Wedtech chipped in another $140,000 for expenses. Chinn allegedly gave Guariglia $100,000 in cash, which Guariglia agreed to accept in lieu of the $200,000 check he'd originally been promised.

With the public offering completed, the campaign to get John Mariotta completely out of the way resumed in earnest. There were seven members of the board of directors beside Mariotta. Neuberger, Moreno, Guariglia, and Chinn were sure votes against Mariotta. That left one other "inside" director, Alfred Rivera, and two "outside" directors, Gen. Richard Cavazos and Paul Halling-by, Jr.

Rivera, the company treasurer and board secretary, was an employee, so the anti-Mariotta forces could use direct pressure to influence him. In fact, he was told they would "get his ass" if he didn't go along. Rivera knew what was best for him. He also concluded that, given the level of animosity, Mariotta couldn't continue to run the company. His vote was firm.

General Cavazos wasn't hard to convince. He had witnessed Mariotta's tantrums, his rambling two-hour monologues. To Cavazos, Mariotta seemed increasingly like Little Caesar, the character played by Edward G. Robinson in the memorable 1930 film. To seal the issue, the Gang of Four apparently used the Big Lie technique: Cavazos was told that Mariotta had called the navy's Captain de Vicq "a dumb son of a bitch" to his face. Cavazos hadn't been out of the army long, but he was familiar enough with the business world to know that you couldn't treat your customers that way and survive. For Mariotta to insult the pontoon program manager was irresponsible and couldn't be condoned. What Cavazos didn't know was that the incident apparently never happened. De Vicq insists Mariotta never swore at him.

Paul Hallingby, Jr. was the final outside director and the biggest name on the Wedtech board. The sixty-six-year-old Hallingby, a general partner at Bear Stearns, was one of the most powerful investment bankers in New York City, with a reputation as a brilliant and forceful dealmaker. He had a co-op apartment on Park Avenue, a home in the Bahamas, and holdings worth some $1.5 million. He sat on seven corporate boards other than Wedtech's.

Although he was head of Wedtech's audit committee, Hallingby apparently paid little attention to the internal workings of the company. He had seen enough of Mariotta, however, to realize that the unpredictable tool- and die-maker wasn't up to running a New York Stock Exchange corporation. Hallingby readily accepted the Gang's assertions that Wedtech's growth had created the need for more structure, modern management techniques, and a passing of the baton on the board.

Now that the board members were aligned against Mariotta, all the Gang needed was a pretext to bring his ouster to a vote. When a special meeting of the board convened on February 7, ostensibly to appoint various board committees which were to oversee compensation, defense products, and the like, Guaraglia was ready. Waiting for just the right moment, he revealed that Mariotta had signed an amendment to Dr. Pinkhasov's employment contract.

Guariglia pointed out that the amendment had never been brought before the board for approval, as was required by corporate by-laws. He moved that the amendment be declared void. Taking the matter a step further, he moved that a special three-member committee be appointed to investigate the unauthorized agreement and to recommend how such occurrences could be avoided in the future. Both motions were direct slaps in the face to Mariotta, both were approved by the board.

Mariotta, not feeling particularly welcome at the 595 Gerard headquarters any more, began spending most of his time at the coating laboratory in Mount Vernon. Shortly after the board meeting, Guariglia, Moreno, and Chinn visited the facility. There, the three confronted Pinkhasov. As the discussions became heated, Mariotta, in the next office, overheard them. He came charging to the rescue of his protegé.

"What are you doing to this poor fellow?" Mariotta demanded. "You are handling him like you are Gestapo. This guy here is the most important thing that we have in this corporation. You are treating him like he was back in Siberia."

Chinn and Guariglia told Mariotta to butt out. Volatile under the best of circumstances, Mariotta became enraged.

"I'm still chairman of the board!" he shouted. "You people get out of here!"

With that, Chinn said that as far as he was concerned, Mariotta was fired. Guariglia echoed the sentiments. The trio departed to spread word of the latest Mariotta outrage to their fellow board members.

The Wedtech board met again on February 11, 1986. It was a wintry day in New York City—six inches of sleet and snow snarled traffic and closed La Guardia Airport to incoming flights. Coming on top of a five-inch snowfall three days earlier, the new storm transformed the city into a sea of slush. Neither snow nor sleet, however, would keep the Wedtech board from convening its special meeting.

As dusk settled over midtown, the directors trudged to the landmark Fred F. French building in midtown Manhattan, passed through the gilded archway, and took elevators to the twenty-third-floor offices of Squadron Ellenoff. The eight directors were joined by five non-board members. They gathered in a conference room just down the hall to the right of the reception area. At the far end of the room, two windows afforded a westward view across

Fifth Avenue, with the black International Paper Company building looming in the background. On the walls were two large posters depicting mountain climbers scaling snow-capped peaks.

As if to underscore the importance of the board meeting, Howard Squadron, the firm's senior partner, was among those taking a seat at the table.

As soon as Mariotta called the meeting to order, a motion was made to have Neuberger, the vice-chairman of the board, run the meeting. The motion was quickly seconded and adopted. Mariotta abstained. Neuberger then administered the *coup de grace*. He moved that Mariotta be fired as chairman of the board and chief executive officer. Neuberger seemed saddened, even regretful. He said he was sorry it had come to this, but the situation had grown intolerable. Mariotta had simply become impossible to work with.

Mariotta, accompanied by his wife and his personal lawyer, Schwarz, listened intently. He pleaded with the members of the board, asking that the matter be reconsidered. He was told there was nothing more to discuss. No one seemed to care that just a few months earlier, an agency of the U.S. Department of Commerce had named him its Minority Entrepreneur of the Year.

All the directors except Mariotta voted in favor of Neuberger's motion. Neuberger was then elevated to chairman and chief executive. Moreno was promoted to vice-chairman. Mariotta no longer had a job with the company he had founded twenty-one years earlier.

"Oh my God, what have they done?" Mariotta wailed. As he started to leave, he added ominously, "You'll be hearing from my attorney."

Outside, darkness had settled over Fifth Avenue. The snow was tapering off. When John Mariotta, the hero for the eighties, left Squadron Ellenoff's conference room that dreary February day, he was, literally and figuratively, out in the cold.

# 22

# The Gang Takes Over

**T**he Gang had finally succeeded in ousting Mariotta. They now controlled the company and its destiny. But even the most optimistic among them couldn't be certain it wasn't a pyrrhic victory.

They were reasonably confident Mariotta wasn't going to blow the whistle on them. No rational man would expose himself to criminal prosecution, or jeopardize a $450,000 severance payment and millions in stock, to exact revenge. Still . . . John Mariotta wasn't always rational. It wasn't inconceivable that he would try to cut a deal with the authorities. It wasn't inconceivable that he would pursue a strategy of "burn and return"—bring down the company, then attempt to reclaim his mantle of leadership.

Even more worrisome, Mariotta owned an enormous block of Wedtech stock—2,122,770 shares, to be precise. This represented 23.1 percent of all of the publicly traded stock. Although there were limits on the amount the ousted executive could sell in a given time, he might be able to have the restriction lifted. Any move by Mariotta to dump his stock was bound to reduce its price substantially. Even the very threat of such an unloading could hang over the stock like a dark cloud.

The most immediate consequence of Mariotta's firing, however, was to put Wedtech's eligibility for the 8(a) program in extreme

248

jeopardy. Wedtech was scheduled to "graduate" from the program in October 1986; Mariotta's departure seemed certain to accelerate that. Even though the company still had hopes of winning the maintenance vehicle contract, it had never demonstrated conclusively that it could compete successfully in the real world.

In typical fashion, Wedtech didn't immediately notify the Small Business Administration of the change in control, as required by the regulations. SBA officials learned of Mariotta's ouster the same way as the rest of the world—they read it in the *Wall Street Journal.*

The day after the board meeting, Wedtech had issued a brief press release about its "management realignment." No explanation was given for the changes. In an effort to offset any negative fallout, Wedtech also announced that Verne Orr, the former secretary of the air force, had been elected to its board of directors. The morning after that announcement, the *Journal* carried a brief article on page 23 stating that Neuberger had been named to succeed Mariotta at Wedtech but giving no further details.

After learning this news, the new SBA district director, Bert Haggerty, promptly sent a letter to Wedtech demanding that the company "show cause" as to why its eligibility for the 8(a) program should not be revoked. Down in Washington, Tom Trimboli at the House Small Business Committee also read the article with interest. Rep. Parren Mitchell fired off a letter to SBA Administrator Sanders demanding immediate review of Wedtech's 8(a) status.

Wedtech wasn't going to give up its 8(a) certification without a fight. The company had fooled the SBA bureaucrats before; maybe it could fool them again.

On February 20, Moreno wrote to Haggerty arguing that Wedtech ought to retain its 8(a) certification. When Mariotta was fired as chairman and chief executive, he wasn't kicked off the board, Moreno noted. As a result, Moreno contended in his letter, five minorities still controlled the nine-member board: Mariotta, Moreno, Rivera, Cavazos, and Chinn. (Actually, neither Cavazos nor Chinn had been certified as disadvantaged minorities.) The same five "control the majority of Wedtech common stock," Moreno added. (This was simply untrue.)

On March 19, Ehrlich followed up with an eighteen-page memorandum of law to Haggerty. Ehrlich deserved credit for his nerve, if nothing else. The lawyer's argument as to why Wedtech was eligible to stay in the 8(a) program was an astounding agglomeration of irrelevancies, half-truths, and outright lies. Ehrlich claimed that Mario Moreno controlled Wedtech's daily operations and parroted Moreno's false assertion that "51 percent of the voting stock of Wedtech is controlled by certified minorities." Even Ehrlich must have realized he was on shaky legal ground, however, because he proposed a deal: if the SBA would help Wedtech get one last suspension kit contract from the U.S. Army Tank Automotive Command in Michigan, Wedtech would voluntarily withdraw from the 8(a) program.

Back at the SBA, Ehrlich's memo was reviewed by Augustus C. Romain, an assistant to Haggerty. Romain noted, quite correctly, that Chinn and Cavazos were not certified minorities, and even if they were, Wedtech was still ineligible because it was not owned and controlled by *disadvantaged* individuals. And so, the game was over.

Wedtech decided to end the charade in characteristically arrogant fashion. In the spirit of "you can't fire me, I quit," the board met on March 27 and voted to withdraw from the 8(a) program. That day Moreno sent a supercilious letter to Haggerty:

> WEDTECH CORP. is proud to report that it is prepared to accelerate its graduation from the SBA's 8(a) program. This premature departure is based upon two factors: (1) ... the Company will have substantially achieved the goals of its business plan; (2) the Company believes it has attained the ability to compete in the market place.

Wedtech held off making any public announcement that its participation in the program accounting for 95 percent of its revenues had come to an end. First, the corporate officers had some unfinished business to attend to.

To their dismay, the executives hadn't been able to use the cover of the January public offering to sell the Wedtech shares they'd just gotten back from Mariotta. In fact, the underwriters had forced them to agree not to sell any shares for at least sixty days after the January 23 offering. That meant Neuberger, Moreno, Guariglia, and Shorten had to hold their Wedtech stock until at least March 24, 1986. Fortunately for them, Mariotta's ouster hadn't caused the stock price to plunge. In fact, a Bear Stearns analyst had put out a research report calling the founder's firing "a positive development that clears the air . . ."

On March 24, Wedtech issued a press release. Making no mention of its imminent departure from the 8(a) program, the release trumpeted the company's record revenues ($117.5 million) and record net income ($9.7 million) during 1985. Both figures were, of course, fabrications. Company officials were quoted as predicting continued growth for 1986. That day, Wedtech's stock closed at 11 1/8, up 1/8. The following day, John Mariotta resigned from the board of directors. The company didn't say a word to the public about that, and the stock rose another 1/8 to 11 1/4.

On March 26, working with Chinn, the Gang of Four began to sell. Neuberger dumped 38,334 shares at $11.25 a share, receiving a total of $431,258. Moreno and Guariglia each unloaded 33,333 shares at the same price, collecting $374,996 apiece. The next day, Shorten got into the act and sold 2,500 shares at $11.25, or $28,125.

This hardly represented all of their stock, but was calculated as just enough to prevent the supply from overwhelming demand and driving down the price.

On April 2, the company issued another press release, with still no mention of its decision to leave the 8(a) program. This release had to do with a new $2.9 million contract from the U.S. Postal Service. (Also unmentioned was the fact that Wedtech had paid a $10,000 bribe to a postal official, Jerrydoe E. Smith, in April 1985 to obtain the original post office contract and another $10,000 bribe in March 1986 to obtain this latest contract.)

Throughout April, the insiders' selloff continued. On one day, April 9, Moreno alone sold 101,167 shares for nearly $1 million. By the end of the month, Moreno and Neuberger had each sold stock worth $2.1 million. Guariglia's take for April was $377,539; Shorten's was $662,167.

It wasn't until April 17, well into the sell-off and after a news report, that Wedtech publicly announced its "graduation" from the 8(a) program. On May 6, the company finally got around to announcing Mariotta's resignation from the board.

Soon after his ouster, John Mariotta began looking for ways to reclaim his company. Mariotta was a persistent man; "I keep coming back like a cockroach," he would tell people. He approached the investment banking firm of Shearson Lehman Brothers Inc., where he inquired about a leveraged buyout of Wedtech. Mariotta didn't fully understand what an LBO was, but Vallone had mentioned it the previous year and it was in the news frequently as a fashionable technique for corporate acquisitions.

The investment bankers at Shearson told Mariotta he didn't control enough Wedtech shares to swing an LBO alone, but if he teamed with the other big stockholder, Fred Neuberger, the two of them might be able to do something. Mariotta, unaware that Neuberger had advocated murdering him in January, invited his ex-partner to meet with the investment bankers. Neuberger, perhaps just wanting to know what Mariotta was up to, came to a meeting and listened. He decided not to get involved.

In early April, Mariotta apparently heard that his ex-cronies were bailing out; he decided to sell, too. Within a couple of weeks he sold 342,650 shares for $3.64 million. He also retained Shearson for financial advice and to help sell his remaining 1.78 million shares.

It didn't take long for word of the insiders' huge sell-off to reach investors and analysts. They called the Wedtech executives to find out what was going on. Did they know something the outsiders didn't? At least one investment firm had noticed that the "receivables" figure—the amount of money shown on the financial statements that the government supposedly owed Wedtech—was suspiciously large.

Guariglia, Shorten, and Neuberger were ready with reassuring excuses. It was Mariotta who was driving the stock price down. They had announced their intention to sell in the preliminary prospectus for the January public offering. The sell-off had nothing to do with current events at the company. The officers were just executing decisions made months earlier.

Stock analysts bought the excuses. In fact one newsletter, written by Joseph A. Walker, touted Wedtech as the Stock of the Month in its April 13 issue. In late April, a Bear Stearns analyst released a report predicting higher sales and earnings. The report reassured investors that the insiders' stock sales should not be viewed "as a signal that the company's fundamentals are worsening."

A month later, the respected Wall Street brokerage of L. F. Rothschild, Unterberg, Towbin, Inc. issued a research report recommending purchase of Wedtech stock. The report predicted rapidly growing profits and a "big swing to positive cash flow" during 1986.

The actual picture was very different. At the rate Wedtech was going through money, the $16.6 million from the public offering wasn't going to last very long. Expenses were out of control. Phone

252

bills were about $44,000 per month—employees used company phones to call their relatives and friends in Puerto Rico, Morocco, Belize, India, Poland, and other faraway places. Premiums on life insurance policies for corporate executives were almost $49,000 per month. The company was leasing thirty-four cars for its officers and employees. Even Ehrlich's wife, Maggie, was driving a Wedtech Mercedes.

There would be no new 8(a) contracts to help pay all these bills. The coating division still wasn't producing revenues, and by May the company had received its final payment for the previous pontoon orders. Under those orders it still owed the navy $23.7 million worth of pontoons. It also owed $17.8 million in engines and $7.7 million in parts for the M–113 personnel carrier. In other words, the company had received nearly $50 million for products it still had to produce and deliver for no additional payment. On its books, however, the company was showing that the government owed it more than $100 million.

The company's best hope was to get an order for more pontoons. It needed the navy to exercise the 1986 options.

A year earlier, the uniformed navy officials in charge of the pontoon program, Admiral Hughes and Captain de Vicq, had begun a campaign to put the 1986 option up for competitive bidding instead of awarding it to Wedtech. The company's miserable performance, Hughes warned, had resulted in "a very real degradation" of the capabilities of the rapid deployment force.

The company was confident, however, that its friends on the civilian side of the navy—Pyatt and Arny—would overrule the recommendation. Moreno, in fact, boasted to another Wedtech executive that "Pyatt is in my back pocket. He'll do anything I want him to." Sure enough, Pyatt and Arny turned down the competitive bidding proposal.

Hughes then tried a new tack. What if the navy gave Wedtech part of the 1986 order and found a second source for the other part? This time, Pyatt and his staff agreed. A few months later, however, budget cuts in the pontoon program made it uneconomical to set up a second supplier. The navy was still stuck with Wedtech as its only source of pontoons.

De Vicq, feeling tremendous urgency to get pontoons out to the fleet, had tried every tactic he knew to get Wedtech to produce. He had begged, pleaded, cajoled, and threatened . . . cementing his position at the top of Wedtech's enemies list in the process. The

253

Wedtech officials began working hard—not to produce quality pontoons on a timely basis, but to get rid of de Vicq.

At first, Hughes resisted pressure from Pyatt and Arny to remove de Vicq as program manager. In late summer of 1985, however, the admiral decided de Vicq had mishandled some suggestions from the Atlantic Fleet about making modifications to the pontoons. De Vicq was ordered to leave his post five months later, in January 1986.

As de Vicq was preparing to leave, Hughes revealed to him that Wedtech had "had the nerve" to offer him a job. Hughes had been furious with Wedtech ever since the company took out a bizarre, full-page ad in *Seapower* magazine thanking him and de Vicq for having "piloted this minority-owned defense contractor through heavy seas of competition, setting the course for safe passage and contract fulfillment." Hughes had turned them down flat.

"How much did they offer you?" de Vicq inquired.

Hughes quoted a big number. De Vicq, who had been losing weight and sleep during his dealings with Wedtech, was feeling more lighthearted now that burden was about to be lifted.

"Gee, admiral, they offered me twice as much," he deadpanned.

Hughes exploded, calming down only after he realized de Vicq was joking.

As it turned out, a few months after he left the navy, de Vicq got a phone call from Richard Ramirez, the former navy official who'd been Wedtech's paid mole. Ramirez was now running a "consulting" business out of a swank Capitol Hill townhouse. He asked how de Vicq was enjoying retirement. Then he got to the point. "The folks at Wedtech—"

"Stop right there," de Vicq interrupted. "You have to be kidding."

Wedtech could not have been more pleased with de Vicq's replacement as program manager, Capt. Tim Kelley. Kelley, it turned out, was a friend of Jim Jenkins, the former deputy White House counselor turned Wedtech consultant. The two knew each other through the San Diego Society, an organization of former navy officials. In yet another coincidence, Wedtech consultant Jim Aspin (brother of Representative Les Aspin) was a close childhood friend of Kelley's brother. Even more remarkably, Kelley and Attorney General Ed Meese were neighbors in the Virginia suburbs.

Although there is no evidence that Wedtech planted Kelley in the job, he clearly took a very different approach to dealing with the company than did de Vicq. Where de Vicq was a tough protector of the navy's interests, Kelley seemed to regard it as his job to assist Wedtech.

One of Kelley's first acts was to recommend that the 1986 options be awarded to Wedtech by the unusual "letter contract" method—the one de Vicq had earlier called "a license to steal." But then Col. Don Hein, commanding officer at the Defense Contract Administration Service in New York, insisted that a survey of Wedtech be conducted before the options were awarded.

The results of the survey were startling. The Defense Department auditors concluded that Wedtech had "a tremendous cash flow problem" and should not get the options.

Guariglia and Moreno were undoubtedly stunned. While accustomed to dealing with questions about the company's manufacturing capabilities, or lack thereof, it was a new experience to have Wedtech's financial viability questioned. The DCAS auditors' charges were particularly unsettling because they were true. If Touche Ross, the company's auditors, and the investment community became aware of Wedtech's desperate financial straits, the pyramid would collapse.

The Wedtech executives howled about the pre-award survey results and threatened to sue Colonel Hein for $10 million. They submitted an entirely new cash flow analysis ostensibly showing the company had the financial wherewithal to build the pontoons. The DCAS auditors quickly picked apart the new analysis and again concluded Wedtech had severe negative cash flow. Without a new line of credit, there was no way the company could produce more pontoons.

At this point, Captain Kelley came to the rescue. He told Colonel Hein that Wedtech's financial situation was none of his business. Kelley then persuaded Hein's boss to conduct a second pre-award survey. Hein told his boss they were surrounded by crooks; his boss thought he was paranoid and agreed to a new survey.

This new survey was conducted in only four days, including the weekend. Wedtech helpfully provided 123 pages of revised financial information to the survey team. Four days later, DCAS recommended awarding the 1986 pontoons options to Wedtech, offering no explanation for its change of heart. The next day, May 21, the navy signed the $48.6 million contract.

Public announcement of the good news was left to Sen. Al D'Amato, who was running for re-election. In his May 30 statement,

255

the New York Republican hailed Wedtech as "a growing and dynamic company." The contract award, D'Amato declared solemnly, was "a victory for the American taxpayer."

Wedtech was also exploring ways to get taxpayers in other countries to buy its products. With the 8(a) program a fond memory and the U.S. government getting wise to its production problems, the company began looking for overseas sales to add to its shrinking backlog of orders.

These initiatives led Wedtech to the Middle East. A long-time Wedtech consultant, Tim Whitaker, held some preliminary discussions with sales agents in Dubai about selling pontoons and M–113 parts to Saudi Arabia and Kuwait. As the discussions continued, Guariglia asked Ed McCarthy, by now the company's vice-president for legal affairs, to fly to Dubai to check out the situation.

McCarthy and Whitaker met the agent, Zikar Shureih, at his plush offices in the Hyatt Regency hotel complex. Among other amenities, the desert resort featured an ice-skating rink. Shureih was in his mid-thirties, about five-foot-five with a mop haircut and Western-style dress. He seemed obsessed with death, convinced he wouldn't live to forty-five. He quickly sized up his visitors from the Bronx as being somewhat unsophisticated in the ways of international arms deals.

Shureih billed himself as a managing partner of something called the Dubai Commercial Services Center. He told McCarthy and Whitaker he had excellent contacts within the Saudi and Kuwaiti governments to whom he'd be able to broker Wedtech's products. Unfortunately, these contacts weren't available at the moment to meet with them. However, if they wanted the contracts, they'd have to move fast. To get started, Shureih would need $450,000 in "operating expenses."

Guariglia and Shorten sent the money. Shureih, pleased to get the $450,000, said he would stay in touch. McCarthy and Whitaker returned to New York. None of the hoped-for contracts ever materialized, and the money, together with Shureih, disappeared. McCarthy felt badly about being conned until the Iran-Contra scandal revealed that the U.S. government had also been snookered by Middle East arms dealers.

The experience didn't sour Wedtech entirely on the Middle East market, however. Later in the year, Moreno and Jim Aspin tried to interest a Saudi prince in Wedtech's cooling and suspension kits. To entertain him, they took the Saudi to Atlantic City, where he quickly dropped $150,000 at the gaming tables. The casino, recognizing a high roller, installed the prince in one of its largest, most gaudily decorated suites.

With a gambler's penchant for throwing good money after bad, the Saudi was determined to keep playing and turned to Moreno for cash. Moreno first borrowed $40,000, then $20,000, against his own credit line and gave the money to the prince, who quickly lost it. Taking $12,000 from his pocket, Moreno handed the money to the prince. The result was the same. The prince then borrowed $1,500 from Aspin with predictable results.

Still, the money advanced to the prince appeared to have been a good investment when, using a blackjack table as a desk, the Saudi signed a joint venture agreement. However, the agreement was no more valuable than had been the one with Shureih. The prince was last seen in a limousine heading for Kennedy Airport; he was never heard from again, and Wedtech never realized a nickel from the agreement.

More desperate than ever after the novel experience of being on the other end of a scam, the Gang immediately began negotiating with a group of banks to obtain an expanded revolving credit line and a loan. Chemical Bank acted as lead bank in a consortium of Citibank, Bank of New York, and Irving Trust.

After extended negotiations, Guariglia was able to persuade these banks to offer slightly more than $60 million—$33 million in a revolving credit line and $27 million in a term loan. The banks naturally insisted that the company put up virtually all of its assets as security. Since those assets were shown on the balance sheet as being worth more than $85 million, the bankers probably thought they were adequately secured. In fact, the assets had a value, net of mortgages and unpaid balances, of less than $20 million.

Wedtech played no favorites in its choice of targets for its Ponzi scheme. The company had now conned some of the largest commercial banks in the United States, just as it had conned the government, Big Eight accounting firms, and investment banking houses. The Gang understood all too well that behind the famous institutional names were ordinary people. People who could be corrupted or fooled by a veneer of respectability.

Even after the bank financing was arranged, Tony Guariglia was still dissatisfied. He wanted more money and fewer restrictions on

257

what the company could do with it. With a kitty of cash, maybe Wedtech could buy an established, profitable company and hide its own problems—"bury the garbage," as Moreno put it—in the consolidated income statements and balance sheets.

Since Wedtech had just completed an equity offering, it was time to sell junk bonds. Technically, these bonds are called senior subordinated debentures. Junk bonds were then all the rage, and Bear Stearns was anxious to show it could be just as aggressive as the firm that dominated the junk bond market, Drexel Burnham Lambert. The new offering was to be nearly as large as the three previous offerings put together: it would raise $75 million.

As preparation of the prospectus began, some problems arose almost immediately. Bear Stearns and Touche Ross were concerned that the backlog of government contracts was getting too low and, especially now that Wedtech was no longer eligible for 8(a) set-asides, that the company might be running out of work. Guariglia and Shorten had a ready solution to both problems. They fabricated a telex, supposedly from the U.S. Navy, indicating that Wedtech was going to receive another $30 million in pontoon orders. The phony telex was then shown to the auditors and underwriters to allay their concerns about Wedtech's ability to get new work. The auditors and underwriters accepted the forged telex as genuine, never thinking to confirm its veracity with the navy.

Another glitch occurred when Squadron Elenoff discovered the $1 million payment to London's company in connection with the January stock offering, an apparent violation of SEC rules. When the lawyers put Guariglia and his cronies on the spot by demanding to know what the payment was all about, their solution was to frame John Mariotta. In one of his crazy moments, the Gang maintained, Mariotta had promised London a million dollars if he could get Sumitomo to sign a deal with the coating division. Mariotta had of course made no such promise, but he was no longer around to dispute what was being said about him. The payment would be explained away in the new prospectus as being "primarily for consulting services related to the development of the Company's coatings business, as well as for certain financial management services."

With these various problems so neatly taken care of, preparations continued for the big bond offering. Then, over the course of a few weeks in June and July, some surprising new problems landed at Wedtech's doorstep, problems not to be so easily disposed of: subpoenas from three separate law enforcement offices.

258

# 23

## Closing In

**I**t was inevitable that some law enforcement agency would begin investigating Wedtech. Given the scope and duration of the company's criminal activities, the remarkable thing is that it took so long. Most criminals operate under the assumption they're not going to get caught; so it was with the Wedtech crew. Their success in deflecting the Mitchell committee investigation had fed their delusions of invulnerability. This time, however, they were up against tougher opponents.

At first glance, Steve Cossu wouldn't seem to be much of a threat to the multinational, politically powerful corporation Wedtech had become. A personable, pleasant-looking, and pudgy father of three boys, Cossu had worked fifteen years as a detective with the New York–New Jersey Waterfront Commission. The bistate agency had been set up to police New York Harbor, a notorious hotbed of organized crime.

By the mid–1980s, Cossu was getting bored. Despite his reputation as a bright and aggressive investigator, the work of the commission was winding down and his career was close to a dead end. He hadn't gone into law enforcement to become a clock watcher. In the fall of 1985, at the age of thirty-five, he decided to leave the commission and take a position as a special agent with the U.S. Department of Labor's Office of Labor Racketeering.

259

Not long after Cossu joined the Labor Department, he was speaking with an informant in another case. The informant—a New York City developer who was upset about having been muscled away from a land deal in the Bronx—told Cossu about a machine shop in the South Bronx with ties to Rep. Mario Biaggi. Curiously, the shop, which had been nearly bankrupt a couple of years earlier, was now receiving huge defense contracts. It was called Wedtech.

Informants' stock-in-trade is information. They tend to pass on a lot of it, most of it useless. A good investigator develops the ability to know almost instinctively which tidbits are junk and which merit follow-up. Cossu was a good investigator; he had honed his instincts during the years he spent working the waterfront. These instincts told him the informant's tip was worth looking into.

On the wall behind his desk, Cossu kept a poster of Sam Spade, private eye. But whereas Sam Spade developed his leads in barrooms and bedrooms, Cossu took a more sophisticated and true-to-life approach. He began in the library. Because Wedtech was a public company, there was a wealth of information contained in the material it had been required to file with the Securities and Exchange Commission. With the informant's tip in mind, Cossu focused on information about the company's construction projects in the Bronx.

Buried in the June 22, 1984 prospectus for the first debt offering was some information about the pontoon plant on 149th Street. "The Company is required to expend at least $2,800,000 to make improvements to the Property," Cossu read.

A while later, combing through the prospectus for the January 23, 1986 stock offering, Cossu read that through September 30, 1985, the company had spent $7,418,000 on improvements to the pontoon plant.

To an experienced investigator like Cossu, the numbers practically jumped off the page. In New York, overruns on construction projects are favorite hiding places for padded costs and kickbacks. A cost overrun of more than 150 percent on the renovation of a building in the South Bronx gave off a strong odor.

Plowing on through the public documents, Cossu spotted other anomalies. The stock transfer to Mariotta seemed fishy, especially considering that the law firm of Biaggi & Ehrlich was involved. Known more for its contacts than the quality of its legal work, Biaggi & Ehrlich was an odd choice for a public company's counsel. Then there were the 112,500 shares of stock that had been given to Richard Biaggi. Cossu knew that Richard Biaggi had been a member of the bar for only a short time. Why would he be given a huge block of stock, Cossu wondered, unless he was a nominee for the old man?

In March 1986, armed with nothing more than the informant's tip and his own gleanings from the public documents, Cossu ran his suspicions past his boss. Before delving deeper, they decided to see if any other agency was looking into Wedtech. A call to the Defense Criminal Investigative Service, the Pentagon agency that conducts the major criminal probes for the armed services, revealed that DCIS had also received tips about Wedtech, but the case didn't seem to be going anywhere.

Cossu went to the DCIS office in Queens to swap information with Mike Raggi, the DCIS investigator who'd been given the Wedtech file. Normally, investigators from separate agencies are wary of each other and protective of their own turf. But Cossu and Raggi hit it off immediately. Both were Italians who'd grown up in Greenwich Village and had belong to the same boys' club.

DCIS had received tips suggesting Wedtech had bribed, or attempted to bribe, low-level Defense Department contract administrator. There were also a suspicious number of auditors leaving their government posts for jobs with Wedtech. Cossu noticed one common thread in both his information and the files at DCIS—Gen. Bernard Ehrlich.

"If you follow Bernard Ehrlich, there's your case," Cossu predicted.

The investigators still didn't have much to go on, but a case potentially involving a United States congressman and a National Guard general had to be brought to the attention of the United States Attorney's Office for the South District of New York, which includes the Bronx, Manhattan, and six other counties. Raggi took the sketchy information about Wedtech to Benito Romano, the executive assistant to U.S. Attorney Rudolph Giuliani. Romano assigned a young assistant U.S. attorney, Mary Shannon, to work with Cossu and Raggi on the case.

Just shy of thirty, Mary Shannon had joined the U.S. attorney's office in early 1985. With her blond hair, pug nose, and pert good looks, she could have been a model for the prosecutor later played by Susan Dey on the television series "L.A. Law."

Shannon had grown up in Nevada, gone to college in San Diego, and graduated from New York University law school in 1982. When she became a federal prosecutor, in a sense she was going into the family business: her father was with the Internal Revenue Service, assigned to Las Vegas to work on organized crime matters.

Bright and energetic, Shannon suffered fools poorly and had a quick temper. When irritated, her blue eyes would radiate an icy glare. She had zero tolerance for mistakes, and colleagues who felt her wrath would joke that they'd been "Shannonized."

Initially, the investigators thought they were dealing largely with corruption among Defense Department employees, "just another bullshit white-collar case," as one prosecutor later put it. As to whether there was high-level political corruption, it was impossible to say. Shannon, who had once worked as an aide in the office of Nevada Sen. Howard Cannon, knew that lawmakers often go to bat—legitimately—for constituents and businesses in their home districts. Even if Mario Biaggi had done favors for Wedtech, the relationship was not necessarily corrupt. Not unless, that is, it could be proved that the congressman received personal financial rewards in return for his help.

At first, the investigators hoped to do a covert operation. Maybe they could "flip" a Defense Department employee suspected of taking bribe money and use him to provide evidence against others. Maybe they could develop a source within the company. For a while, Cossu and Raggi even staked out Wedtech headquarters at 595 Gerard to see who was coming and going.

Unknown to Cossu, Raggi, and Shannon, two other investigative offices—the Bronx district attorney and the U.S. attorney in Baltimore—were also starting to sniff around Wedtech.

As often happens in criminal investigations, the Bronx D.A. had stumbled across Wedtech while looking for something else. In early 1985, Bronx D.A. Mario Merola had asked one of his assistants, Philip F. Foglia, to check into delays in wiring the borough for cable television. The D.A.'s office subpoenaed the records of Cablevision, the cable TV franchise holder. The records showed large contributions by the company to Bronx politicians and Democratic Party organizations.

Following the trail, Merola's office then subpoenaed records from Borough President Stanley Simon and the Bronx Democratic Party. Those records showed large contributions from a corporation called Wedtech. Although Wedtech was now one of the largest private employers in the Bronx, neither Merola nor Foglia had ever heard of it. Their curiosity piqued, they decided to request Wedtech's financial records.

By the spring of 1986, a series of major New York City corruption scandals was beginning to come to light. The most dramatic headlines appeared as Donald Manes, the Queens borough president, twice attempted suicide. The first time, Manes slashed his left wrist and survived; the second time, he died after plunging a kitchen knife into his chest. Manes's death came in the wake of a new series of investigations.

As the probes spread to the Bronx, Foglia was cross-designated as an assistant U.S. attorney. In the course of discussing the various investigations, Shannon and Foglia discovered their mutual interest in Wedtech.

Foglia mentioned that the Bronx D.A.'s office was starting a file on Wedtech. The Bronx investigators were particularly interested in the company's contributions to Stanley Simon, and whether those had anything to do with Wedtech's access to the parking lot at One Loop Drive. Foglia disclosed that a businessman named Henry Thomas had come to Merola several months earlier complaining about his eviction from the site. Still, compared to everything else, Wedtech didn't look like particularly fertile ground.

Shannon was concerned. While double-teaming a target is sometimes helpful, it's hard for one team to run a covert operation if the other isn't making any effort to hide its investigation. She explained the situation to Foglia. He understood the sensitivity. They agreed to add Wedtech to the list of investigations on which the Bronx D.A. and U.S. attorney would work together.

Efforts to conduct the investigation covertly went nowhere. The investigators then began questioning high officials at DCAS, the office at which Wedtech's defense contracts were administered. This tactic—"shaking the top of the tree," Cossu called it—started to bear fruit. Some DCAS employees apparently welcomed the opportunity to discuss the favored treatment Wedtech always seemed to be getting. Others, sensing the pyramid was about to collapse, were looking to avoid being trapped in the rubble. When the U.S. attorney's office started getting inquiries as to what was going on, the investigators sensed they were onto something.

In Baltimore, meanwhile, Assistant U.S. Attorney Gary P. Jordan had also tripped across Wedtech. Jordan—along with the IRS, FBI, and the Drug Enforcement Administration—had been investigating a major drug dealer named Melvin Williams. Williams, it turned out, had financial ties to State Sen. Clarence M. Mitchell III.

In April 1986, Jordan's office subpoenaed the bank records of the law firm Mitchell, Mitchell & Mitchell. The records revealed $110,000 in deposits from Wedtech; that made Wedtech the firm's biggest customer by far. The records also showed disbursements to one Anthony Loscalzo, a person familiar to the FBI.

Following the trail, the U.S. attorney's office in Baltimore issued a grand jury subpoena to Wedtech on June 25, 1986, asking for the company's records related to the Mitchell firm. Before the subpoena was delivered to the company, however, Mary Shannon caught wind of it and called Jordan.

"I'm investigating Wedtech," she said. "Why are you investigating Wedtech?"

Jordan explained, and he and Shannon agreed they would work together in a parallel fashion.

By July 1986, then, prosecutors in Manhattan, Baltimore, and the Bronx were all starting to look at Wedtech. And all had served subpoenas on the company or on its long-time law firm, Biaggi & Ehrlich.

At 595 Gerard Avenue, the Gang received the subpoenas with concern but not panic. Through bribes and bluster, the company had escaped from hot water many times. The looming investigations certainly did not cause enough concern to slow down the Gang's thievery. Through the summer of 1986, they took another quarter of a million dollars out of the F.H.J. account. At the same time, they instituted a major layoff in mid-July. In a memo to Wedtech employees, Guariglia asserted that the layoff decision was "not the result of business setbacks" but instead "reflects the continued growth of the company." The workers responded two days later with a memo of their own. Its anonymous author wrote:

> Every employee at Wedtech is aware of the financial set backs that are occurring. By stating that this is not the reason for cutbacks is both a myth and you are insulting the intelligence of your employees.

To escape from their latest financial crisis, Wedtech needed to complete the planned $75 million junk bond offering. It would be difficult to sell the bonds, however, if investors knew that the company was under investigation. Therefore, the first decision was to conceal the subpoenas from Squadron Ellenoff, which was preparing the prospectus for the bond offering. If the firm didn't know about the subpoenas, it couldn't feel obligated to disclose them in the prospectus. To handle the New York investigation, the company retained Stephen E. Kaufman, a former head of the criminal division in the U.S. attorney's office.

Bob Wallach, meanwhile, took the lead in finding counsel to represent Wedtech in connection with the Baltimore probe. Having fallen out with Howard Squadron after Wallach was appointed the U.S. representative to the United Nations Human Rights Commission—a position Squadron had sought for himself—Wallach was now hanging his hat at the Washington, D.C. firm of Dickstein, Shapiro & Morin. Wallach and Leonard Garment of Dickstein Shapiro had worked together on Meese's confirmation hearing, which led to an "of counsel" arrangement giving Wallach use of an eighth-floor office at the firm. (Dickstein Shapiro partners, who tended toward understated office decor, watched in amazement as Wallach began adorning the office with an Oriental rug and expensive, elaborate furniture. The *pièce de résistance*, however, was the pair of ceramic English spaniels that flanked the door. As if his decorating had not called sufficient attention to himself, Wallach sponsored a "Name the Dogs" contest within the firm, the prize being dinner for two at the restaurant in the swank Four Seasons Hotel. The winning entry suggested the names of FDR's dog, Fala, and Nixon's dog, Checkers.)

At Wallach's urging, John Kotelly of Dickstein Shapiro was retained to deal with the Baltimore investigation.

Despite the subpoenas from the Bronx and two U.S. attorneys offices, the final prospectus for the junk bond offering carried not a word about any investigation. On the grounds that it would be improper to divulge a grand jury investigation, the investigators who knew about the bond sale made no effort to block it or contact the SEC. The effect of this decision was to allow Wedtech to perpetrate its biggest fraud yet on the investing public. In August, the bonds were sold, giving Wedtech $72.4 million in new capital and Bear Stearns $2.6 million in underwriting fees.

# 24

## The Headlines Begin

**I**n early September, the crowd of investigators sniffing around Wedtech was joined by the Manhattan district attorney's office. Since early in the year, John W. Moscow, deputy chief of the investigations division, had been looking into Citisource Inc., a scandal-ridden company partly owned by the Bronx Democratic leader, Stanley Friedman. (Larry Shorten had once brought 700 shares of Citisource stock, thus making him a part-owner of New York City's two most notorious companies.) Citisource records included checks made out to another company, called Porta Tech Enterprises. The only information available about Porta Tech was that it had been incorporated on behalf of one Richard Biaggi. On September 2, the Manhattan D.A. subpoenaed Porta Tech's business records. When the records were delivered, the investigators "cracked up" laughing. The complete financial records of Porta Tech consisted of eight checks—three in, five out. One of the "in" checks was a $5,000 payment from Wedtech to Porta Tech for "consulting work." The day after it had received this check, Porta Tech had paid $5,000 to a man who turned out to be the driver for Maj. Gen. Vito Castellano.

The investigators knew immediately that Porta Tech was a money laundry. Now they had to figure out whose money it was laundering and for whom.

Morgenthau's office called in Steve Kaufman, a prominent criminal attorney who was representing Biaggi & Ehrlich in addition to Wedtech Corp. Reviewing together the Porta Tech "records," Moscow asked Kaufman what this "Wedtech" entity was. Kaufman told him Wedtech was a defense contractor in the Bronx and that Mary Shannon of the U.S. attorney's office already had a subpoena out on the company. At that point, the paths of the U.S. attorney, the Bronx D.A., and the Manhattan D.A. intersected.

Like sports, entertainment, and business, criminal justice in the Big Apple is a highly competitive field, populated by individuals who are talented, driven, ambitious, and egocentric. The incumbents of three top positions—Rudolph Giuliani, the crusading U.S. attorney for the Southern District of New York; Robert Morgenthau, the long-time New York County (Manhattan) district attorney; and Mario Merola, the veteran Bronx County district attorney—were no exceptions. All three had crossed paths in the past. All were publicity conscious and strident in defending their turf.

Giuliani's office and Merola's office had agreed to work together on Wedtech—in August, twenty-nine-year-old Ted Planzos of the Bronx D.A.'s office was assigned to the investigative team—but relations between Giuliani's office and Morgenthau's office were at an all-time low. The two had clashed repeatedly over which would handle the sexy Citisource case. Now, with Wedtech starting to look like a potentially major scandal, the bad blood was simmering again. The U.S. attorney's office quickly expressed the opinion that the Manhattan D.A. had no jurisdiction over a Bronx company involved with federal officials. Nonsense, replied Morgenthau's office: We uncovered the Porta Tech–Wedtech connection. Biaggi & Ehrlich is a downtown Manhattan firm. It's our case.

With that, it became obvious that Giuliani and Morgenthau were going to compete, not cooperate, on what was shaping up as a headline-grabbing case. And in mid-October, the headlines began.

Throughout Wedtech's history, the press had been a helpful dupe. Early on, Mariotta and Neuberger had discovered that journalists were easy marks for their heartwarming tales. Two favorable stories about Wedtech had appeared in the usually skeptical *Forbes*. The *New York Times*, the *Daily News, Inc.* magazine, and *Nation's Business* also had run articles about the South Bronx "success story." Each article in such respected publications added another layer to the veneer of respectability.

In the summer of 1985, however, two young graduates of the Columbia School of Journalism, Richard F. Burns and Todd Jacobs, began work on a Wedtech story for the *Village Voice*. This was not going to be a puff piece. The reporters knew Mario Biaggi was involved with the company and had picked up hints of high-level influence-peddling in Washington. They sent some two dozen Freedom of Information Act requests to various government agencies.

Word of the requests quickly reached the Wedtech gang and their lawyer, Howard Squadron. Coincidentally, Squadron had been outside corporate counsel for the *Voice* when it was owned by his client Rupert Murdoch. Squadron called *Voice* editor-in-chief David Schneiderman to express concern about the way the FOIA requests were worded, particularly those that made reference to possible criminal activities involving Wedtech.

Schneiderman agreed that the letters were inappropriately worded and could have left the publication exposed to a libel suit. He dropped the inexperienced young freelancers. The story died.

It took another fifteen months for the press to pick up the trail again. This time, however, the media would go after Wedtech with a vengeance.

Ironically, the onslaught began with an October 14 story in the Murdoch-owned paper, the *New York Post*, titled "Biaggi's Son Owns Stock in Defense Firm." It was written by Charles Lachman. The next day both the *Daily News* and the *Post* ran articles about the suspicious stock transaction that had allowed Wedtech to retain its 8(a) eligibility. In the following days, the *Daily News* pulled ahead of the pack, as reporter Marilyn W. Thompson broke a succession of stories about the Biaggi & Erhlich law firm and the investigations of Wedtech.

At Wedtech headquarters, the newspaper articles were causing more of a reaction than the subpoenas: something close to panic. The stock price had dropped below $5 a share. Important customers and creditors demanded to know what was going on, as did Squadron Ellenoff, which had been kept in the dark about the investigations. The *Daily News* had to be stopped, the Gang decided.

On October 22, the Wedtech officers, apparently at the behest of Wallach, directed Squadron Ellenoff to file a libel suit against the *News*. The suit defended the legitimacy of the stock transfer and sought $400 million in damages. To their credit, Thompson and her editors at the *News* refused to be intimidated. In the weeks that followed, Thompson, joined by Josh Barbanel of the *New York Times*, continued to dig into Wedtech's shady dealings and political connections.

Within the company, the lower-level managers were in the dark about the state of affairs. The first press reports were largely a source of amusement—much ado about nothing was the prevailing sentiment. As the reports continued, the mood shifted to outrage. Not at upper management, but at the press and prosecutors. Most employees believed the company was being victimized by publicity-hungry prosecutors who, lacking evidence that would stand up in court, were trying the company in the press.

Ed McCarthy was the in-house counsel designated to deal with the growing requests for information from the investigators. Occasionally, Moreno and Guariglia would stop by to give him a pep talk. "We're going to beat this," they would vow. "You can take this to the bank—we've never done anything wrong." Because they had never asked McCarthy to hide or destroy anything, he felt reassured.

On October 27, McCarthy circulated a memo urging managers to keep an upbeat tone and refer any inquiries to in-house counsel. "It is expected that after all the facts have been put before the different grand jury panels, no further action will be taken," the memo stated.

Meanwhile, Guariglia and the rest of the Gang were scrambling for a way to offset the negative publicity and prove to the investment community that the company was sound. Guariglia thought he had a solution. Even before the headlines had started, Wedtech had been attempting to acquire a profitable company with a lot of cash. The cash and profits from the acquired company would, it was hoped, enable Wedtech to finish its government contracts and mask its own insolvency. Wedtech's search for such a company had taken it to White Engines Inc. of Canton, Ohio.

White, a seventy-year-old engine manufacturer, had annual sales of about $100 million—mainly truck engines to the Pentagon—and a backlog of orders of approximately $120 million. Even more impressive to Guariglia, White had forty straight quarters of profitability, an unused $11 million line of bank credit, no long-term debt, and about $10 million in cash with another $4 million excess in the pension fund account.

On September 18, Guariglia had written to Paul Hallingby, Jr., the investment banker at Bear Stearns who sat on Wedtech's board of directors. The letter requested Hallingby's assistance in obtaining the $51 million needed to acquire White Engines. Four days later, and well before the deal was announced to the public, Hallingby purchased 13,000 shares of Wedtech's common stock at $7 a share.

Hallingby maintains there was no connection between his stock purchase and the White deal, which he considered "a dead duck from day one." He says he bought the stock because he thought Wedtech was "going to break out on the upside" and because he thought it important for directors to have an equity stake. If Hallingby was trading on inside information, he was in for a rude surprise. Wedtech stock was headed straight down.

On October 27, more than a month after Hallingby bought his stock, Wedtech issued a press release stating that it had signed a definitive agreement to buy White for $51 million in cash. At the time, Wedtech was also negotiating to acquire a majority stake in the railroad products division of Abex Corp. Guariglia and his cronies thought they were on the verge of pulling off an eleventh-hour miracle. (Guariglia and Moreno have testified that they were so optimistic about the White deal, and possible contracts at the coatings division, that they paid $240,000 to reacquire 120,000 stock options they had earlier kicked back to Chinn and London.) At the wake for his father, who had died just as the headlines started, Guariglia told a group of Wedtech managers that the White and Abex acquisitions were on track. Within a year, Wedtech would have sales of close to $500 million and be a member of the Fortune 1000, predicted Guariglia. Now all they had to do was raise the money to complete the acquisitions.

This wouldn't be easy. The Gang quickly discovered that the newspaper reports had scared off mainline banks and investment funds. Guariglia offered a crony $2.5 million if he could come up with the money from Security Pacific Business Credit Inc. When even that inducement proved futile, he turned to financial brokers in England who, for a fee, promised to try to put a deal together.

Simultaneously, Guariglia was trying to work out a sale and leaseback of all of Wedtech's assets (which the financial statements showed as being worth more than $85 million). His first approach was to Chrysler Capital Corp., the financing arm of the number-three automaker. Chrysler Capital indicated initially that it was prepared to buy Wedtech assets for about $25 million and lease them back to the company. With the spate of publicity about Wedtech, however, Chrysler Capital soon got cold feet. The Wedtech executives, never ones to concede defeat easily, decided to take their case to the top: Chrysler Chairman Lee Iacocca.

Guariglia and Moreno spoke with their friendliest Italian-American, Rep. Mario Biaggi, and explained the situation. (Biaggi had begun calling Moreno every morning at seven o'clock to get the latest information on what was happening at the company. It got so bad Moreno told Caridad Vazquez that he was going to quit setting his alarm—he could count on Biaggi to wake him with the morning call.) Biaggi promised to call Iacocca personally to ask for his help.

A short time later, Ehrlich reported to Moreno that the congressman had, in fact, spoken with Iacocca. According to Moreno, Iacocca told Biaggi that Chrysler would be willing to give Wedtech the financing if it settled its legal problems with the Manhattan D.A. and U.S. attorney. When the prosecutors refused to agree to a corporate settlement, the possibility of financing by Chrysler Capital evaporated.

Ehrlich then suggested that Wedtech approach the Teamsters union, which, he claimed, had a great deal of money at its disposal. Ehrlich, Moreno, and a New York Teamsters official identified only as "Carmine" arranged to meet with Jackie Presser, president of the International Brotherhood of Teamsters. Because Carmine was afraid of planes, he and Ehrlich took the train to Teamsters' headquarters in Washington, D.C. while Moreno flew.

When the three converged at Teamster headquarters on Louisiana Avenue, Presser, who had his own legal troubles at the time, came out and hugged Carmine. His response to Moreno and Ehrlich was less enthusiastic, however. When they made their pitch for funding, Presser only shook his head. The rotund Teamsters' president told them that he had no direct control over the Teamsters' investment funds. He mentioned, however, that he had friends who had money overseas. As with Chrysler Capital, the deal went nowhere.

The boost Wedtech hoped to get from the White Engines announcement was short-lived. Early in November, the *Daily News* learned about the progress payment fraud of the early 1980s. While Squadron Ellenoff did its best to downplay the importance of the fraud, the impact was devastating. When the story ran, the world learned that people still involved in running Wedtech had fabricated invoices to cheat the government.

For nearly a month, Jack Kehoe, Wedtech's outside investor relations counsel, had steadfastly defended the company against the various allegations being raised. When he learned about the progress payment fraud from the reporter preparing the story, however, Kehoe realized his position was indefensible. Even if the government hadn't lost any money, Kehoe recognized, the episode was absolutely a "material event" that should have been disclosed to investors. After an agonizing weekend, on November 10, Kehoe submitted a letter of resignation to Guariglia.

Guariglia tried to convince Kehoe to stay, attempting to make him feel guilty ("I thought I could count on you") and blaming John Mariotta for all the company's troubles. Even though his firm was owed $40,000 by Wedtech, Kehoe walked away.

Despite these setbacks, Guariglia tried to maintain a calm exterior. Aside from one brief memo in which he concluded that "we have done nothing wrong," the employees were provided no details as to what was going on. At one point, the vice-presidents were assembled in the conference room of the 149th Street building to hear Stephen Kaufman explain that the situation was under control. The lawyer urged that no one make any comments to the press; Guariglia underscored the point by saying that he would delight in firing anyone discovered saying anything other than "no comment" to a reporter.

Without any hard information or explanations, rumors ran rampant through the corridors. The central clearinghouse for the latest gossip was the hallway outside the switchboard operators' cubbyhole. Employees would stop there on their way to and from the coffee room to exchange information and speculation. The switchboard operators talked to the executives' secretaries frequently and handled most of their calls. Information from them was generally regarded as reliable.

Many employees believed the furor would soon subside; the belief was based in part on information from the switchboard operators that the executives weren't even in town. Guariglia and Shorten were in London much of the time; Moreno and Neuberger were also frequently absent. If the situation wasn't serious enough to warrant their full-time attention, the reasoning went, then it couldn't be too grave.

Actually, the Gang of Four was taking steps to prepare for the worst. In the summer of 1986, according to Guariglia and Shorten, they had each paid John Tartaglia $125,000 in cash to set up dummy companies and bank accounts in Panama and Curaçao. They had also set up a third company that had bank accounts in London and Liechtenstein. In the fall, they set up two more companies in London and began moving their own money into these accounts along with money transferred directly from Wedtech's accounts. For Guariglia, Shorten, and Moreno, it came to $200,000 from Wedtech's accounts and almost $800,000 in money from the F.H.J. account. Then there was another account in London they shared with Fred Neuberger; in the fall of 1986, they transferred $180,000 to it from Wedtech operating capital.

By mid-November, employee uneasiness within the company was growing again. The newspaper articles continued unabated, and it was obvious the reporters had very good sources of information. The libel suit against the *Daily News* was beginning to look like an irrational act. Very little work was getting done. The company was floundering, lacking direction from above and increasingly distracted by the events swirling around it outside. Workers could be seen gathered in little groups, passing on rumors and speculating about who the source of the information could be.

When, on November 16, the *Daily News* ran an article headlined "Wedtech Bigs Knew When to Sell Shares," the shift in sentiment was almost palpable. The article detailed the massive stock sales by the senior executives six months earlier. (Paradoxically, the *New York Times* ran a chart the same day listing Wedtech among "low priced stocks with sound fundamentals.") The employees had tended to side reflexively with management, believing that any infractions of government regulations were at least partially justified by the extraordinary difficulties of running a company in the South Bronx. The article made it clear, however, that the senior executives had an agenda quite different from the one they espoused for public consumption. The realization began to set in that the company might not survive, and that senior management, far from working diligently to protect the company and its employees, may have been the cause of the current crisis. The siege mentality of "us against the press," with its gallows humor and sense of common purpose, gave way to bitterness and despair.

For the blue-collar workers, many of whom spoke English only haltingly and read it not at all, the situation was particularly distressing. They didn't even have the advantage of being able to read

273

the newspaper articles; all of their information was obtained through word of mouth. Particularly for the workers at 595 Gerard, Wedtech was in a very real sense their community. They shared with their co-workers a common heritage and language, went to the same church, lived in the same neighborhoods. For them, the prospect of the collapse of Wedtech, brought about by only dimly understood crimes and deceit, was a catastrophe.

Daily, the number of begrimed workers climbing the steps from the factory floors to the administrative offices on the third floor grew. There, obviously ill at ease, they would seek out the personnel manager, a Puerto Rican woman active in the Pentecostal movement. Since Mariotta left, she was one of the few people on the corporate staff with whom they felt comfortable. She would patiently explain, over and over again, that she didn't know what was going on, she didn't know what was going to happen. Still, she along with everyone else had to realize that something was wrong, seriously wrong.

Just when the Wedtech employees thought nothing else could shock them, another bombshell exploded. They learned that Fred Neuberger's wife, Eileen, had disappeared.

Neuberger's marriage to Eileen Vanora had been no more successful than his previous two, despite Neuberger's obvious attraction to her striking looks. Eileen's jet black, shoulder-length hair contrasted dramatically with the unnatural pallor of her face, which she achieved through liberal applications of makeup and powder. Her taste in clothes and adornments also ran to the dramatic—flashy clothes and an abundance of heavy, flamboyant jewelry. If she was trying to achieve a look of stylish wealth, she was generally unsuccessful. She struck one acquaintance as looking like "a $500-a-night call girl" and another as "a 20th century Cleopatra."

Just as Neuberger and Mariotta were an odd couple in business, he and Eileen were an odd couple in marriage. Eileen was taller than her husband, and nearly twenty years younger. Fred would look rumpled in one of Savile Row's finest; Eileen would look exotic in a housedress.

Appearances aside, Eileen was not a stable person. She had been hospitalized for a nervous breakdown in the psychiatric ward of Mount Sinai Hospital in New York for a number of weeks in early

1985. Later that year, she was found in the East River, having tried to commit suicide. At the time, she was carrying a pocketbook full of charge cards under the name Mary O'Connor. Asked why she tried to kill herself, she said she was having "ideations" to murder the couple's adopted children, ages one and two then. She felt it better to spare their lives and take her own, she explained.

By the following year, the Neubergers had moved from their Upper East Side condominium to the townhouse they purchased on fashionable Sutton Place. Renovating the townhouse (with Italian marble and hundreds of thousands of dollars in other improvements) and running her own cosmetics business apparently were not enough to make Eileen happy. In January 1986, she was again institutionalized, having taken an overdose of barbiturates and other pills. That summer she made a third attempt on her life and was again institutionalized.

Being married to Fred Neuberger was no comfort. Neuberger had women all over the world, several of whom he supported to one degree or another, never really bothering to hide his peccadillos. In fact, he seemed to get some sophomoric glee from his reputation as a skirt chaser. In his desk, Wedtech's chairman and chief executive officer kept pictures of his girlfriends, some of them nude shots and at least one including Neuberger naked as well.

When Eileen was released from the hospital in the summer of 1986, she retained a divorce lawyer. If anything, taking action worsened her mental condition. She took to calling the other executives at home in the middle of the night, complaining bitterly and incoherently about her husband. She showed up at the somber wake for Guariglia's father attired in a silver-trimmed pantsuit studded with black rhinestones, and created a scene by howling about an expensive ring she lost, and then found, in the ladies' room. She started going to the Nineteenth Precinct police station house almost every day to report that she had been robbed or attacked or that people were watching her and were going to kill her. She was going regularly to a Park Avenue psychotherapist.

Given Eileen's condition, Neuberger hired nannies to care for the couple's adopted son and daughter. Eileen had become so paranoid, however, that she fired the women almost as fast as her husband could hire replacements.

Eileen Neuberger was last seen on November 9, 1986. In the middle of the night that she disappeared from the Sutton Place apartment, she called the housekeeper and asked to speak to the children, perhaps to say goodbye. As of this writing, she has not been heard from again.

Neuberger filed a missing-person report and hired a private detective to look for his wife. He did not, however, appear to be overcome with grief: not long after Eileen disappeared, his latest girlfriend moved in with him and the children.

Most investigators, citing Eileen Neuberger's history of mental illness, concluded that she disappeared of her own volition and probably committed suicide. She had become such a regular at the Nineteenth Precinct, in fact, that when Neuberger reported her disappearance, the police at first refused to take his report. When they did, they treated it as a missing-person case, not a potential homicide.

Some investigators and defense lawyers argued that Neuberger may have killed his wife to prevent her from talking to the authorities just as the investigation was breaking open. As one veteran prosecutor sarcastically put it: "It was suicide . . . She was telling everyone she was going to talk. She called Fred and said she was going to talk . . . To me, that was suicide."

Those who believed that Neuberger was a literal ladykiller pointed out that he was known to have a gun, that his previous wife had met a violent death, that he had proposed murdering Mariotta as a way of handling a potentially threatening witness, and that he had good relations with a union leader who apparently could arrange for a contract "hit." The morbid joke became that Eileen Neuberger ended up "in one of the pontoons."

The truth about Eileen Neuberger's disappearance may never be established. She may have flung herself again into the East River, she may be one of the thousands of anonymous homeless who populate New York's streets, she may have fled and set up a new life using an alias. Or she may have been murdered, and her body disposed of by experts.

Whatever the case, Eileen Neuberger was another victim of the Wedtech scandal. Wedtech and her husband may not have caused her mental problems, but the simultaneous collapse of her fragile state of mind and the company's reputation seem more than coincidental.

# 25

## All Fall Down

**A**s the headlines continued and the prosecutors closed in, the jockeying among investigators paled next to the confusion among the various lawyers for Wedtech and its top executives.

By late fall, Biaggi and Ehrlich were fading rapidly from the picture. Representative Biaggi was under investigation, and soon to be indicated, for his dealings with another New York City defense contractor, Coastal Dry Dock & Repair Corp. of Brooklyn. That investigation revealed Diaggi had accepted a Florida spa vacation in late 1985 from Meade H. Esposito, a Brooklyn Democratic boss whose company sold insurance to Coastal. Embarrassingly, the sixty-eight-year-old congressman had been accompanied on the trip not by his wife, Marie, who was seriously ill, but by his forty-five-year-old girlfriend, Barbara Barlow, a redhead Manhattan divorcée.

Ehrlich, meanwhile, was a broken man. With the allegations mounting against him, he had been stripped of his general's rank in the New York National Guard. As General Ehrlich, he had been arrogant and insufferable. The loss of his cherished position and the charges of misconduct were too much for his fragile psyche to handle. He became depressed and suicidal and considered fleeing to London.

Among the remaining lawyers, a power struggle was shaping up between Wallach and Squadron Ellenoff. Squadron Ellenoff was still Wedtech's corporate counsel, but Wallach had appointed himself as "coordinating counsel" with the responsibility of keeping the company advised of "all matters affecting the full range of the subjects under inquiry." Steve Kaufman, in addition to being Ehrlich's attorney, was representing Guariglia and Moreno as well as Wedtech Corp. in connection with criminal investigations. John Kotelly at Dickstein Shapiro was still handling the Baltimore investigation. Fred Neuberger had retained the Manhattan firm of Pollner, Mezan, Stolzberg, Berger & Glass to represent his own interests.

Surveying the confusion from the U.S. attorney's office, Mary Shannon threw up her hands, refusing to deal extensively with any of the lawyers. All except Pollner Mezan had, in her opinion, some conflict of interest or were potential witnesses themselves. As the allegations mounted, Wallach began campaigning to have himself and Dickstein Shapiro, the Washington firm with which he was now affiliated, take the lead role in Wedtech's defense. Squadron Ellenoff, naturally, was becoming increasingly upset at Wallach's efforts to supplant its role as corporate counsel. The partners there were also distressed that the Wedtech executives had kept them in the dark about the original subpoenas the company had received. Siskind made it clear he wasn't taking orders from Bob Wallach.

In mid-November, Wallach went to the U.S. attorney's office for an unsworn interview. The atmosphere was tense, because the attorneys knew they were questioning the close friend of their boss, Ed Meese. Wallach denied that he or the company had done anything wrong. Shannon and her colleagues thought he was lying, but Wallach reported back to the Gang that he'd gotten the investigation under control.

In the struggle for control over the defense strategy, Wallach held the upper hand by virtue of his friendship with Meese. The Gang of Four viewed the Wallach-Meese connection as its trump card. As Guariglia later put it, "We thought Mr. Wallach would deliver Mr. Meese in helping to put a stop to the investigation."

Ira Lee Sorkin, a partner at Squadron Ellenoff with a more clearheaded view of how the world works, advised Guariglia that he was "dead wrong" if he thought that Wallach was going to be able to call Meese and Meese would then call Giuliani and kill the investigation. Guariglia remained unpersuaded.

By early December, Squadron Ellenoff decided it could no

longer represent Wedtech. The U.S. attorney's office had opined that it would be a conflict of interest for the firm to continue as corporate counsel. On December 1, Wedtech paid $317,799 in legal fees owed to Squadron Ellenoff.

Two days later, three of the partners—Squadron, Siskind, and Sorkin—met with Guariglia and Moreno in Squadron's office to break the news of the firm's resignation. Squadron announced the decision. The executives hadn't been forthright, he complained. He and his partners were tired of playing catch-up, of finding out what was going on by reading the newspapers.

Squadron then gave Guariglia and Moreno some parting counsel: Bob Wallach was giving them bad advice. He had bad judgment. He wasn't doing the right thing by them.

Moreno jumped to Wallach's defense.

"It is my ass that is facing ten years," he declared, cutting to the heart of the matter. "Wallach is my compadre."

With that, the meeting ended.

Five days later, on December 8, Wedtech formally asked Dickstein Shapiro and Wallach to serve as general counsel. The Dickstein Shapiro partners in charge of the case were Seymour Glanzer and Jack Griffin. Glanzer was a heavyweight Washington lawyer who'd represented Edwin Wilson, the ex-CIA operative who'd been convicted of smuggling arms and explosives to Libya. Griffin was a former Securities and Exchange Commission staffer and an expert in securities law. The various lawyers representing the company and its principals gathered at Dickstein Shapiro offices in New York for an urgent strategy discussion chaired by Glanzer.

The next day, Dickstein Shapiro received a check for $500,000 as a retainer drawn on Wedtech's operating account at Chemical Bank.

Jack Griffin had been reluctant to take on the Wedtech case. His instincts told him things were seriously amiss, and the company was close to financial meltdown. Wedtech was a sinking ship, and everyone was jumping off. The navy pulled the plug on the pontoon contract ("terminated for default" in bureaucratic jargon), citing Wedtech's failure to deliver the products on time. Touche Ross resigned as auditor and announced that Wedtech had a negative net worth of at least $90 million. The stock price plunged to less than $1 a share. The company's coffers were all but empty.

Griffin's concern intensified at 5 P.M. on December 10 when Moreno replaced the original retainer with a $500,000 bank check from Banco Popular. Griffin asked a bankruptcy lawyer who'd been brought in whether Banco Popular was one of the company's "line banks." The lawyer said it wasn't. With that, Griffin returned to Washington determined to extract Dickstein Shapiro from the developing fiasco.

With the roof caving in, Guariglia and Moreno met privately with Wallach. Moreno, contemplating fleeing abroad, had asked Wallach to find out which foreign countries didn't have effective extradition treaties with the U.S. Guariglia and Moreno decided it was time to play their trump card: according to the two executives, they each offered Wallach $100,000 if he could keep them out of jail. Guariglia's description was clear: "It wasn't an offer to represent us. It was an offer for him to get on a plane, get to Washington, and talk to Ed Meese. That was it. It was not an offer to engage him as attorney to represent me. It was an offer, if you get it done, I will give you a bonus of $100,000."

As it turned out, Wallach didn't have to get on a plane to see Meese. On December 10, Meese came to New York to speak at a United Jewish Appeal dinner at the Sheraton Centre Hotel.

The next morning, the attorney general was to be interviewed at NBC studios in Manhattan on the fast-breaking Iran-Contra scandal. Meese's press secretary, Terry H. Eastland, flew to New York from Washington to prepare his boss for the interview.

When Eastland arrived at Meese's L-shaped suite at the Sheraton, Meese was closeted in the inner room. After cooling his heels for a while, Eastland asked the FBI agent what was keeping Meese. The agent told him that Bob Wallach had showed up unannounced at the hotel room; the two had adjourned to a private discussion. By the time Wallach and Meese emerged from the inner sanctum, only five minutes remained in which to brief Meese for the interview.

What was said at the meeting remains a mystery. Wallach later denied he had received any offer from the Wedtech executives to kill the investigation. Meese said he had no specific recollection of the meeting, but it was "probable" that the two discussed what was happening at Wedtech.

That same morning in Washington, the senior partners at Dickstein Shapiro had made a final decision not to represent Wedtech. They were suspicious about the Banco Popular check and had been told Wedtech couldn't make its payroll if the check was cashed. Wallach's long involvement with Wedtech and his association with the law firm raised the specter of a conflict of interest. Glanzer and Griffin got on the speakerphone to break the news to their clients in New York.

Guariglia, Moreno, Neuberger, and Ehrlich had gathered once more at the Dickstein Shapiro offices on Madison Avenue. The outcome of the meeting was tipped off right away. A relatively junior member of the firm made a perfunctory show of playing host—offering coffee, chatting about the weather, and the like. As the gathering imperceptibly turned into a meeting, it became clear that no senior member of the firm planned on attending in person, a not-very-subtle indicator that Dickstein Shapiro was having second thoughts about representing Wedtech. In fact, the Dickstein Shapiro participation, other than the use of the offices, was limited to the speakerphone.

To an outsider, it would have been a rather bizarre scene: the Wedtech executives—men who controlled a multimillion-dollar company and the jobs of workers from the South Bronx to Israel—gathered around a small, rectangular speakerphone box, hunched over it in an almost supplicating posture.

What Glanzer and Griffin told them through the box was not what they wanted to hear. The box told them that it did not want to be their general counsel anymore. The box explained that since Bob Wallach was associated with its law firm, and since Bob could himself be a potential witness, there would be the appearance of a conflict of interest if Dickstein Shapiro served as Wedtech's general counsel.

The box's pronouncement was devastating. It announced to all those in the room that the game was over. There would be no corporate plea, no avoiding bankruptcy. Mario Moreno just shook his head and looked away. The experiences of the past several weeks had left him shaky; now he paled visibly and seemed to sag.

The box had just told the Gang that Wedtech was going to take a fall, a fall so far and so bad that being anywhere in the vicinity of Wedtech would not be worth half a million dollars. They knew this because the box announced that it was going to return to them the $500,000 retainer check.

The dirty work having been done, the box became almost avuncular. Chin up, fellows, swallow the bankruptcy medicine and you'll land on your feet, ready to build another company. But Neuberger was not ready to throw in the towel so quickly. He demanded to know why bankruptcy was unavoidable. Because the investigations and the dismal performance on previous contracts would make it impossible for Wedtech to get any new government contracts, replied the box. Not a problem, growled Neuberger. Just yesterday, he explained, he had talked with a man about using that man's company as a front to bid on defense contracts which, once won, the other company would subcontract to Wedtech.

There was an embarrassed silence. Neuberger had just described a plan to commit a felony. Even worse, he had done so over an open phone line at a time when every prosecutor and investigator on the East Coast was eager to count coup on those in the room. To top it all off, Neuberger's comment meant that in the coming months, his judgment was not going to be reliable.

After an awkward moment, the conversation picked up from where it was before Neuberger's suggestion. No use trying to explain the situation to Fred. Neuberger, however, had not survived the Nazis, British counterintelligence, and the South Bronx by being easily discouraged. If the box wouldn't listen, he'd talk to his partners; they'd been through a lot together. He called Guariglia over to a corner of the room and coaxed Moreno and Ehrlich out of their chairs. With his arms around the shoulders of the closest two, he said, "We've got to delay this for at least thirty days. You know why. I've got my reasons for needing to delay it." But it was too late, the others argued. Bankruptcy couldn't be delayed, even to allow Neuberger the opportunity to pull off a few more scams.

As the Wedtech executives pondered their next step, Bob Wallach entered the room. Dapper as always, he joined the circle around the box, which quickly gave him the bad news and added some pablum about the problem being one of appearances rather than actual conflict of interest.

Wallach quickly grasped the implications of what he was being told. He made a halfhearted attempt to convince the box that resigning as Wedtech's general counsel was not necessary, but it was no use. Even though Wallach knew that his last, best hope for steering the investigation away from himself was gone, he was not a man to waste time on futile pursuits. Quickly pulling himself together, he assessed the state of the Gang and took charge of the meeting.

Wallach's first step was to try to convince Guariglia not to make a final break, to take it easy and not do anything rash. But as soon as Wallach was out of earshot, the Gang decided the hell with him, and the hell with Dickstein Shapiro. They were going to take their business to the firm of Pollner Mezan.

Before he left the Dickstein offices and jumped into a cab, Guariglia instructed one of the corporate vice-presidents to return to 595 Gerard and "lay off everybody." The executive, believing that he hadn't understood the instructions, sought clarification. Guariglia impatiently repeated the instructions, adding that the $500,000 retainer that Dickstein had just returned might enable the company to make payroll the following day, but there was certainly no money to make payroll the following week.

Meanwhile, back in the Bronx, chaos reigned. Law enforcement officers were staking out the headquarters at 595 Gerard to determine if any records were being removed or if any suspicious fires were being set. (Unknown to the officers, Ceil Lewis, at the instructions of Moreno and Guariglia, was busy destroying records of the F.H.J. slush fund.) Many of the two hundred fifty or so workers from the 149th Street plant who had been laid off the previous week when the navy had cancelled the pontoon contract were in the street in front of 595 Gerard Avenue. They had been told to report today to pick up their final paychecks. It was chilly and gray, and the process of paying them was slow. Forced to stand in the cold for several hours, many had started drinking, either down the street at Glacken's or from bottles wrapped in brown paper bags. They were understandably upset about being laid off, particularly right before Christmas.

The mood of the previously laid-off workers was not helped by their perception that they and their families were the innocent victims of management's greed and corruption. Soon scuffles started, and it became difficult for people to pass through the mob going to or from the main entrance to the building. The police were called. They, the television cameramen, and reporters joined the increasingly vocal Wedtech employees milling around on the sidewalks and in the street. Particularly to those inside the building, it seemed as though Wedtech were under siege.

The employees still at work knew something had to happen soon. Over the past two weeks, the tension had become almost unbearable. Very few people made more than a pretense of doing their jobs. The uncertainly made it impossible to concentrate; be-

283

sides, the company had been without direction since October and people no longer knew what to do.

Guariglia's layoff announcement was delayed until mid-afternoon: it was feared that when the factory workers on the lower floors learned that they, too, had been laid off, they might be tempted to let their alcohol-inflamed union brothers into the building, creating an ugly scene.

At 3 P.M., the supervisors were called into the conference room and informed of Guariglia's directive. Although the news was not unexpected, people were still stunned. They were especially unhappy that no one had any information about the future—whether the layoffs were temporary, whether medical benefits were still intact. As Thursday was the normal payday, they received their paychecks on the way out of the building. But then, as if to add insult to injury, the payroll manager realized that the money that had been returned by Dickstein Shapiro would not be credited to the payroll account until the following day. So as the workers were walking slowly through the parking lot to their cars, they heard over the public address speakers in the lot the announcement that they could not cash their paychecks until the following day.

After leaving Dickstein Shapiro, the Gang took a cab to the offices of Pollner Mezan to make arrangements to retain them as the company's general counsel. Headed by Martin R. Pollner, a former federal prosecutor and deputy assistant secretary of the Treasury, the firm was small by New York standards but highly regarded for its work in the area of white-collar crime. Pollner Mezan had done some personal work for Neuberger over the years and had represented him in the autumn as the investigations unfolded. Martin Pollner agreed to become general counsel, to help find a new lawyer for Neuberger, and to get clearance from the U.S. attorney's office that there would be no conflict of interest.

The meeting was interrupted by an urgent phone call from Ed McCarthy back at Wedtech headquarters. Mary Shannon was sending trucks to Wedtech to haul away all the subpoenaed documents and files. Pollner called Shannon and assured her the records would be safeguarded under twenty-four-hour scrutiny, and none would be removed from the premises. Shannon called back the trucks.

It didn't take Pollner long to recognize that the company was going to have to file for protection under the federal bankruptcy laws. He moved quickly to retain bankruptcy counsel for Wedtech, recommending the firm of Angel & Frankel, with whom Pollner Mezan had worked on another bankruptcy case. John H. Drucker, a partner at Angel & Frankel, would assume direct responsibility for the Wedtech case. Drucker, a Brooklyn native, was young but had a growing reputation in New York bankruptcy circles as a tough and skilled attorney. Combining common sense, a detailed knowledge of the bankruptcy code, and the ability to assimilate details quickly, Drucker was an ideal choice for the incredibly complicated Wedtech case.

Early on Sunday, December 14, Moreno and several of the Wedtech vice-presidents assembled in Angel & Frankel's conference room at 366 Madison Avenue. Pollner, Max Stolzberg, and Michael S. Etkin from Pollner's firm and Bruce Frankel and Drucker from Angel & Frankel led the team of lawyers that met far into the night, preparing the petition that had to be filed with the federal bankruptcy court.

About four o'clock on Monday morning, the petition and supporting documents, some one hundred pages in all, were ready. The petition showed assets of $218,592,000 and liabilities of $151,563,000; the assets were to prove to be largely illusory, the liabilities grossly understated.

Exhausted, Drucker and Frankel went to a nearby twenty-four-hour coffee shop for a bit of breakfast and then home to snatch a couple of hours' sleep. A few minutes past nine o'clock that same morning, they met at the United States Courthouse on Foley Square in lower Manhattan. Passing the columns, bronze doors, and marble halls, they went to the second floor, where the temporary offices of the clerk of the bankruptcy court for the Southern District of New York were located. There they handed the paperwork to the clerk on duty. After a quick review and a few questions, the clerk logged it in and assigned it case number 86 B 12366.

Wedtech, the General Motors of the Bronx, one of *Inc.* magazine's 100 fastest growing companies, the star of the SBA's 8(a) program, was now officially bankrupt.

# 26

# The Gravy Train Derails

**D**uring the weeks leading up to Wedtech's collapse, the company's Washington connections had been coming more clearly into focus. Late one afternoon, Donna Merris, a law assistant in the U.S. attorney's office, was plowing through a stack of documents in the "war room" that had been set up on the eighth floor of the high-rise at One St. Andrew's Plaza. She found a letter from White House aide Pier Talenti to a top army official indicating that the White House wanted Wedtech to get the army engine contract. It was the first hard evidence of a White House connection.

Not long afterward, also in the stacks in the war room, Merris located an even more significant document: the April 8, 1982 letter from Nofziger to Meese in which Nofziger stated that it would be a blunder not to award the contract to Wedtech. This letter would later be used as evidence that Nofziger had not waited a year, as required by the ethics law, before lobbying his old agency.

With these discoveries, the investigators' imaginations began to run wild. Maybe this was another Watergate. Maybe it went all the way to the top. Maybe the whole thing was a Reagan-Meese operation. But Steve Cossu, whose judgment would prove uncannily reliable throughout the investigation, kept his feet on the ground. The indictable offenses, he predicted, would stop with Nofziger.

The investigators now realized the paper trial led from 595 Gerard Avenue in the South Bronx to 1600 Pennsylvania Avenue in Washington. After delicate negotiations with the White House counsel's office, they were granted permission to inspect certain of Meese's files from his days as White House counselor.

The day after Wedtech declared bankruptcy, Mary Shannon, Benito Romano, and Ted Planzos, joined by Tom Walsh of the FBI, went to Washington. They assumed it would be a one-day trip. As they began reading the files stored on the fourth floor of the Old Executive Office Building adjacent to the White House, however, they discovered there was more Wedtech-related material than they had anticipated.

Around 1 P.M., Shannon called Donna Merris in New York. "You and Cossu," she barked. "Get your asses down here!"

As Shannon and the three others then combed through the files, the previously hazy Wallach-Meese-Wedtech connection came into sharper focus. It became clear that Meese had been aware of the engine contract. Romano was struck by Nofziger's blunt and free-wheeling literary style. They began marking documents to photocopy. In their enthusiasm, they went beyond the limits of their original search request.

That night, the White House staffer who had been assigned as their point of contact reviewed the documents the group had marked. He reported to Jay B. Stephens, the deputy White House counsel, that Shannon and the others seemed to be looking into areas for which they hadn't asked permission.

The next morning, before they were allowed to resume their search, Stephens called the investigators into his office. Cossu and Merris had joined the group; Romano had returned to New York on business. Stephens went around the room asking the investigators to identify themselves and to justify their presence. He seemed displeased to learn from Planzos that the Bronx D.A.'s office was involved; Merola had supervised the unsuccessful prosecution (or persecution, as the White House thought of it) of former Labor Secretary Raymond Donovan.

Stephens seemed even more displeased that the team had gone beyond the bounds of its original request. "What's relevant about this?" he asked, waving one of the documents the team wanted.

"What relevant about that?" he said, indicating another. Stephens suggested that the team go home.

Mary Shannon, having gotten her foot in the door, was not about to let it slam shut. Mustering all her powers of persuasion, she tactfully but forcefully stated her case. The White House wouldn't want to be seen as obstructing an important investigation, would it? If she had to, she could get a grand jury subpoena for all the documents *that very day.* Stephens relented. The group was allowed to stay and retroactively file an expanded request.

Despite the tantalizing new leads the investigators brought back from Washington, they were feeling frustrated. There were legal restrictions on how far they could follow the Washington trail; because Meese was their boss as head of the Justice Department, any information about his involvement would ultimately have to be turned over to an independent counsel. Meanwhile, the case in New York wasn't going anywhere without information from Neuberger, Moreno, Guariglia, and Shorten. Although the investigators had evidence implicating Mario Biaggi and Stanley Simon, without the cooperation of the Gang of Four they probably didn't have enough for convictions. And they weren't making a great deal of progress in finding the pressure point that would crack the Gang. In fact, about the only criminal conduct they could prove was the progress payment forgeries in the early 1980s.

Making matters even more frustrating from the Shannon team's perspective were Manhattan D.A. Morgenthau's continuing efforts to carve out a role for his office in the headline-making case. Why should the Wedtech executives cut a deal with Giuliani and Merola if they still faced indictment by Morgenthau? When Morgenthau told Merola that the Manhattan D.A.'s office was going to indict Ehrlich in connection with the $5,000 Porta Tech payment, Merola was livid.

Around Christmas, the senior people in the U.S. attorney's office were getting impatient with the progress of the Wedtech investigation. Giuliani said he wanted to see an indictment against the company in thirty days. Get it done, he ordered. To Planzos, the unspoken threat was that if they didn't get results soon, they'd be given other things to do.

Shannon usually went home to Las Vegas to visit her family at Christmastime; this year, she stayed in New York, working day and night, trying to pull the pieces together. She and her team faced a formidable challenge. Her boss had set the clock ticking, and the Wedtech executives were clearly tough adversaries, con artists used to living on the edge and surviving. If she was going to break the case she had to do something fast.

Shannon had learned enough about Wedtech's history to realize that John Mariotta might be a very valuable source of information. Mariotta had passed most of 1986 trying to figure out ways to reclaim his company; according to one source, he spent upwards of $500,000 talking to various investment bankers, including associates of Ivan Boesky.

When Mariotta decided to dump his remaining shares, he used the Shearson brokerage house. For reasons that remain murky, the Shearson employee responsible for executing the trades didn't put the sell orders through immediately but instead let the stock sit in a house account. The employee may have thought the stock was headed upward; or he may have been involved in some type of buy-back scheme with Mariotta. Whatever the case, by the time the employee attempted to execute the trades, Wedtech's stock price had collapsed. Shearson lost $980,000; the employee lost his job.

Shannon had hoped that Mariotta's hostility at being fired would give him the incentive to cooperate with the investigation. In mid-October the prosecutor had approached Mariotta through his attorney, Jeffrey Glekel of Skadden Arps, giving Glekel a list of topics the investigators were interested in learning more about. If Mariotta's answers were consistent with the facts that had already been uncovered, Mariotta would be offered complete immunity from prosecution.

After a few weeks, Glekel passed along Mariotta's answers to the investigators' questions. Shannon was disappointed and angry. The information Mariotta provided was wholly inconsistent with what the investigators knew to be the case. With that, the government's offer was off the table. If Mariotta wasn't going to tell the truth, he wasn't going to get immunity.

The Gang had been right about Mariotta. He believed in his own myth. The hero for the eighties wasn't going to admit his criminal guilt—even if it meant he could escape the consequences of his many crimes. In fact, Mariotta didn't believe he had done anything wrong. And as long as he was convinced of that he wasn't going "to bear false witness" against those who had helped build Wedtech.

Of the Gang, Guariglia in particular was urging his confederates to hang tough. If all the U.S. attorney's office had was the progress payment fraud, they could beat the rap, he argued. The prosecutors knew the Gang would argue that their only offense was to speed up the payment of money to which the company was ultimately entitled. Given that argument, it was questionable whether a jury would return a guilty verdict.

Early on, the investigators had concluded that the Gang of Four must have had an illegal slush fund into which it was diverting stolen money and making payoffs. However, the investigators hadn't been able to identify the slush fund account with certainty. They had photocopied Wedtech checks written to suspicious accounts and had posted the photocopies on the wall of the war room. Based on the Main Hurdman work papers, Shannon thought the slush fund was the F.H.J. account. But whether it was used for more than union payoffs, she really didn't know. Still, if she could prove the existence of the slush fund, she would have her case.

Pollner's firm was talking with Shannon fairly regularly, trying to persuade her not to indict the company on racketeering charges. As Guariglia and his cronies were still the senior management of Wedtech, Pollner was reporting to them on his conversations with the U.S. attorney's office. Shannon used that line of communication to execute an enormous bluff. Right around New Year's Eve, she told one of Pollner's partners, John Lang, that the government was "aware" of the F.H.J. account.

Lang, making notes, returned to his office with the initials *F.H.J.* written in large letters on his note pad. Meeting with Guariglia, Lang left the pad visible on the table, and Guariglia saw the initials. Seeing Lang's note and believing that it meant that Shannon had discovered that F.H.J. was the slush fund, Guariglia figured that his luck had run out. He was also aware that the U.S. attorney in Baltimore had broken Jerrydoe Smith, the postal service employee to whom Guariglia had personally paid a $10,000 bribe. It was time to consider negotiating the best deal he could with the U.S. attorney.

Not knowing exactly what a cooperation agreement entailed, Guariglia decided to talk to Pollner and Lang. They went to the Domenico restaurant on Fortieth Street, near Pollner's offices, and found a table all the way at the back where there was a separate room that was usually unoccupied. Over the meal, Guariglia asked what the advantages of cooperating with the government were. Pollner and Lang responded at some length. They mentioned that if he cooperated he might escape indictment under the Racketeering Influenced and Corrupt Organization (RICO) statute. Without a RICO indictment, the government might not be able to seize all of his assets. They added that cooperation might afford him some say in who the sentencing judge would be, and that the prosecutors might make a recommendation for leniency if he cooperated fully. They also pointed out that if he made a deal with the U.S. attorney, he might be able to ensure that any jail sentence he received be served in the comparatively plush federal prison system rather than in a brutal state prison. The meeting lasted into the small hours of the morning.

Guariglia was still nervous about how some of the tough characters he'd been dealing with might react to his becoming a government cooperator. But he believed that Shannon had found the F.H.J. account and that he was going to be indicated for bribing a post office employee. Pollner's explanation of the advantages of cooperating had been persuasive. Guariglia arranged for Moreno to meet with Pollner and Lang the next day, and Neuberger and Shorten soon afterwards.

Those at Wedtech who thought the bankruptcy filing would produce dramatic changes were disappointed. Nothing happened, at least on the surface. About forty office workers had been called back to work and were kept busy producing lists and data and projections (only to be laid off again two days before Christmas). But there were no management changes, no pronouncements about the company's future, no indication of what was happening.

Wedtech was now operating under Chapter 11 of the United States Bankruptcy Code as what is known as a "debtor-in-possession." When a company operates as a debtor-in-possession, the management stays in place, attempting to make the changes necessary to enable it to pay its creditors and become profitable, while a committee of the creditors and the bankruptcy court monitors management's performance. Thus, for Wedtech as a debtor-in-possession, Neuberger remained the chairman of the board and chief executive, Moreno the vice-chairman, Guariglia the president and chief operating officer, and Shorten the executive vice-president.

When Wedtech went into bankruptcy, most people believed it was basically a sound company with a profitable core business. In December and January, only the Gang of Four and certain allies had any idea of the full extent to which the company was riddled with corruption and its reputation built on lies. Pollner, along with much of the rest of the world, believed that Wedtech and the jobs of hundreds of minority workers could be saved if the company was properly reorganized.

When Pollner explained the advantages of cooperating to the Gang, he had the interests of his client, Wedtech Corporation, in mind. He knew from his conversations with Shannon that she was strongly considering indicting the company on racketeering charges. She had indicated the only thing that would dissuade her from doing so would be the agreement of the executives to step down, plead guilty, and cooperate. Thus, Pollner believed his first step in revitalizing the company was to obtain the voluntary resignations of the four executives. If he didn't, and Wedtech was indicted under RICO, the company would almost certainly be forced out of business and its assets would be sold.

Pollner convinced the Gang of Four to resign as officers and directors of the company. Late in the afternoon of January 13 the Wedtech vice-presidents gathered around a speakerphone in Guariglia's office at 595 Gerard. Neuberger, Moreno, and Guariglia (Shorten was in London working on deals for himself and Guariglia) announced from Pollner's office that they had resigned. No reasons were given other than it was "for the good of the company." By now, most illusions were gone, but there was a feeling of resentment at the way the resignations were announced. "If they had come in and shook our hands, I would have believed them," said Ed McCarthy. "When they didn't have the decency to come out and instead made the announcement over a speakerphone, it put an awful taste in my mouth."

Working feverishly, Pollner addressed himself to the problem of reconstituting management and the board of directors. It was not an easy task. Wedtech's reputation was ruined. Most experienced businessmen had no interest in associating themselves with a scandal-plagued company or becoming entangled in lawsuits with disgruntled investors. But Pollner believed the company could survive if it could restore relations with its principal customer, the Department of Defense. He turned to someone whose reputation and credibility with the Pentagon were unquestioned. He asked Gen. Richard Cavazos to serve as Wedtech's chairman of the board.

Although he had been a member of the Wedtech board for almost two years, Cavazos was untouched by the scandals. Within the army he was still widely respected as a soldiers' general, a man whose values were unimpeachable and whose leadership ability was extraordinary. But Cavazos was reluctant to accede to Pollner's request. He lived in Texas and had no intention of relocating to New York. He didn't want to prolong his association with an organization that had developed a severe case of "corporate herpes." But Pollner kept at it, trying to convince him that the company needed someone with his reputation and credibility if it was going to have any chance of surviving. He reminded the general that hundreds of jobs in the South Bronx depended on the continued existence of Wedtech. Finally, Cavazos agreed.

With the old officers out and a reconstituted board of directors in, Pollner met with Giuliani to urge that the company itself not be indicted on racketeering charges. Pollner also arranged for each of the Gang of Four to retain a criminal attorney to handle the negotiations. Neuberger's personal lawyer was Kal Gallop; Guariglia's were Norman Ostrow and Lawrence Bader; Moreno's was Arthur Christy; and Shorten's was Karl Savryn. All were experienced criminal attorneys who knew when to bargain and when to dig in their heels.

Shannon now had to convince these new criminal attorneys that their clients should cooperate. And the clock was ticking. It was now getting close to mid-January. She had about two weeks left to make her case.

Shannon met with Norman Ostrow, Guariglia's lawyer, in her eighth-floor office. Ostrow said that if all the government had was the progress payment fraud, it was a case that could go either way at trial. Shannon pointed out that the government also had evidence that a couple of government officials had been bribed. Shannon was really referring to lower-level types like Gordon Osgood and Jerrydoe Smith, but if Ostrow wanted to think she was referring to heavyweights like Mario Biaggi or Stanley Simon, she wasn't going to dissuade him. After some more banter back and forth, Ostrow again allowed that his client didn't think the government had a very good case. Shannon repeated her earlier bluff, this time with emphasis: "If he's so sure, why don't you ask him about F.H.J.?"

Not long after this conversation, Moreno's attorney, Arthur Christy, scheduled a meeting for Friday, January 16, in Shannon's office. The curly-haired Christy was a distinguished member of the New York legal establishment. Educated at Yale and Columbia, he was himself a former U.S. attorney for the Southern District and special prosecutor in Washington. Christy knew his way around the criminal justice system. Now he knew it was time to make the best deal he could for Moreno.

The day of the meeting, Steve Cossu predicted Moreno was ready to cooperate; Shannon and Planzos were skeptical. Around 2:30 P.M., Christy walked into Shannon's small, cluttered office. After some initial chitchat, Christy came to the point: he was not there to ask for immunity. He understood they had information about bribery of federal officials. If they were willing to drop the racketeering charge, Moreno might well be willing to cooperate. In fact, all four officers might be willing to cooperate.

Shannon struggled to mask her elation. A deal along those lines might well be possible, she allowed. She told Christy he had ten days—until the Monday after Super Bowl Sunday—to arrange to bring in all the lawyers to cut deals for their clients.

In less than fifteen minutes, the meeting was over. Months of work, of late dinners and missed Cub Scout meetings, of sifting through thousands of pages of documents, of withstanding the bureaucratic infighting, had culminated in Christy's announcement. Shannon and her team had done it. They were on the verge of breaking the Gang.

When Christy was safely out of earshot, Shannon spiked a notebook to the floor like a football player who has just scored a touchdown. She and Planzos went into the hallway, exuberant. Planzos let out a victory yelp; Shannon shook her fist triumphantly, then ran down the hall to the war room. She grabbed Cossu and hugged and kissed him.

The investigators understood that they had probably just found the thread to unravel one of the biggest political scandals since Teapot Dome. It was, without question, the high point of their professional lives. That night, they all went out drinking.

Shannon and the others had told their superiors as little as possible about the details of the investigation. The less the superiors knew, the less chance there was of interference. But when Giuliani reminded them that the indictment was due within days, Shannon had no choice but to reveal that Moreno, and possibly the others, seemed ready to cooperate.

At that point, Howard Wilson, head of the criminal division at the U.S. attorney's office, took charge of negotiating the plea agreements. Wilson insisted that the lawyers for the Wedtech executives be brought in promptly to hash out the deal. Shannon was upset—she had told Christy he had until Monday, January 26, and Giuliani was in California for the Super Bowl. But Wilson told her it couldn't wait until after the weekend.

Before they would discuss a plea, the prosecutors demanded to know what information the Gang would provide and how reliable the information was. In turn, before telling all they knew, the four wanted to extract some agreement from the government as to what criminal charges they would have to plead guilty to and in what jurisdictions they would plead.

While the negotiations were developing, Guariglia and Shorten were in London, supposedly working on huge arbitrage deals that they claimed had the potential to net them as much as $100 million. In reality, they were also moving money among their overseas accounts and making arrangements to obtain phony passports in case the negotiations fell through. Fiddling while Rome burned, they stayed in $600-per-day hotel suites in London and flew first class back and forth. Moreno had been to Panama and Colombia in late December; he is said to have hidden between $500,000 and $1.5 million in secret overseas bank accounts and with relatives. In mid-January, Moreno went to Sweden to buy a phony passport.

Guariglia faced the hardest decision: whether to cooperate or whether to become a fugitive. Of all the officers, he was the one who had dealt most closely with Simone and Tartaglia. According to Guariglia, Simone and Tartaglia had urged him to flee to Switzerland. There would be money waiting for him there, and his family would be provided for. Guariglia knew he could get hurt if he copped a plea and became a government cooperator. After wavering back and forth, he boarded a plane in London and returned to New York.

The formal meetings between the defense lawyers and the prosecutors began on Saturday, January 24, in Howard Wilson's large corner office on the seventh floor, overlooking the Brooklyn Bridge. Behind Wilson's desk was an American flag and a cast-iron City of New York seal from the old West Side Highway.

Wilson was feeling a sense of déjà vu: on Super Bowl weekend a year earlier, he and Giuliani had been negotiating a deal with a key witness in the city Parking Violations Bureau scandal. It was hard to imagine that Wedtech would eclipse that scandal, but Kal Gallop, the lawyer for Neuberger, told Wilson: "The facts that will

295

be revealed by our clients will make the PVB case look like the minor leagues."

The dress code was casual—sweaters, jeans, and sweatsuits. The atmosphere, however, was anything but relaxed. The prosecutors and the attorneys for the Gang of Four quickly got down to business. One by one, the attorneys described what information their clients could provide. No names were mentioned. They would say things like, "My client can give you a state politician on a silver platter" or "We can give you two or three federal politicians." The attorneys would also describe what the basis for the information was—direct cash payment, payment to shell companies, etc. The prosecutors struggled to get specific information; the defense attorneys tried not to give away too much of their bargaining leverage.

Planzos was sitting next to Guariglia's lawyer, Norman Ostrow. Ostrow's office had prepared for him a typed list of the names of the people whom his client was offering to testify against. By rocking back in his chair, Planzos could see over Ostrow's shoulder and read the list. After an hour or so of fencing with the defense attorneys, everyone took a break. During the break, Planzos told Shannon and Wilson the names of the people that Guariglia was going to be fingering: Biaggi, Simon, Ramirez, Osgood. The names confirmed what the government already suspected. At least one name, however, was something of a surprise—Rep. Robert Garcia of the Bronx.

The next day—Super Bowl Sunday—the prosecutors and the attorneys met again to determine which criminal charges the Gang of Four was going to plead guilty to. Because the New York Giants were in the Super Bowl for the first time in years, the football fans in the room wanted to wrap things up before the kickoff. They started the meeting at 10 A.M. with the expectation that they'd be done in plenty of time to get home for the 6 P.M. start.

Soon it was evident that the negotiations were not going to be easy. Some of the defense lawyers wanted to wait until a judge with a reputation for leniency was available to take the pleas. Others weren't satisfied that prosecutors in other jurisdictions, particularly Morgenthau, would go along with the deal. Wilson was on the phone frequently to Giuliani, who was in California to see the game in person.

Finally, late in the afternoon, the deal was struck. Neuberger and Moreno would plead guilty to three felonies apiece and could

296

be sentenced to fifteen years in jail. (Moreno took an extra felony count to spare his sisters from being prosecuted. His brothers-in-law, however, would still face charges.) Guariglia would plead guilty to two counts and face ten years in jail. Shorten would plead to one five-year felony. In return, the Gang would cooperate fully with the government's investigation.

Around 5 P.M. Planzos called Phil Foglia, the assistant Bronx district attorney, to fill him in. Just before kickoff, Foglia passed the news to his boss, Mario Merola. Merola was shocked when he heard the names of the people who were going to be implicated. The veteran district attorney and long-time Bronx politician found it hard to believe that four unknown con artists working in the South Bronx could be at the center of the huge network of corruption that had just been described to him. "You've ruined my Super Bowl," he told Foglia.

The feeding frenzy had come to an end. But it had been a grand feast while it lasted. Wedtech had received federal contracts with a total value of $494 million and had sold $160 million in worthless securities to the public. In just a few years, Mariotta and the Gang of Four had stolen more that $5 million from Wedtech, had made at least another $15 million selling their stock, and had lived like royalty at the company's expense. Not bad for a group that had a lot in common with the gang that couldn't shoot straight. Even more incredibly, these small-timers had compromised some of the most prestigious members of the United States' financial community, and their trail of criminal enterprises led from the South Bronx to the executive wing of the White House.

Benito Romano, an assistant to Giuliani who was both Hispanic and a Bronx native, felt a particular sadness about discovering the truth behind the Wedtech myth.

"It was such a wonderful story," he said. "I wanted it all to be true."

# Epilogue:
# The People, the Law, the Company

**W**hile hundreds of minority workers lost their jobs when Wedtech collapsed, the scandal proved to be something of a full-employment act for New York's legal community. The company's rapid demise spawned a spate of criminal and civil cases that will take years to resolve.

Criminal investigations in New York, Washington, and Baltimore produced charges against more than twenty individuals. Many of the indictments were based on information provided by the Gang of Four.

**John Mariotta** failed in his efforts to get his company back. In June 1987, he was indicted on racketeering and conspiracy charges. Testifying in his own defense at his trial, Mariotta denied any criminal wrongdoing, contending he was simply an illiterate "minority figurehead" who was kept in the dark by the "intellectuals" who were really running the company. Mariotta's credibility was shredded under cross-examination by Mary Shannon. The Wedtech founder claimed, for example, that he didn't know his wife had bought sixty pounds of gold in April 1987.

Mariotta was convicted on eleven criminal counts, including racketeering, mail fraud, income tax evasion, and bribery. At his sentencing on November 18, 1988, Assistant U.S. Attorney Edward

J. M. Little argued that Mariotta was "no victim" and that he knew what he was doing when he stole nearly $12 million.

Mariotta made an emotional, rambling plea to Judge Constance Baker Motley. Approaching the lectern, he began to speak but was interrupted by the pealing bells of nearby St. Andrew's Church. Closing his eyes tightly and taking a deep breath, Mariotta began again, "I call myself Chauncey the gardener . . ."

Mariotta went on to say he was handicapped by his illiteracy, had been deceived by his partners, and was guilty only of ignorance. "Next time," he concluded, weeping, "I just stay a simple tinsmith and stay at my bench."

Judge Motley replied that Mariotta had an exceptional dedication to the advancement of his people, but he knew he was associating with thieves and allowed his company to be abused. She sentenced Mariotta to eight years in prison and imposed fines totaling $291,550.

On January 7, 1989, thirty-seven former Wedtech employees braved a snowstorm to attend a testimonial dinner for Mariotta at an Italian restaurant in Westchester County. Two days later, the hero for the eighties reported to Allenwood Federal Prison Camp in Montgomery, Pennsylvania.

**Fred Neuberger** pleaded guilty on January 30, 1987, in U.S. District Court for the Southern District of New York to charges of conspiracy to bribe federal, state, and city public officials; conspiracy to defraud the Defense Department, the SBA, and purchasers of Wedtech securities; and mail fraud. On February 10, 1987, Neuberger pleaded guilty in State Supreme Court to bribing Richard Bluestine. Three days later, he pleaded guilty in Bronx County Criminal Court to grand larceny for stealing more than $500,000 from Wedtech through the F.H.J. account.

Awaiting sentencing, Neuberger began selling rebuilt alternators and starters for a company in Long Island City, Queens. He maintained an active social life, joined a singles' club, and made regular trips to Atlantic City.

Testifying as a government witness in federal court, Neuberger perjured himself by trying to conceal a secret bank account he had opened. In May 1989, Neuberger was sentenced to two years in prison on his initial plea and another three months on the perjury count. Serving his sentence at the federal prison in Danbury, Connecticut, Neuberger was assigned to supervise the facility's machine shop.

The 1974 shooting death of Neuberger's second wife, Helen, was re-examined by the Nassau County district attorney's office, which found nothing to indicate it wasn't suicide and closed the file. At this writing, Neuberger's third wife, Eileen, who disappeared in November 1986, is still missing.

**Mario Moreno** pleaded guilty in Federal Court to two conspiracy charges and mail fraud. In State Supreme Court, he pleaded guilty to bribing Vito J. Castellano, the former state National Guard commander. In the Bronx, he pleaded guilty to grand larceny in connection with the F.H.J. account. In late 1988, Moreno asked that his bail be revoked, and he began serving time at the Metropolitan Correctional Center in Manhattan. In April 1989, Moreno was sentenced to eighteen months for his crimes.

**Anthony Guariglia** pleaded guilty to two conspiracy counts in the Southern District, grand larceny in Bronx County, and bribery in New York County.

**Lawrence Shorten** pleaded guilty to one conspiracy count in the Southern District and conspiracy to commit bribery in Bronx County.

Moreno, Guariglia, Shorten, and Neuberger were all key government witnesses against Biaggi, Mariotta, Simon, and other officials. Their credibility as witnesses was undermined by revelations brought out under cross-examination that they continued to gamble heavily, move money in their overseas accounts, and live extravagantly even after their plea-bargain agreements. Their credibility was also damaged when it was shown that they had made minimal restitution to the victims of their crimes.

**Mario Biaggi** refused to enter into any plea-bargain negotiations, even though it might have led to immunity for his son. At trial, prosecutors referred to him as "a thug in a congressman's suit." He was convicted in August 1988 on fifteen counts in the Wedtech case, including racketeering, extortion, bribery, mail fraud, making false statements, filing false tax returns, and perjury. The day after the Wedtech verdict, he tearfully announced his resignation from Congress.

Five weeks after his conviction, hundreds of Bronx residents, local union leaders, and a marching band turned out at a rally to honor Biaggi for his fifty years of public service. "People love him because he was a pro-neighborhood congressman," explained one attorney. "Politics is a tawdry, rotten system and all he did was play the game." Through a quirk in the election law, Biaggi's name remained on the ballot on the Republican line in the November election; he got about 30 percent of the vote.

Biaggi appeared for sentencing in November 1988. In a memo to Judge Motley, U.S. Attorney Rudolph W. Giuliani laid out the case against Biaggi: "For almost ten years, Biaggi engaged in a blatantly corrupt and criminal relationship with Wedtech and its chief officers. Using first his law partner, Bernard Ehrlich, and later his own son, Richard Biaggi, Congressman Biaggi deliberately and repeatedly extorted money from Wedtech in the guise of legal fees. More seriously, he sold his congressional office for several millions dollars in stock and fees, and he betrayed the public trust."

Biaggi, wearing a double-breasted, navy pinstripe suit, hobbled to his feet, limped to the lectern, and pleaded for mercy. His left hand trembling and his ruddy right cheek twitching, he said he "loved to be loved" and "died a little bit every day" during the trial. He continued to deny wrongdoing, saying he had passed a lie detector test and was "still of the belief that I'm innocent." As he continued, his voice cracked and he began to sob. "Do what you want with me," he concluded. "My time is done. Don't hurt my family."

Judge Motley sentenced the former congressman to eight years in prison and fines of $242,750, saying the sentence was needed for "general deterrence" and would have been substantially longer if not for Biaggi's age and poor health. Biaggi was allowed to remain free pending appeal.

Biaggi had been previously sentenced to two and a half years in prison and fined $500,000 as a result of his conviction in the Coastal Dry Dock case for accepting an illegal gratuity and obstructing justice. His appeal in that case was rejected, and he began serving his prison sentence on April 10, 1989. Shortly before Biaggi reported to prison, his wife of forty-eight years, Marie, filed for separation.

**Bernard Ehrlich** was convicted on eleven counts in the Wedtech case, including racketeering, extortion, receiving a bribe and a gratuity, mail fraud, and demanding a gratuity. Ehrlich's sentencing was delayed as he was twice institutionalized for mental illness. On January 10, 1989, Ehrlich appeared before Judge Motley. "I feel sick over what I've done," he said in a quivering voice. He was

301

sentenced to six years in jail and fined $222,550. "You were doing the bidding of Mario Biaggi and you corrupted Mr. Neglia," the judge said.

**Richard Biaggi** was convicted on five counts, including bribery, receiving a gratuity, mail fraud, and filing false tax returns. His lawyer argued for probation on the ground that Richard Biaggi was "a gentle, law-abiding person" who would never have gotten involved with Wedtech if not for his special relationship with his father. Prosecutor Edward Little said Richard Biaggi could have told his father not to accept bribes. Richard Biaggi was sentenced to two years in prison and fined $71,250.

**Stanley Simon,** in an effort to save his pension, resigned as Bronx borough president in March 1987, shortly before he was indicted. At trial, he was convicted of charges that included racketeering, extortion, perjury, and income tax evasion. He was sentenced to five years' imprisonment and fined $70,350. He reported to the Allenwood Federal Prison on January 9, 1989, where he has been teaching John Mariotta how to write.

**Peter Neglia** was convicted on four counts, including racketeering, bribery, and obstruction of justice. At sentencing, the former Small Business Administration official said he was sorry for his actions, which brought dishonor to his profession and betrayed the public trust. He was given three years in prison and fined $30,200.

**Ronald Betso** was acquitted of charges that he took Wedtech stock options in Neglia's name.

**Clarence Mitchell** and **Michael Mitchell** were convicted of mail fraud and impeding a congressional inquiry. Each was sentenced to two and a half years in prison. Michael Mitchell was fined $7,000; Clarence Mitchell was fined $6,000. The Reverend Jesse Jackson appealed to U.S. Attorney General Richard Thornburgh to help free the Mitchells while they appealed their convictions. Jackson pointed out that several white defendants convicted in Wedtech-related cases were allowed to remain free pending appeal, while the Mitchells, who are black, were denied bail.

**Richard Strum** pleaded guilty to conspiracy to impede a congressional inquiry and was returned to prison.

**Lyn Nofziger** was found guilty on February 11, 1988 of illegally lobbying his White House friends on behalf of Wedtech and two other clients. It was the first conviction under a 1978 government ethics law designed to prevent former high-level officials from cashing in on their influence soon after leaving office. He was sentenced to ninety days. His conviction, however, was subsequently overturned on the grounds that the government had not proved criminal intent.

**Mark Bragg,** Nofziger's partner, was acquitted of charges that he aided and abetted Nofziger's illegal lobbying.

**Edwin Meese** announced his resignation as attorney general on July 5, 1988. On July 18, a report by independent counsel James McKay was released; it concluded that Meese and his staff were "instrumental" in helping Wedtech win the army engine contract, but that "currently available evidence does not show any criminal wrongdoing" by Meese in relation to Wedtech. McKay also reported finding no evidence that Meese was aware of questionable trading practices by his investment adviser, W. Franklyn Chinn.

Though not charged with criminal misconduct, Meese came under continued fire for sloppy ethics. At the trial of Mario Biaggi and his co-defendants, Prosecutor Little, with authorization from Rudolph Giuliani, called Meese "a sleaze." In January 1989, the Justice Department's own office of Professional Responsibility concluded that Meese's dealings with Wallach and Wedtech created at least the appearance of impropriety: Meese's conduct "should not be tolerated of any government employee, especially not the attorney general of the United States. Were he still serving as attorney general, we would recommend . . . that the president take disciplinary action."

**E. Robert Wallach, W. Franklyn Chinn,** and **R. Kent London** were convicted on August 8, 1989, on racketeering and fraud charges. Even after his conviction, Wallach continued to maintain his innocence and that of his close friend Ed Meese.

**Congressman Robert Garcia,** his wife, **Jane Lee Garcia,** and Puerto Rican attorney **Ralph Vallone, Jr.** were indicted November 21, 1988, on charges of conspiracy, extortion, bribery, and the receipt of illegal gratuities. All pleaded not guilty; their trial was to begin September 5, 1989.

**Stephen Denlinger** lost his job as head of the Latin American Manufacturers Association. He pleaded guilty to tax evasion.

**Reynaldo Berney** and **Moe Yaghoubi,** brothers-in-law of Mario Moreno, pleaded guilty to income tax evasion.

**Frank Casalino** and **Richard Stolfi,** officials of Teamsters Local 875, were convicted of racketeering and receiving payoffs, kickbacks, and cash payments. Stolfi was sentenced to six years in prison, Casalino to four. They were fined a total of $374,700.

**Richard Ramirez** pleaded guilty to one count of conspiracy in connection with a $60,000 payment from Wedtech and two counts of filing a false tax return. Ramirez also admitted accepting bribes from a black-owned company for helping to steer contracts to it.

**Jerrydoe Smith,** a contract specialist with the U.S. Postal Service, pleaded guilty to bribery conspiracy charges.

**Major General Vito J. Castellano,** former commander of the New York State National Guard, pleaded guilty to tax evasion and falsifying business records in connection with his acceptance of $58,000 in bribes from Wedtech to lobby for research contracts. He was sentenced to one to three years in prison.

**Steve Cossu** received the 1987 Federal Executive Employee of the Year Award from the Federal Executive Board for his role in breaking the Wedtech case. **Mary Shannon** left the U.S. attorney's office after the Biaggi trial to go into private practice. She and fellow prosecutor, **Edward Little,** were married March 11, 1989.

As is usual after a major scandal, Congress moved to "reform" the law that enabled the scandal to occur. Wedtech was simply the most spectacular of the many scams inspired by the 8(a) program. And as the unfolding Pentagon procurement scandal of the late 1980s demonstrated, graft and corruption in the defense industry were by no means limited to "minority" companies.

The reform legislation, enacted in late 1988, attempted to wall the 8(a) program off from politics. Penalties for setting up "front companies" were increased; competition among qualifying firms was mandated for the larger contracts; companies were limited to nine years in the program and required to wean themselves gradually from set-aside contracts. Morality still can't be legislated, however, so it remains to be seen whether the new law will be any more effective than previous "reforms."

In the wake of the Wedtech scandal, the judiciary began taking a harder look at the philosophical underpinnings of minority set-aside programs, In *Richmond v. Croson,* the U.S. Supreme Court declared that any government program favoring one race over another is "highly suspect" and must be subjected to "strict scrutiny." Many commentators called the decision the beginning of the end for rigid affirmative action programs.

While the trials of the various people connected with Wedtech continued to make headlines, the victims of their crimes quickly disappeared from public view. For a few weeks after the company filed for bankruptcy, the New York papers and television stations ran stories about the workers in the South Bronx who were laid off. But the shelf life of a human interest story is very short, and New York City is never short of victims.

After the Gang of Four resigned, Wedtech's new management struggled to preserve some part of the company. But the odds against them were overwhelming. The corrupt Wedtech executives had paid such scant attention to running the business that basic management data was not available. Without it, it was impossible to tell whether any part of the business was, or could be made, profitable. To make matters worse, Wedtech had received such large progress payments that the contracts it still had couldn't be completed except at a loss. On the engine contract, for example, the company had delivered only 4,892 of the 13,100 engines it had contracted to build, but it had received about $22 million of the $27.7 million contract price. Given these circumstances, it was hardly surprising that it was impossible to obtain new financing or new contracts.

Wedtech's caretaker managers had little choice but to limp along, finishing the few contracts on which the company might make small profits while they tried to find buyers who would keep parts of the company alive. The subsidiary on Long Island, Euclid Equipment, was sold to a group led by its president and was able to keep most of the seventy workers employed, at least in the short run.

Pinkhasov and most of the employees of the coating division found investors who believed in much-touted LTAVD process. In its first year, the new company, Vapor Technologies Inc., replowed the ground that Wedtech tilled so thoroughly and achieved the same results: no profitable contracts. The subsidiary in Israel, Carmo, was forced into receivership by the Israeli banks; at last report all of its employees had been laid off. The closest thing to a success was the subsidiary in the Upper Peninsula of Michigan. Its assets were purchased by a regional company that retained Bob Rotundo. Rotundo had run the facility for Wedtech and was one of the few competent manufacturing managers in the company. Rotundo was able to bring back on the payroll about fifty of the almost three hundred workers who were laid off in that economically depressed area.

In the Bronx, the news was uniformly bad. A halfhearted attempt to revive manufacturing at 595 Gerard Avenue failed before it ever really got started. The Wedtech sign that overlooked the Major Deegan Expressway blew down in a windstorm; there was no money to replace it. The navy put the pontoon contract up for bids. It was won by a company in Mississippi. One Wedtech engineer managed to get a job with the new contractor. The machinery that John Mariotta was so proud of was sold in a series of three auctions. The buildings in which hundreds of workers were employed were sold; two were virtually empty—one was being used as a wholesale grocery distribution center, and the other as a self-storage warehouse.

For many of the minority workers in the South Bronx, the ones whom Mariotta made the focal point of his Spiel, it was off Wedtech and on welfare. Some of the unemployed went back to Puerto Rico, others were able to find jobs only as unskilled laborers—security guards, hospital orderlies, etc.—at wages a fraction of what they used to make at Wedtech. New York City made an effort to provide job training to teach them skills in demand in the area. About a half-dozen former Wedtech employees, inspired by Mariotta's entrepreneurial bug, attempted to start companies of their own.

Wedtech's shareholders, investors, and creditors were also victims. Including the bondholders, claims against the company reached almost $300 million. It appears unlikely that Wedtech will ever be able to pay more than a few cents on each dollar owed. The shareholders will probably receive nothing.

Not only did these people lose enormous amount of money, the domino effect was tragic. Some companies, believing what they were being told about Wedtech, extended it too much credit. When Wedtech collapsed and was unable to pay its bills, these companies couldn't survive. They, too, declared bankruptcy. Some people invested in the bonds because they needed the high rate of return to make ends meet. Others bought what they were led to believe was a growth stock for their retirement accounts. For these people, the collapse of Wedtech had an impact at least as personal as the loss of a job.

The people in between—the lawyers, accountants, investment bankers, bureaucrats, and politicians—generally suffered momentary professional embarrassment but no long-lasting personal consequences. Yet it was these people who made it all possible. For the most part they had no criminal intent; they simply didn't do their jobs very well. They helped the Wedtech crooks disguise their frauds or they failed to detect and report them. For this they received millions of dollars in fees, salaries, and bonuses.

Human nature being what it is, crooks steal. But how these crooks—Mariotta, Neuberger, Guariglia, Moreno, and Shorten—could so easily co-opt some of the most prestigious members of United States' financial and legal communities is one of the most disturbing aspects of the Wedtech story. Perhaps the whole scandal is eloquent testimony to the "greed is good" ethic that pervaded Wall Street and Washington during the Reagan presidency. In an ironic sense, John Mariotta *was* a symbol of the eighties.

Wedtech is gone now, leaving only a trail of litigation in its wake. In the South Bronx, it is almost as if the company never existed. Poverty, crime, drugs, and AIDS still ravage the community. The areas around the former Wedtech plants are still grimy and decaying. It doesn't seem right that there isn't something to mark the extraordinary hopes and enthusiasm and promise that Wedtech once symbolized. But there isn't. The feeding frenzy consumed it all.

307

# Notes on Sources

This book is nonfiction. None of the events or conversations depicted are products of the authors' imaginations. Quite the contrary, we expended a great deal of time and effort to ensure that the book be as accurate as a historical reconstruction can be.

Having said that, it is important to remind the reader that truth is sometimes in the eye—and ear—of the beholder. In the course of our research, we frequently encountered different versions of the same event. We dealt with this situation in several ways. Where the differences between versions were inconsequential, we glossed over them. Where it was possible to make a decision about which version was most likely to be accurate, we exercised our judgment. Where the differences were important and all versions were equally plausible (or implausible), we incorporated differing accounts in the text.

We attempted to double-check all of the information we used. We reviewed tens of thousands of pages of documentary evidence. In cases in which more than one person was involved in an event, we solicited each participant's version. However, many of the participants, for various reasons, chose not to be interviewed. To omit all events for which we could not obtain corroboration from multiple sources would have severely distorted our account of the Wedtech scandal. Therefore, we have included some information from only one source but have tried to make it clear to the reader where we have done so.

In the course of our research, we developed strong opinions on a number of subjects and drew conclusions based on our interpretation of the facts.

These opinions are interspersed throughout the book. We believe it is clear to a reasonably attentive reader which material is factual and which is our opinion or conclusion. We recognize that some readers may draw different conclusions from the same set of facts.

The factual skeleton of the book is based on more than twenty thousand pages of sworn court testimony and trial exhibits, personal interviews, reports by a congressional committee and an independent counsel, documents obtained through the Freedom of Information Act, documents released by the National Archives and various federal agencies, and files made available to the authors. In cases where significant information was taken from secondary sources such as newspaper and magazine articles, the source is indicated in the narrative or in the chapter notes below.

To provide firsthand descriptions, the authors spent many days in courtrooms and visited most of the sites described in the book. Moreover, as described in more detail in the preface, each author played a role, albeit small, in the Wedtech story—Harrison as an executive of the company in its final months, Sternberg as a journalist who reported on the company both before and after the scandal erupted. We believe these experiences gave us unique insights into the Wedtech story.

To flesh out the human drama outlined in the documents, hundreds of hours of interviews were conducted with more than seventy-five persons involved in the Wedtech story. Many of these interviews were tape recorded and are on the record. A few were conducted on a "background" basis, meaning the information could be used but the source could not be revealed.

None of the dialogue in the book was manufactured by the authors. All comments contained within quotation marks were spoken in interviews, or were expressed as remembered dialogue, presumably to the best of the interviewee's recollections; or they were contained as direct quotations in court transcripts or other documents. In a number of cases, however, the dialogue does not reflect the recollections of *all* parties to a conversation. In those cases, the authors used their professional judgment to gauge the reliability of differing sources.

To maintain the narrative flow and enhance readability, the authors have attempted to minimize the use of attributions in the text itself. More detailed attributions are contained in the chapter notes below.

### Chapter 1

Details about the "Salute to Victory" dinner were obtained from newspaper accounts; an interview with Charles A. Gargano, the chairman of the dinner; Federal Election Commission reports; interviews with the decorator for the dinner and with employees of the Waldorf-Astoria; and *Presidential Documents*, The Administration of Ronald Reagan, 1984. Information about John Mariotta's reaction came from an interview with Mariotta and from two persons who saw him on the late-night news.

309

## CHAPTER 2

The brief history of the Bronx was compiled from newspaper articles, Jill Jonnes' book *We're Still Here: The Rise, Fall & Resurrection of the South Bronx* (Atlantic Monthly Press, 1986), and the transcript of a WNET/Channel 13 program titled "South Bronx/Work in Progress."

Details about Mariotta's early life and the founding of Welbilt Electronic Die Corporation came largely from an interview with him and his wife and from his trial testimony. The description of Neuberger's early life came from interviews with people who know him, his trial testimony, his lawyer's remarks at his sentencing, and an article in the December 1981 issue of *Inc.* magazine.

Some of the tales about the early days of Welbilt were taken from a column by Michael Daly in the *Daily News* on September 24, 1980. Information about the relationship between Fred and Helen Neuberger, and the death of Helen Neuberger, came from interviews with Mariotta and law enforcement officials.

## CHAPTER 3

Contacts with the Carter White House were disclosed in documents made available to the authors. Background on Mario Biaggi was obtained from newspaper profiles, comments made by his attorney at Biaggi's sentencing, and an interview with Robert Blancato, Biaggi's former administrative assistant. The story about black limousines outside Biaggi's congressional office came from the sworn court testimony of Mario Moreno. Mario Merola's belief that Biaggi may have gotten away with murder was confirmed by two former assistants to the late district attorney. Mario Biaggi did not respond to requests made through his lawyer for an interview.

Background on Moreno was obtained from his resume, testimony at various trials, and the authors' impressions based on dealings with him. Moreno declined to be interviewed for this book.

Descriptions of the area in which the Welbilt facilities were located and of the facilities themselves were based on the authors' observations and on comments by former employees. A report about the dedication of the new headquarters was published in the *Daily News*. Characterizations of morale and the atmosphere at the company at the time came largely from an interview with Edward McCarthy.

## CHAPTER 4

Much of the chronology of the six-horsepower engine contract was drawn from "A Report Prepared by the Subcommittee on Oversight of Government Management of the Committee on Governmental Affairs, United States Senate," dated May 1988 (hereafter referred to as the Senate Report).

Neuberger's reaction to the decision to pursue the engine contract was related in a conversation with Neuberger. The bloody fight between Mariotta and Neuberger was described in Moreno's trial testimony and the interview with Mariotta.

Information about Jose Aceves came from an interview with Aceves and people who know him. Background on Thomas Keenan came from a biography provided by his office. The investigation of Keenan was described in interviews with David Epstein and Harold Lipset, an article in *California Business* (October, 1987), and trial testimony.

Background on E. Robert Wallach and his first visit to Welbilt came from a press conference he held in Washington; numerous newspaper and magazine articles, especially ones by James Traub in *The New York Times* magazine, Steven Brill in *The American Lawyer*, and Hershel Shanks in *Moment* and the transcript of an interview between Wallach and Senator Carl Levin. Wallach declined requests for an extensive interview.

The activities of Dickey Dyer were described in newspaper articles, documents made available to the authors, and the Senate Report.

White House involvement in the engine contract was detailed in the "Report of Independent Counsel *In Re* Edwin Meese III" (hereafter the Meese Report).

CHAPTER 5

Anecdotes about the atmosphere at Welbilt in the early 1980s were obtained through numerous interviews with former employees. The "King Kong" story was related to the authors by a former employee who witnessed the incident.

Information about the F.H.J. account came from trial testimony and documents made available to the authors. Information about Gordon Osgood and his companies was detailed in trial testimony by the former Welbilt executives, documents made available to the authors, and an interview with Osgood.

The progress payment fraud description derived largely from Mario Moreno's testimony at the trial of Mario Biaggi and six others (hearafter the Biaggi Trial). Information about the ownership of Welbilt and Caridad Vazquez' no-show job also came from trial testimony.

Details about Neuberger's third marriage came from the wedding invitation and documents made available to the authors. Facts about Neuberger's humanitarian award came from a 1986 interview with him and were confirmed by a spokesman for the Albert Einstein College of Medicine.

Mariotta's unusual religious and gambling practices were disclosed in an interview with him, interviews with former Wedtech employees, and trial testimony. Information about Jennie Mariotta's no-show job came from trial testimony by Moreno and documents made available to the authors. The description of the Mariottas' house was obtained during a visit in 1988.

311

The story about the mystery parachutist was told to a source by Pier Talenti and was confirmed by John and Jennie Mariotta. The City of Yonkers Police Department, however, could find no record of the incident.

### CHAPTER 6

The varying versions of why Michael Cardenas was fired were obtained from a report in the *Daily News*, an interview with James Sanders, and the Senate Report.

The story of Mariotta's presentation in Atlanta came from the interviews with Mariotta and Epstein. The account of Mariotta's visit to the White House was based on Mariotta's recollections, photographs, and interviews with others who attended. The comments by President Reagan were based on Mariotta's recollection. Mariotta's seeming fixation with Chauncey the Gardener was mentioned by several persons, including an attorney for the company and a government prosecutor.

Background on Lyn Nofziger came from press clippings; background on James Jenkins came from his resumé and the authors' observations. Information about the role of Nofziger, Bragg, and Jenkins in connection with the engine contract came largely from the Meese Report, the Senate Report, and trial testimony.

Details about Reagan's plan to visit Welbilt came from Ed McCarthy and other former employees and were confirmed by documentary evidence.

### CHAPTER 7

Background on Larry Shorten came from his resume, trial testimony, and the authors' contacts with him.

Information about discovery of the progress payment fraud came primarily from trial testimony by Moreno, Shorten, and Anthony Guariglia. Details about the trip of Mariotta and Bluestine to Japan, and the offer to Bluestine, came from records made available to the authors, from comments made on background by a source with first-hand knowledge of some of the events, and from trial testimony. Through his attorney, Bluestine declined comment.

Information about Main Hurdman's response to learning of the progress payment fraud, and efforts by Bernard Ehrlich and Peter Neglia to paper it over, was obtained primarily from trial testimony. Ehrlich refused to be interviewed; Neglia did not respond to requests for comment.

Background on Anthony Guariglia and his decision to join Welbilt came from his resume, his trial testimony, and the authors' personal contacts with him.

### CHAPTER 8

Information about Moseley Hallgarten's retention came from the Meese Report and a former executive of the firm.

Wallach's controversial legal fees were disclosed in articles by William Carlsen in the *San Francisco Chronicle*. Information about the contacts among Meese, Wallach, and Judge Eugene Lynch came from articles in the *Chronicle* and the Log of Contacts Between Edwin Meese III and E. Robert Wallach (Jan. 1981 - April 1987) released by the United States Department of Justice Office of Professional Responsibility. Information regarding Wallach's arrangements for compensation came from trial testimony, the Meese Report, the *Moment* magazine article, and documents made available to the authors.

The selection of Squadron Ellenoff as the new general counsel for Wedtech was described in trial testimony, articles in several newspapers and magazines, and interviews with members of the law firm.

Mario Biaggi's ethnic slur against Wallach was reported by Moreno in his testimony at the Biaggi trial. Biaggi's demands for stock in Welbilt were detailed by Wedtech executives in their testimony at the Biaggi trial. Background on Richard Biaggi came from trial testimony and exhibits.

### Chapter 9

Information on the $500,000 cash loan came primarily from Moreno's testimony at the Biaggi trial. An article in the *Riverdale Press* provided some of the background on New York National Bank and Serafin Mariel. Impressions of John Tartaglia were based on personal contacts and interviews with people who had dealt with him. Efforts to arrange interviews with Tartaglia and Pat Simone were unsuccessful. Through a spokesman, officials at New York National Bank declined comment.

### Chapter 10

Several former Wedtech employees provided information about Mario Rosado's efforts to obtain money from workers. The authors were unable to locate Rosado to interview him.

Information about payments to Richard Stolfi and Frank Casalino, and approval of the 1983 labor contract, came from testimony at their trial. Neither Stolfi nor Casalino would comment.

The account of the EDA loan subordination issue was drawn from trial testimony, particularly that of Mario Moreno; the Meese Report; newspaper articles; and an interview with Carlos Campbell. Information about Campbell's fate came from the interview with him and an article in the *Chicago Tribune*.

Anecdotes about Mariotta's conduct on the "road shows" came from trial testimony and a conversation with a former executive of Moseley Hallgarten. Information about the division of proceeds from the public offering came from filings with the Securities and Exchange Commission and trial testimony and exhibits. The story about the Mercedes comes from Shorten's testimony at the Biaggi trial and the interview with Mariotta.

## Chapter 11

Information about the bribe of Richard Ramirez came from testimony by Moreno and others at the Biaggi trial, and Ramirez's plea agreement. Background on Ramirez came from his resumé and a 1986 interview with him.

Details about Wedtech's efforts to stay in the 8(a) program came from the Meese Report, the Senate Report, trial testimony, and interviews with Sanders and Robert Saldivar.

Information about the participation of Squadron Ellenoff in the Mariotta stock transfer was obtained from trial testimony and interviews with Arthur Siskind and a government prosecutor. Neuberger's attitude toward the IRS was reported in an article in *Inc.* magazine in December 1981. The comments about Mariotta's personality were based on an interview with Mariotta and perceptions of many of his associates.

Information concerning efforts to make the Navy award the pontoon contract under the 8(a) program came from an interview with Captain David de Vicq, the Senate Report, and the Meese Report.

Information about the efforts of Wedtech's competitors came from the Senate Report, an article in the *San Francisco Chronicle*, an interview with James Sanders, trial testimony, and documents made available to the authors.

## Chapter 12

Information on the revival of the F.H.J. account and kickbacks from Henry Zeisel came from trial testimony and documents made available to the authors. The firing of Bluestine was recalled in court testimony and by former Wedtech employees.

Information about the 149th Street facility, Jofre Associates, and Pat Simone's role came from financial documents, documents made available to the authors, trial testimony, and an interview with one of the prosecutors. Simone's comment that he "owned" Mario Biaggi was related by Guariglia at Biaggi's trial. Information about the kickback scheme related to improvements to the 149th Street building came primarily from Guariglia's court testimony.

Details about Stanley Simon's role came from trial testimony, an interview with one of the prosecutors, an interview with Henry Thomas, and statements made at Simon's sentencing.

Information about Robert and Jane Garcia and Cross Roads Tabernacle came from newspaper articles, an interview with one of the prosecutors, the government's indictment of the Garcias, trial testimony, and a source with detailed knowledge of the PTL scandal.

## Chapter 13

Details about the acquisition of the shipyard in Michigan came from a 1986 interview with Richard Ramirez; interviews with Representative

Robert Davis and his administrative assistant, Mark Ruge; and trial testimony.

Information about the $300,000 payment to Wallach following the shipyard acquisition came from the Meese Report, trial testimony, and comments by a former Wedtech manager. The Consultants Supreme scam was described in Guariglia's court testimony and by a prosecutor.

The description of conditions at the 149th Street facility derived from interviews with former Wedtech employees, documents made available to the authors, the interview with de Vicq, and the Senate Report.

Information about the awarding of the 1985 option came from the Senate Report and the interview with de Vicq.

## CHAPTER 14

The narrative about the Mitchell investigation was drawn from testimony at the trial of Clarence and Michael Mitchell; interviews with Thomas Trimboli, Gary Jordan, and James Sanders; documents obtained from the House Small Business Committee; and documents made available to the authors. Background information on the Mitchell family came from newspaper articles.

## CHAPTER 15

The Wedtech executives' activities at the inauguration were detailed in trial testimony and exhibits, interviews with two of the participants, and documents made available to the authors.

Details about the Wedtech executives' assets and lifestyles came from their trial testimony, an interview with one of the prosecutors, an interview with a former Wedtech employee, the interview with the Mariottas, the authors' observations, and documents made available to the authors.

## CHAPTER 16

The description of the wildcat strike came from interviews with several former Wedtech employees, trial testimony, and the interview with Mariotta.

The story about the dogs and rats at 350 Gerard was related by three former Wedtech employees. Information about the problem with the carpenters union came from trial testimony, documents made available to the authors, an interview with one of the prosecutors, and recollections of former Wedtech employees.

Labor problems at the 149th Street facility were described in documents made available to the authors, an interview with one of the prosecutors, and an interview with a former Wedtech employee.

Information about the Ambassadors' Ball came from the Meese Report and documents made available to the authors.

315

CHAPTER 17

Information about Main Hurdman's performance as Wedtech's auditors came from trial testimony, financial statements and press releases, documents made available to the authors, and interviews.

Information about the retention of Touche Ross came from documents made available to the authors and interviews. Gil Tenzer's analysis came from documents made available to the authors. Information about Samuel Cohen's report came from an interview with Cohen.

CHAPTER 18

Information about the maintenance-vehicle contract came primarily from documents made available to the authors, an interview with Samuel Cohen, and exhibits at the Biaggi trial.

Background about Vito Castellano came from trial testimony and a column by Jimmy Breslin in the *Daily News* of December 8, 1987.

CHAPTER 19

Information about the LTAVD process came from documents made available to the authors, personal observations made by the authors, recollections of several former Wedtech employees, and published financial reports.

Background on Eduard Pinkhasov came from documents made available to the authors, an interview with Pinkhasov in January 1988, and conversations with Mariotta and Neuberger.

CHAPTER 20

The story about Mariotta filling out Lotto tickets at a board meeting came from the trial testimony of Guariglia and Mariotta. The discussion about finding a white, Anglo-Saxon Protestant executive was related by Guariglia in trial testimony.

Information about Wallach's self-promotion and his relationship with Meese came from newspaper and magazine accounts, trial testimony, and the Justice Department summary of Meese-Wallach contacts.

Background about Chinn and London came from the Meese report, trial testimony, interviews with their acquaintances, comments made by Guariglia to a federal agent, documents made available to the authors, and newspaper articles. Particularly helpful were profiles of Chinn and London by Katherine Bishop in *The New York Times* of June 22, 1987, and a profile of Chinn by Douglas Frantz and Dan Morain in the *Los Angeles Times* of March 13, 1988. Though their attorneys, Chinn and London declined requests for interviews.

Information about Chinn's questionable trading practices came from the Meese Report and from an affidavit by Robert L. Charboneau, an IRS

316

agent. Information about financial arrangements with Chinn and London came from Guariglia's court testimony.

The description of the struggle for control of the company was based on trial testimony, interviews with a former attorney and a former consultant for Wedtech, and the authors' observations.

Information about Mariotta's signing the rescission agreement came from trial testimony, documents supporting a lawsuit prepared on behalf of Mariotta, and an interview with Siskind.

Information about Neuberger's suggestion to have Mariotta murdered came from trial testimony and an interview with a former prosecutor. The "Boy Scouts" quote is Moreno's recollection of what Neuberger said.

## CHAPTER 21

Details concerning the January 1986 sale of stock came from financial documents, the Meese Report, trial testimony, and documents made available to the authors. Information about the "in-house" sales meeting came from a Wedtech employee who participated in the event and documents made available to the authors. Information about the Meese-Wallach-Chinn-London lunch, and the $100,000 kickback to Guariglia, came from the Meese Report.

Details about the Kennedy airport meeting to discuss the murder of Mariotta came from trial testimony and interviews with prosecutors.

The description of Mariotta's ouster was based on a draft lawsuit prepared on behalf of Mariotta, documents made available to the authors, trial testimony, financial documents, interviews with the three "outside" directors, and an interview with an attorney who was present at the February 11, 1986 board meeting.

## CHAPTER 22

Facts about the SDA's reaction to Mariotta's ouster were obtained from trial testimony, SBA documents obtained through the Freedom of Information Act, and documents released by the House Small Business and Committee.

Details about the insider sale of stock came from filings with the SEC, a chronology of Wedtech press releases, and an interview with a former prosecutor.

Information concerning the 1986 pontoon option came from the Senate Report, trial testimony, the interview with Captain de Vicq, and a press release issued by Senator D'Amato's office. Moreno's comment that he had Pyatt in his "back pocket" was related by William W. Pearsall, president of a former Wedtech subsidiary.

The stories about Wedtech's unsucessful efforts to sell products in the Middle East came from the interview with Ed McCarthy, documents made

317

available to the authors, Moreno's trial testimony, and an interview with a former Wedtech executive.

Information about the phony Telex for pontoon orders, and the framing of Mariotta for the payment to London's company came from trial testimony.

## CHAPTER 23

The account of the origins of the Wedtech investigations was a synthesis of interviews with Steve Cossu, Mike Raggi, Mary Shannon, Phil Foglia, Gary Jordan, Ted Planzos, and Donna Merris.

Mariotta's purported talks with the Ivan Boesky organization was mentioned by McCarthy.

## CHAPTER 24

The *Village Voice's* aborted investigation of Wedtech was described in *National Law Journal* of July 18, 1988.

Wedtech's efforts to purchase White Engines and Abex were detailed in documents made available to the authors. Information about Paul Hallingby's purchase of Wedtech stock came from a letter by Guariglia to Hallingby, a filing with the Securities and Exchange Commission, and an interview with Hallingby.

Information about Wedtech's efforts to locate financing—including the overtures to Lee Iacocca and Jackie Presser—came from trial testimony and documents made available to the authors.

Information about payments to John Tartaglia came from court testimony by Shorten and Guariglia. The depiction of the situation within the company came from the author's recollections.

Information about the disappearance of Eileen Vanora came from trial testimony, interviews with people who knew her, and interviews with law enforcement authorities.

## CHAPTER 25

The description of Bernard Ehrlich's personality and mental state in late 1986 came from trial testimony and an interview with a prosecutor.

Details about Squadron Ellenoff's role came from trial testimony, an article in *Manhattan Lawyer*, documents made available to the authors, interviews with prosecutors, trial testimony, and an interview with Siskind and Ira Lee Sorkin of Squadron Ellenoff.

Information about the hotel room meeting between Wallach and Meese came from the Meese Report, an interview with Terry Eastland, and comments made by Wallach. Details about Wedtech's relationship with Dickstein Shapiro came from documents made available to the authors, the Meese Report, interviews with three lawyers at Dickstein Shapiro, trial testimony, and the recollections of the authors.

The filing for bankruptcy was reconstructed from interviews of participants in the activities and recollections of the authors.

## CHAPTER 26

The description of the investigators' trip to the White House was based on interviews with several of those who were present. Foglia provided the description of Merola's reaction to Morgenthau's decision to indict Ehrlich. Information about Shearson's big loss in connection with the sale of Mariotta's shares was confirmed by three sources.

Information about Guariglia's decision to consider cooperating after he believed the F.H.J. account had been discovered came from trial testimony and interviews with Planzos, Shannon, Martin Pollner, and John Lang.

Details about the January 16 meeting in Mary Shannon's office came from interviews with Arthur Christy, Shannon, Planzos, and Cossu.

Information about plans by Moreno, Guariglia, and Shorten to flee the country came from their testimony at the Biaggi trial.

The description of the events of Super Bowl Weekend came from interviews with Howard Wilson and several of the other prosecutors and defense lawyers who attended the meetings.

# Acknowledgments

The authors are indebted to a number of people for their encouragement and support. Arnold Goodman, our literary agent, was largely responsible for bringing about this collaboration. He provided sound advice and guidance throughout. Donald Hutter, our editor with Henry Holt and Company, gave us direction and made many suggestions that improved the manuscript.

Our sources, several of whom knew they would be portrayed less than favorably, took many hours from their busy schedules to discuss the events recounted in these pages.

Special thanks go to Ray Lawhon, Stan Kolanowski, Eli Levy, Andy Healey, Esther Gonzalez, and Carol Tschudi. They have had the sad duty of liquidating Wedtech, a duty they have performed with skill and diligence. Their encouragement of our efforts to write the story of Wedtech has been gratifying. We would also like to thank Steven Wegman, who guided us through the sometimes mysterious world of personal computers. His efforts made the job of writing and exchanging drafts far less tedious.

Bill is indebted to his parents, Lawrence and Audrey Sternberg, for their unflagging encouragement, and his in-laws, Lloyd and Anita Haas, for putting him up (and sometimes his large, hairy dog) during his many research trips to New York. Diane Haas, Stephen Kesselman, and Margery Fischbein are also owed special thanks for their hospitality.

Matt is also indebted to his parents, Matthew and Roberta Harrison, for their support and enthusiasm. Thanks are due to Bob Cresci for his efforts in reviewing the early drafts, suggesting ways to make the story more compelling, and providing advice on how to treat such difficult subjects as initial public offerings, financial statements, and accounting principles.

Finally, we would like to thank our wives, Ellen Sternberg and Judy Harrison, and our children, Scott Sternberg and Cecily and Page Harrison. They have made the major sacrifices involved in writing this book; without their love and support we could not have done it.

# Index

321